GOOD HEARTS

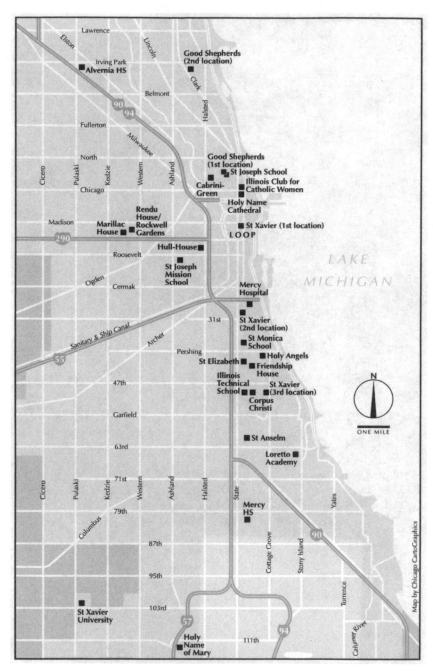

Chicago Locations Referred to in *Good Hearts*

SUELLEN HOY

Good Hearts

CATHOLIC SISTERS IN CHICAGO'S PAST

UNIVERSITY OF ILLINOIS PRESS

URBANA AND CHICAGO

Front cover photos: *From top, clockwise,*
St. Xavier's Academy, where Chicago's Mercy Sisters
    lived until the 1871 fire. Courtesy of the Sisters of
    Mercy, Chicago.
Six of the seven Franciscans who demonstrated in front
    of the Illinois Club for Catholic Women, July 1963. As
    published in the Chicago Sun-Times, Inc. © 2006 Chi-
    cago Sun-Times, Inc. Reprinted with permission.
Sister Catherine Sullivan saluted the flag with two stu-
    dents at St. Thomas the Apostle School in Hyde Park,
    1962. Courtesy of the Sinsinawa Dominicans.
Sister Marie Dorothy Delaney attempted to comfort a
    child at St. Rose of Lima parish, circa 1940. Courtesy of
    the Sisters of Mercy, Chicago.

Back cover photo:
Sister Mary William Sullivan presented the John F. Ken-
    nedy Award to Martin Luther King Jr. for his courageous
    leadership in the cause of justice at the annual dinner
    of the Catholic Interracial Council of Chicago, October
    1964. Courtesy of Sister Mary William Sullivan, DC,
    and the Daughters of Charity, St. Louis.

© 2006 by Suellen Hoy
All rights reserved
Manufactured in the United States of America
∞ This book is printed on acid-free paper.
1 2 3 4 5 C P 5 4 3 2 1

Library of Congress Cataloging-in-Publication Data

Hoy, Suellen M.
Good hearts : Catholic sisters in Chicago's past / Suellen Hoy.
p.   cm.
Includes bibliographical references and index.
ISBN-13: 978-0-252-03057-4 (cloth : alk. paper)
ISBN-10: 0-252-03057-5 (cloth : alk. paper)
ISBN-13: 978-0-252-07301-4 (pbk. : alk. paper)
ISBN-10: 0-252-07301-0 (pbk. : alk. paper) 1. Nuns—Illinois—
Chicago—History. 2. Chicago (Ill.)—Church history.
I. Title.
BX4220.U6H69   2006
271'.90077311—dc22   2005022121

For
The Other nÓg

"It was certainly done with a good heart and a sincere intention."

—Sister Mary William Sullivan, DC
  Chicago, 1963

Contents

Acknowledgments

How sweet it is—frosting on the cake, to be honest—to pause at the end of a long project and thank the many institutions and individuals who made the past ten years especially rewarding. First of all, I am grateful to the University of Notre Dame's Cushwa Center for the Study of American Catholicism, which assisted me at both the beginning and end of this project. A Hibernian Research Award, along with a research grant from the Irish American Cultural Institute, enabled me to make good use of the year I spent in Ireland. In 2004, the Cushwa Center again came to my assistance, through a grant that enabled me to obtain a map and additional photographs for this book. During the course of the project, I also received funding from the Spencer Foundation (1996–97) and the Louisville Institute (1999) and now thank them both. I am grateful to the Conference on the History of Women Religious for the numerous opportunities it provided me to present my work and discuss my findings.

All of the chapters in this book, except Chapter 7, were previously published as individual essays (although they have been updated and, in some instances, expanded for this collection). In each case, my submissions received careful attention from editors at *Chicago History, Journal of Illinois History, Journal of Urban History, Journal of Women's History*, and Loyola Press. I am grateful to them for permission to reprint these articles and for the consideration shown me by editors Rosemary K. Adams, Emily M. Holmes Nordstrom, and William B. Tubbs, along with my current editor at the University of Illinois Press, Joan Catapano.

This book would not exist if it were not for the assistance and generosity of archivists, especially those in convents and motherhouses of religious communities in Ireland and the United States. In Ireland, I acknowledge the sister-archivists at Baggot Street (Mercy), Cabra (Dominican), Callan (Mercy), Carlow (Mercy), Castleisland (Presentation), Cobh (Mercy), Cork (Ursuline), Ennis (Mercy), Drogheda (Dominican), George's Hill (Presentation), Kinsale (Mercy), Lucan (Presentation), Milltown (Charity), Naas (Mercy), Terenure (Mercy), and Tralee (Presentation). I am also indebted to David Sheehy, Dublin Archdiocesan Archives, and Rachel O'Flanagan, All Hallows College Archives. And I thank historians and others whom I met in Ireland and who helped me while I was there: Mary Broderick, Caitriona Clear, Seamus Enright, Jack Hennessy, Eileen Hogan, Sheila Lunney, Elizabeth O'Toole, Jacinta Prunty, Rosemary Raughter, Maryann G. Valiulis, and the Nolan and Prendiville families of Castleisland, County Kerry.

While living in Dublin, I contacted many sister-archivists in the United States who assisted me expeditiously through airmail letters and packages: Chicago (Mercy); Cincinnati (Mercy); Erie, Pennsylvania (Mercy); Dubuque, Iowa (Charity of the Blessed Virgin Mary and Presentation); Houston, San Antonio, and Victoria, Texas (Incarnate Word); Latham, New York (St. Joseph); New Orleans (Dominican); Pittsburgh (Mercy); Rochester, New York (Mercy); Sacramento, California (Mercy); and San Francisco (Mercy and Presentation). I was grateful to all of them in 1991–92 and remain so.

Once my attention turned to Catholic sisters in Chicago, I made new friends among librarians and archivists. Very important to me were those at the University of Notre Dame, especially Wendy Schlereth and Sharon Sumpter, as well as those at the Joseph Cardinal Bernardin Archives and Records Center of the Archdiocese of Chicago, particularly John J. Treanor and Julie A. Satzik. Many staff members at the Chicago Historical Society came to my aid, but I am most indebted to the late Archibald Motley Jr., who knew the collections intimately and directed me to treasure after treasure. I am also grateful to Dolores Madlener and Tom Sheridan, at the *Catholic New World,* who allowed me to roam through their photographic files.

Equally indispensable were those sister-archivists who welcomed me (oftentimes more than once) and assisted me time and time again through the mail. I thank them personally: Sisters Marjorie Buttner (Sinsinawa Dominicans); Reparata Clarke and Reginald Gerdes (Oblates of Providence); Joella Cunnane and Patricia Illing (Mercy); Corinne Dais (School Sisters of St. Francis); Juliana Dusel (IBVM, Toronto); Anita Therese Hayes (BVMs); Elvira Kelley (Dubuque Franciscans); Genevieve Keusenkothen and Lois Martin (Daughters of Charity); Mary Lourdes Langenfeld (Good

Shepherd); Maria Espiritu McCall and Therese Misencik (Blessed Sacrament); Margaret Phelan and Mary Louise Gavan (Sacred Heart); Joseph Plewa and Gemma Wacek (Holy Family of Nazareth); Mary Lonan Reilly (Rochester Franciscans); Charlene Sullivan (St. Joseph); Margaret Valois and Alice Marie Henke (Servants of Mary); Marian Voelker (Joliet Franciscans); and Alice Whitehead (IBVM, Chicago). I also am grateful to Valerie Gerrard Browne, Women and Leadership Archives, Loyola University, Chicago; the late Brother Michael Grace, Loyola University Archives, Chicago; the late Father Peter Hogan, Josephite Archives, Baltimore; and Marcia C. Stein, Society of the Divine Word Archives, Techny, Illinois.

During the course of my research, I interviewed many individuals, and all of them were generous with their time and thoughts. I thank them: Margo Anderson Butler; Marie Davis; Sister Brenda Finnegan; Sister Marilyn Freking; Sister Irene Gavin; Sister Ignace Garvey; the late William Hogan; the late Sister Eleanor Holland; Sister Mary Benet McKinney; Father Dan Mallette; Sister Elizabeth Mallon; the late Ed Marciniak; Mary Louise Higgins Mims; Sister Kate Moriarty; Richard Morrisroe; Sister Anastasia O'Connor; Sister Margaret Ordway; Sister Martin de Porres Orford; the late Sister Mary Gene Partridge; Sister Callista Robinson; Sister Therese Rooney; Francis Rothluebber; Warner Saunders; Ann Seng; Sister Mary Simpkin; Gwen Smith; Mary Sparks; Sister Colette Srill; Sister Helen Strueder; Sister Mary William Sullivan; Father Anthony J. Vader; Sister Alice Whitehead; Sister Janvier Williams; Sister Lucy Williams; Pauline Lewis Williams; John Woodford; and Maudine Wordlaw.

For sharing experiences of their own, for sending me newspaper clippings or copies of journal articles, for giving me tips on books to read and archival collections to consult, and for sincere expressions of interest, I am grateful to: M. Christine Anderson; R. Scott Appleby; Annette Atkins; Charlene Avallone; Steven M. Avella; Joseph C. Bigott; Ernest Brandewie; Anne Butler; Patricia Byrne, CSJ; James Carroll, CFC; Joseph P. Chinnici, OFM; the late Peter D'Agostino; Ivan R. Dee; Hasia Diner; Myrtle Doaks; Jay P. Dolan; Eileen Durkin; Michael H. Ebner; Michael F. Engh, SJ; Charles Fanning; George V. Fornero; Donna Gabaccia; Timothy J. Gilfoyle; Philip Gleason; Christopher Hamlin; Don Hayner; Joan Hoff; D. Bradford Hunt; Jane Hunter; Kathleen Joyce; Edward R. Kantowicz; Christopher J. Kauffman; Patricia Kelleher; Karen Kennelly, CSJ; Linda K. Kerber; Anne Meis Knupfer; Emmet Larkin; Thomas LeBien; Barbara Lockwood; James H. Madison; Deirdre Mageean; Joseph G. Mannard; Timothy Matovina; Lawrence J. McCaffrey; Malachy McCarthy; Dennis McClendon; Theresa McDermott; John T. McGreevy; Margaret McGuinness; Wilson D. Miscamble; Sandra Yocum Mize; Deirdre Moloney; Cecilia Moore; Diane Batts Morrow; Maureen Murphy; Timothy B. Neary; Kevin O'Neill; Anna Nelson; Janet Nolan; James M. O'Toole; Dominic A. Pacyga; Christopher R. Reed; Peggy Roach; the late Martin Ridge; Steve Rosswurm; Lana Ruegamer; Rima Lunin Schultz; Mary Seematter; Amanda I. Seligman; Kathryn Kish Sklar; Eric Smith; Jan Shipps; Catharine R. Stimpson; Ann Stull; Margaret Susan Thompson; Louise Wade; Barbra Mann Wall; Bernard A. Weisberger, and Janet Welsh, OP.

I am extraordinarily grateful to a special circle of women historians who are also cherished friends. I thank them for their good advice, smart insights, and everlasting encouragement: Carol K. Coburn; Kathleen Sprows Cummings; Maureen A. Flanagan; Ann Durkin Keating; Margaret Mac Curtain; Mary J. Oates; and Ellen Skerrett.

Finally, and above all, I thank Walter Nugent, who as always is my editor-of-the-first-instance, best friend, and sustainer.

GOOD HEARTS

Introduction: Catholic Sisters in Chicago's Past

"Convent" is what the small, chiseled sign said. I noticed it one Sunday afternoon not long ago, as my husband and I were walking to our car on Chicago Avenue. I stopped, turned to him, and asked: "When is the last time you saw a sign like that?" We couldn't remember. Convents are hard to find today, even though during much of the twentieth century they numbered in the hundreds. Once familiar anchors of Chicago's neighborhoods, most of them—along with many schools and churches—are now closed or used for other purposes. On a rare occasion, though, you may come across a convent that still houses a few Catholic sisters, like the one we noticed adjacent to Holy Name Cathedral on North Wabash near Chicago Avenue. As late as 1966, twenty Sisters of Charity of the Blessed Virgin Mary (BVMs) lived there and taught more than seven hundred students in the parish school. It had opened its doors in 1904.[1]

The cathedral's school continues to operate a century later, but with a predominantly lay faculty. It is now a campus of the Frances Xavier Warde Schools, named after the American founder of the Sisters of Mercy. In 1846, five of them arrived in Chicago from Ireland (via Pittsburgh) and became the first of many Catholic sisters who would "make the most and best of life" by doing good in the world and contributing to the well-being of generations of Chicagoans. The number of nuns grew rapidly from the first five in 1846 to over 9,000 in 1946. Most were engaged in teaching, health care, and social service. Twenty years later, in 1966, their head count in the United States peaked at about 180,000, with Chicago holding its own at approximately 9,500. When the twentieth century ended, however, their ranks had thinned to 83,000, which included 3,000 women-religious in the Archdiocese of Chicago.[2]

These figures are impressive and should prompt us to ask who these women were and what they accomplished. Although the questions are simple, they cannot be answered simply: the number of sisters is too large and the variety of their achievements too broad. Yet there are some common denominators. Most of the women who entered active reli-gious communities during the nineteenth and twentieth centuries were young and the daughters of working-class immigrant parents. Although they would not have understood or been sympathetic to the notion of "having it all," they sought a fuller life and chose what they considered the best of the limited avenues before them. As nuns, they committed themselves to an extraordinarily wide range of efforts that responded to local needs, only some of which are addressed in this book. They were also a group of women who did not seek attention, who tended to value deeds over words, and whose bent was more toward the practical than the theoretical.

Most importantly, perhaps, Catholic sisters were "good hearts." As Mary Frances Clarke, founder of the BVMs, once observed, they had dispo-sitions that were naturally "pliant to[ward] good." This essential quality, however, did not undercut their ambition and determination to enlarge the scope of their lives through useful service. They carried out their assignments with energy, purpose, and confidence, often commanding attention from people in the street as well as from those in high office. Church leaders regulated and restricted nuns' lives, but "this tutelage was in stark contradiction to the relative self-governance enjoyed by many orders of women and to the real authority that sisters exercised in the schools, hospitals, and other charitable institutions they sponsored."[3]

The Dublin-born Clarke, for example, defended the BVMs' pre-rogatives by refusing a local pastor's request to examine the convent accounts. "Not even our Right Reverend Bishop required that," she told him; "therefore, you will excuse me for positively and finally declining." The young Agatha O'Brien, also an Irish immigrant and the first supe-rior of the Mercy Sisters in Chicago, was hardly reticent when it came to defending her community and its work. Following a visit with Bishop John Henni of Milwaukee and his traveling companion from Pittsburgh, she wrote to a friend that she had "argued strongly" with the latter and "gave him word for word."[4]

To deny women like Agatha O'Brien and Mary Frances Clarke a

legitimate place in American history is a double loss, theirs and ours. Historians of American women made this point long ago, and the research they have done over the past several decades has awarded women agency to such a degree that one eminent scholar recently bemoaned the hackneyed quality of such work. She said that "stories designed to celebrate women's agency . . . seem predictable and repetitious, more information garnered to prove a point that had already been made." Women-religious, however, are undoubtedly an exception, as their agency and activism remain an unwritten chapter in the history of American women.[5]

Who Catholic sisters were and what they did are not engaging topics, particularly to Americans who live in a world where religious commitment is frequently misunderstood, male-dominated structures are instinctively regarded as oppressive, and opportunities and adventures for young women appear nearly limitless. Facing old age and possible extinction, nuns are dismissed as irrelevant, publicly ridiculed, and considered little more than pawns of the Catholic Church's male hierarchy. But those willing to look beyond conventional wisdom will discover that women-religious, who were paradoxically subordinate and privileged, developed a surprising capacity to influence the church to which they had dedicated their lives as well as the city in which they resided. This book of essays, researched over a ten-year period and rooted in a locale, is another attempt to place Catholic sisters in the mainstream of American women's history—to show their "lives and activities to be as complex, varied, and interesting as the lives of their Protestant and secular peers."[6]

Convents and sisters were by no means unique to Chicago. But this city had its own distinctiveness. Besides having a population that was largely Catholic and immigrant from its beginning, it was also the site of the renowned Hull-House, which Jane Addams and Ellen Gates Starr opened in 1889, and other less well-known settlements. Far outnumbering the dedicated residents and volunteers of these centers, however, were thousands of nuns who staffed schools, hospitals, and social-service institutions, not only in Chicago but across America. Yet it is Chicago—with its sizeable immigrant and Catholic populations early on, followed quickly by a heavy influx of black migrants from the rural South—that provides an unusually rich environment in which to examine the range and depth of the benevolent enterprises spearheaded by Catholic sisters.[7]

I offer this collection of essays as a large window through which to glimpse the neglected past of these women. My offering is not comprehensive; many more sisterhoods than those treated in this book have served Chicagoans during the past two centuries. It is strikingly evident, in fact, that until additional primary research has been completed on Chicago and other locales (big and small), it will be impossible to assess the full scope and impact of the sisters' institutional network in the United States.

By the time I finished this study, I had come to agree with historian Leslie Tentler. More than a decade ago, she noted that "had women under secular or Protestant auspices compiled this record of achievement, they would today be a thoroughly researched population." There is not a region in the United States that did not benefit from the presence of nuns. Still, because of "the tendency of historians to ignore religion in general and Catholicism in particular," most of the determined and heartfelt efforts of America's Catholic sisters are only fleetingly recognized and generally unknown.[8]

Although I have known nuns nearly my entire life, both as teachers and as friends, I had never considered writing a book about them. What could they possibly tell me that I didn't already know? Had it not been for an opportunity to spend a year in Ireland with my husband, this project would not have been begun. It started quite simply as an adventure, not as a book. I was interested in religion as a motive for emigration. That interest resulted in an essay (the first in this collection) on the "journey out" of a significant group of Irish women to the United States. Over time my curiosity developed into something more. Back at home, new questions demanded new answers: what happened to those thousands of energetic and purposeful young women after they left Ireland for America? How did they adjust away from home? How well did they do, living and working in American cities? I decided to take a look at Chicago, the place where I was born and a city that continues to please and intrigue me. I knew that early on, Irish Catholics had left their imprint on the urban landscape, "not in words but in stone—Catholic churches, schools, convents, rectories, charitable institutions, and hospitals."[9] Amidst all the bricks and mortar, there were Irish sisters, I felt certain, who had made a difference. That hunch proved correct, as did others. But there were discoveries too.

I found almost immediately that, except for their enthusiasm, Chicago's first Irish sisters did not resemble the nuns who taught me. Because they were few in number, the small band of Sisters of Mercy who arrived in the 1840s could not afford to be specialists such as teachers, nurses, social workers, or administrators. The demands of a developing metropolis coupled with the enormous needs of the Irish community's working poor prevented such luxury. Unrelenting forces of nature and ingrained habits of poverty compelled those nuns to go everywhere and do everything. They were not bound by convent rules or classroom walls; the city was their workplace. Instructed by their Irish founder, Catherine McAuley, "to seek justice, to be compassionate, and to reflect mercy to the world," they chose to provide useful services. They opened orphanages, staffed schools, cared for cholera victims in their homes, nursed the sick and injured in makeshift hospitals, visited prisoners, helped secure employment for the jobless, and sheltered abandoned women. The activism of these pioneering sisters laid a solid foundation for the diversified and specialized undertakings that Catholic sisters of various ethnic and racial origins would undertake during the nineteenth and twentieth centuries.[10]

Nuns were among the earliest women to make substantial contributions to Chicago's rise as a modern city, especially in education, health care, and social welfare. I was surprised to learn that large numbers of them predated by decades Chicago's famous settlement-house workers, remarkable women whom I had learned to admire as a high school student. In fact, Catholic sisters and Protestant settlement workers often lived and acted in similar fashion, despite their markedly different backgrounds and worldviews. But nineteenth-century nuns, who came from the working class, were far more self-effacing and far less critical of institutions. Unlike middle-class reformers, sisters thought that class divisions were likely to endure and therefore "did not imagine an end to the inequitable social and economic system that made charity necessary." Hence they channeled their efforts toward alleviating the symptoms of poverty through personal works of mercy and charitable institutions.[11]

Nowhere did I find a community of women-religious who were submissive servants of the male clergy. Although nuns frequently labored under hierarchical constraints, they also had their advocates—influential clergymen and laymen who shared their views. Without them, the Sisters of the Good Shepherd, for example, would not have succeeded in building the House of the Good Shepherd or the Illinois Technical School for Colored Girls. With them, these private and determined women of the church charted their own course and carried out what they believed to be its mission in America. Their vision for social betterment, though never unified, sprang from deep religious convictions as well as from what they judged to be pressing local needs. During the nineteenth century, Catholic sisters primarily took care of their own, especially the most neglected and forgotten of Chicago's immigrants. As more parish schools were built and as the number of nuns increased, the majority of them curtailed their public outreach and generously contributed years of their lives to educating the sons and daughters of immigrant Catholic families.

Creating a network of private, affordable, and competitive neighborhood schools in a city bedeviled by problems in its public system was no small accomplishment. Good schools where students learn, like happy homes where families thrive, do not happen by accident. They result from the determined and cooperative efforts of many. Yet women, who have almost always played the central and most difficult role, have rarely been adequately recognized or compensated for their successes. A former teacher observed that instructing young people is "an extremely exhausting job: it is like doing a one-woman show, in which you are on stage for about seven hours every day."[12] That, however, aptly describes the lives of most Catholic sisters following the bishops' decision in the 1880s to build a separate system of parochial schools in response to anti-Catholic prejudice. Within two decades, the schoolhouse became "an extension of the convent"; indeed, many young women thought that "being a sister meant being a teacher." Diverted from more public avenues of ministry, they instead left a sizeable imprint as teachers. Remembered (and often mocked) for their strong discipline, Catholic sisters earned a reputation for creating a quiet learning environment, offering a solid foundation in the basics, and leaving no child behind.[13]

This record of achievement, which may be unparalleled in the history of women in the United States, is hardly ever acknowledged. Perhaps it is because an inexpensive, reliable source of labor is generally not valued; or because nuns learned not to look to contemporaries for recognition; or because there is little excitement or drama associated with teaching children. Whatever the reasons, this coordinated "mighty force" of resourceful women-religious had dramatic—even radical—results. Striving "to be the best [they] could be," as one veteran commented, sister-teachers were crucial figures in the parishes of working-class Catholics.[14]

To read and to write was to rise. Nuns not only taught the basics, in addition to giving religious instructions, but they also encouraged middle-class aspirations. By routinely emphasizing hard work, dependability, honesty, and cleanliness, they instilled important values in their pupils while urging them to continue their education. Most students went on to high school (usually Catholic ones); a good many attended normal school or college and subsequently joined the ranks of the middle class. By 1915, so many Catholics were teaching in the city's public schools that Superintendent Ella Flagg Young considered placing a quota on them at Chicago Normal. This effort failed; and their numbers in the teaching force continued to rise and reached 70 percent in 1920, according to Archbishop George Mundelein. A select group of graduates from Catholic high schools also became nuns and priests.[15]

Having witnessed the effects of Catholic schooling on my second-generation father, I trusted him when he advised that "education was money in the bank."[16] But what I did not hear from him or anyone else, despite years in Catholic schools, was a bit of information that stunned me. On a winter day in 1996, I discovered that Catholic sisters had extended their reach long before the 1960s and the modern civil rights movement to non-Catholic people of color who did *not* live in foreign lands. I was, of course, familiar with the church's missionaries to Africa and China, but I knew nothing about the early work of Catholic sisters among African Americans on Chicago's South Side. The first indication I had of this fact was a small, yellowed brochure on the Illinois Technical School for Colored Girls. I found it among some old records at the House of the Good Shepherd, a short distance from Wrigley Field. Over coffee, I asked Sister Mary Lourdes Langenfeld, who is well versed on the undertakings of the Good Shepherd Sisters in Chicago, about the school. She told me where it had been located and for how long; she also mentioned that it had had a contentious beginning. That last comment sparked my curiosity and propelled me forward. Again, new questions demanded answers.

I soon learned about Katharine Drexel (canonized a saint in 2000). An American woman born in 1858 to a wealthy family of Philadelphia bankers, she used her multimillion-dollar inheritance in an extraordinary way. In the 1890s, she founded a religious community of women to live among people of color, Native Americans and African Americans, and to teach their children. The Sisters of the Blessed Sacrament for Indians and Colored People arrived in Chicago in 1912 and opened a school in St. Monica's parish. Like the Sisters of the Good Shepherd, they too had their difficulties; yet they stayed on the South Side (now at St. Elizabeth's), just blocks from where they began. In time, more Catholic sisters quietly and eagerly followed their lead. They moved into black neighborhoods and welcomed black students into their schools. As exceptional as these racially active nuns were—no other group of white women made such a commanding choice and lifelong commitment—their experiences remain unacknowledged and unexplored.[17]

Although historians and social scientists tend to view religious women as "backward" and secular women as "progressive," Catholic sisters were among the few white people who actually lived and worked in black neighborhoods. In Chicago, the most racially tolerant progressives appear to have been white settlement workers. But the majority of them regarded African Americans differently from their immigrant neighbors from southern and eastern Europe. Jane Addams, who was one of the most visionary of the nation's progressive reformers, had working relationships with black leaders, but Hull-House did not "make much of an effort to cross racial boundaries and promote association among different races." Well into the twentieth century, most settlement workers "still thought of their movement as being primarily for whites," despite their belief in "the solidarity of the human race." Celia Parker Woolley, a Unitarian minister and active Chicago club woman, was a unique exception. In 1905, she reached across racial boundaries and invited African Americans into her home, the Frederick Douglass Center.[18]

The center was a three-story stone building situated on the edge of the Black Belt at Thirty-first Street and Wabash Avenue. Woolley and her husband bought it with support from middle-class friends, black and white. Notable among them was another Unitarian and club woman, Fannie Barrier Williams, who had been the first African American elected to the Chicago Woman's Club. She became a director of the Douglass Center and remained intimately involved in its affairs until Woolley's death in 1918.[19]

The Frederick Douglass Center, however, never provided direct assistance to Chicago's poor and uneducated black newcomers. It was not only located too far from most of them, but also was not disposed to assist them. Woolley was aware of their presence, having described them in 1904 as "the hordes of colored people coming up from the South . . . and threaten[ing] the well-being of the whole." The center instead became a meeting place for "the best people of both races," where they regularly came together to enjoy lectures, discussions, recitals, and teas. When criticized for this absence of direct action, Williams responded that the Douglass Center was "not organized to do slum work." Racial uplift was for others—those (white or black) more religiously motivated who lived among the poorest in settlements or missions.[20]

For Catholic sisters, the local parish almost always served as the site of their missionary efforts. Although parish boundaries could be restrictive, they produced benefits as well.[21] An unheralded one is that such organization compelled nuns to live where they worked. At the close of a long, tiring day on the job, they did not leave one neighborhood for another. As a result, this practice made them "proximate and available" to those they sought to help, according to Sister Mary William Sullivan, an activist Daughter of Charity at Marillac House during the 1960s. When Martin Luther King Jr. moved to a four-room apartment on the West Side in January 1966, he underscored this point by remarking: "You really can't get close to the poor without living and being with them." Thus, in the end, "new nuns" (as activists were often described in contemporary accounts) and "old nuns," often separated by years and perhaps by approaches, were bound together in a "ministry of presence"—one in which they chose to serve all God's people by standing "shoulder to shoulder with [those] who are suffering."[22]

After examining the efforts of a large number of Catholic sisters who worked to improve the lives of black Americans in Chicago, I reached a new conclusion about the 1960s. What happened in the civil rights movement was the culmination rather than the beginning of a longer history of nuns linking their lives to those of African Americans. Indeed, what had begun as a trickle in the 1890s amounted to something like a torrent by the mid-1960s. To be sure, not all women-religious joined the movement. In Chicago, a survey of 600 teaching sisters (mostly in elementary schools and mostly from working-class families) in 1966 showed that 23.7 percent still agreed (or were unsure) that "no matter how many advantages the colored attain, they will, as a group, always remain inferior to whites." But three out of four rejected this and other racist propositions. Anecdotal evidence also indicates that a considerable number of Catholic sisters "caught courage" from one another and were especially moved by King's message of nonviolence and Christian unity.[23]

The vision and courage of Katharine Drexel and those who followed her example cannot be overlooked. Well before the Second Vatican Council (1962–65), some sisters opened parish schools for black youngsters; some welcomed African Americans into their white schools and academies; some began adult education centers in black neighborhoods; some spent late-afternoon hours, Saturdays, or summer months volunteering at Friendship House, Marillac House, or the Cabrini-Green housing project. What these nuns did in the first half of the twentieth century was as necessary, deliberate, and striking as the actions of those who joined public demonstrations in Chicago or Selma in the 1960s. Through their uncompromising commitment to racial justice, they forged a bond of solidarity with one another that made them, like Dorothy Day, visible witnesses to God's love for the poor and powerless—a position the Catholic Church as an institution has been slow to adopt.[24]

1 The Journey Out:
From Ireland to America

"Do you think I shall ever be good enough for you *to send me away?*" an Irish girl asked Sister Mary Eustace Eaton, a Sister of Charity and moderator of the Children of Mary Sodality at Our Lady's Hospice, Harold's Cross, in Dublin. For thirty-eight years, from 1868 to 1906, Sister Mary Eustace had heard the same question from hundreds of "pure hearted young girls" who, upon receiving the sodality's medal and blue ribbon, pledged to turn "from worldly pleasures to give themselves to God."[1] Most of these Children of Mary were in their early teens and came from the homes of Dublin's working class. As they grew older and expressed a desire to become nuns, Sister Mary Eustace successfully placed them in convents outside Ireland—ones willing to accept a young woman with little or no dowry.[2] These were located largely in foreign, English-speaking countries to which millions of Irish had fled after the Great Famine (1845–51). By 1905, Sister Mary Eustace had found places for approximately seven hundred women from Harold's Cross, several of whom later bore the name Sister Mary Eustace. About four hundred of these Children of Mary became nuns in the United States.[3]

Sister Mary Eustace's work at Harold Cross is only one example of what had become by 1900 an almost routine pattern of migration—young

Originally published as "The Journey Out: The Recruitment and Emigration of Irish Religious Women to the United States, 1812–1914," *Journal of Women's History* 6–7 (Winter/Spring 1995): 64–98.

Irish women going out to the New World as nuns (professed sisters, novices, postulants, or aspirants). The pattern began in the spring of 1812 when three Ursuline nuns traveled from Cork to New York, where they established the first foundation of Irish women in the United States. They remained only three years, but they initiated a practice that would become commonplace by the end of the nineteenth century. They also represented the first wave of Irish emigrant women who would come to the United States at the invitation of bishops and priests, often Irish, to establish new convents.[4]

The first wave lasted from 1812 to 1881. It consisted of the establishment of sixteen foundations that did endure, ending with the 1881 arrival in Watervliet, New York, of a small group of Presentation Sisters from Fermoy, County Cork. But a second wave, which began in earnest during the late 1860s (and overlapped with the first wave during the 1870s) continued into the twentieth century. Young women, usually not professed sisters or even novices, were recruited by nuns from the United States who regularly launched "major drives" to acquire new members during visits to Ireland in the spring and summer months. In this way, several thousand women journeyed to the United States, where they entered religious orders as postulants and received training for their lifelong work.[5]

Those recruited in the second wave, for the most part, became teachers in the United States' rapidly developing parochial school system. By the 1880s, the needs of the Catholic Church, as defined by its bishops, centered on classroom instruction, and nuns were sought for that purpose. The diverse ministries begun by the pioneers of the first wave—nursing the sick, caring for orphans, housing working women and unwed mothers, and educating adult immigrants—simply lost out to the task of staffing new schools. But over the years the women of both waves, united more by their fortitude and resourcefulness than by their professional work, grew into a capable community of American Catholic women that extended over several generations.

Once the schools were built, bishops and pastors tended to leave day-to-day affairs to the nuns, who from the beginning served as principals and teachers.[6] In both roles, these emigrants became "heroes of their own lives." This was no small achievement for women, especially of the second wave, who once seemed trapped in the deprived and constrained circumstances that were repercussions of the Great Famine. By recruiting, educating, and sustaining one another in religious communities, most of them succeeded in gaining control over their personal lives. Thus, for these emigrants, "the nineteenth century was often a period of triumph rather than subjection."[7]

It is probably not surprising that the story of these Irish women is largely untold. Their journey out is an exceedingly difficult one to trace, for a variety of reasons. During most of the nineteenth century, nuns traveling from Ireland wore secular clothes and used their surnames, as they had during penal times, so as not to call attention to themselves.[8] As members of a church governed entirely by men, nuns experienced the same disregard as other groups of women. Frequently taken for granted, nuns were expected to provide the services to which they had committed their lives in a spirit of meekness, humility, and detachment. Obscurity and invisibility, though not uncommon in the study of women's lives in general, are particularly troublesome when they are sought after and considered measures of success.[9] Because nineteenth-century nuns believed that their good work would be recognized in the hereafter by an all-knowing God, they made little or no effort to preserve records of their comings and goings or the reasons for them. But they did leave traces both in Ireland and the United States, and these help explain how and why the "scattering" of Irish religious women occurred during the nineteenth and early twentieth centuries.[10]

The First Wave

In 1834, Bishop John England of Charleston, South Carolina, succeeded in persuading three Ursuline Sisters and a postulant from his native Cork to establish a school for girls in Charleston. His success, however, had not come easily. Two years before, in a letter written from Dublin, he had mentioned that "a colony of Ursuline Nuns" would return with him to Charleston.[11] But, despite the fact that "His Lordship . . . [seemed] determined that our Superiors should not sleep over his petition," the Ursulines responded slowly to the bishop's imperious pleas. They remembered all too well the difficulties encountered by an earlier group of Ursulines who attempted to found an academy for young women in New York in 1812, only to return disillusioned three years later. Their experience had provided these nuns with "a lesson . . . too dearly purchased to be either forgotten or neglected."[12]

The Ursulines finally agreed to accept Bishop England's invitation, but only after he traveled to make several personal visits to them. His "ardent zeal & insatiable desire for the extension of the Kingdom of Christ" finally convinced them. Although there is no record of the exact "arguments" the persistent bishop used to make his case, the sisters were eventually satisfied of "the large field which such a Mission would open to Ursuline zeal."[13] Bishop England most likely explained the special needs of his diocese, one that he considered "the poorest, the largest, and the most insalubrious."[14] And he probably made known his strong views on the disquieting condition of the church in the United States. In a widely circulated statement in 1836, Bishop England asserted that the loss of faith among Catholic immigrants and their children was "exceedingly great" (over three million in the previous fifty years). Although his assessment has been proven incorrect, he and others believed it and saw in it the tremendous need for priests and nuns.[15] Nearly a million Irish had gone to North American in the half-century before the famine, and a majority had settled in the United States. Thus in the 1830s, following the Catholic Emancipation Act of 1829, the Irish Catholic Church began concentrating its major missionary efforts on this diaspora.[16] Irish clergy—followed by Irish nuns—left family, friends, and country to bring the faith to Irish immigrants in their new homes.

In October 1843, when another Cork-born bishop, Michael O'Connor, invited the Sisters of Mercy in Carlow to Pittsburgh, they responded more expeditiously (and more typically) than the Ursulines. The Carlow nuns were not burdened with memories of a mission that had not endured, nor did they feel uncomfortable with Bishop O'Connor. When he visited St. Leo's convent, the nuns greeted him warmly, accompanied as he was by Father James Maher, a longtime friend of theirs and their founder, Mother Catherine McAuley. Not only had Father Maher been administrator of the parish when the nuns arrived in Carlow in 1837, but he was also the cousin of Mother Frances Xavier Warde, who founded St. Leo's, and the uncle of Father Paul Cullen, then rector of the Irish College in Rome and later Ireland's first cardinal.[17]

All twenty-three sisters at St. Leo's volunteered for the Pittsburgh mission. Mother Frances Warde, who was appointed superior, and six other nuns (among them was Sister Agatha O'Brien, later to become superior of the first group of Catholic sisters in Chicago) left Carlow for Dublin on November 2, 1843—two days short of a month after Bishop O'Connor's last visit. The sisters wore secular clothes (black cashmere dresses) and traveled first-class. Although Bishop O'Connor mingled with other passengers, the nuns kept their own company, especially during the first week, when they became terribly seasick from "the constant rocking & heaving of the good ship," *Queen of the West*. Upon recovery, they "acted as Sisters of Mercy" and visited passengers in steerage and second-class. As much as possible, the nuns followed their regular routine. They prayed, read, sewed, and walked the decks of their "floating convent," remembering St. Leo's.[18]

The Sisters of Mercy, who left St. Catherine's convent in Dublin for

New York City on April 13, 1846, in response to a personal appeal from Bishop John Hughes (also Irish-born), had similar experiences aboard the *Montezuma.* The bishop had returned home, but he sent his priest-secretary to accompany Mother Agnes O'Connor and her party of six nuns, a novice, and a postulant across the Atlantic. They started their trip not long after agreeing to accept the bishop's invitation, they traveled first-class, and they became very sick during the first week at sea. Sister Monica O'Doherty wrote that it was "a real purgatory"; there was "so much sickness and sorrow," she said, as they "parted from all that was dear . . . on earth" and sailed "towards the country of independence and Yankeeism!"[19]

Yet there were aspects of their life on ship that proved pleasurable. These sisters, like those from Carlow, enjoyed their walks on deck, where they made their meditations and said their rosaries. The captain and other passengers treated them with "respect and attention," willing to provide "everything [they wished] for." Although the famine that would send millions of Irish to North America had not yet reached its full force, the nuns did not see a hint of it on their English ship. Food was plentiful, and few hotels could have given them more variety. "We have only to say whether we will have fowl or mutton, beef, etc., after which we always have a very nice pie or pudding," wrote Sister Monica. In another letter, she described the "scented soap of a superior kind" and a large "looking glass in which you can have almost a full length view of your extensive perfections." She wondered if their "spirit of mortification" would "suffer shipwreck in the midst of so many delicacies."[20]

They had little to fear in this regard. Once the first wave of Irish nuns reached the New World, ample hardships and challenges awaited them. Almost all would find the weather troublesome. Mother Agnes O'Connor, who felt New York City's "intense [summer] heat very much," anticipated winter so she could "bask in the frost."[21] The Sisters of Mercy, who arrived in Pittsburgh in December 1843, shivered in the cold and snow; the Dominicans from Cabra in Dublin, who settled in New Orleans in 1860, suffered each year from the "scorching sun," the unrelenting humidity, and the pertinacious mosquitoes.[22] Only the Mercy and Presentation nuns, who traveled to San Francisco from Kinsale and Midleton in 1854, considered the climate a blessing. It may have been their unexpected reward for enduring an extremely arduous trip to San Francisco, one that included crossing Panama on the backs of mules.

In the summer of 1854 the Spanish-born archbishop of San Francisco, Joseph Alemany, had sent an Irish priest, Hugh P. Gallagher, to Ireland in search of nuns. Father Gallagher, who thought it would be easier and cheaper to approach the Mercy Sisters in Pittsburgh, was instructed instead to go to the fountainhead. Thus he began his assignment in Dublin, at the Mercy convent on Baggot Street, and successfully completed his mission at the Mercy convent in Kinsale and the Presentation convent in Midleton. Eight Mercy and five Presentation Sisters journeyed from Cork to California, one of the world's most rough-edged frontiers.[23]

Whether on the frontier or in a city, these pioneer sisters experienced physical hardships unequaled by those who would follow in the second wave. The nuns of the first wave lived and worked in convents and schools that were especially unattractive and often unhealthy. Bad weather—excessive heat or bitter cold—simply heightened their loneliness and discomfort; it also contributed to "the dreadful mortality" among them. In Pittsburgh, three Sisters of Mercy died "in one week and two shortly before" as a result of the change of climate, long hours of hard work, and poor living conditions.[24]

In San Francisco, where a mining-camp mentality unsettled both minds and mores, Sister Mary Clare Duggan became mentally ill and Mother Mary Joseph Cronin physically sick. They and Mother Augustine Keane returned to Ireland only two years after their arrival in the United States.[25] These Presentation Sisters had done "much good" among Catholics and Protestants, but Archbishop Alemany knew their convent was then in desperate straits. In March 1857, in a letter to the president of All Hallows College, Archbishop Alemany said the convent needed "a few more subjects (good) not only to do good, but even to secure the existence of the establishment, which has only 2 professed [sisters]! Of whom one may soon die!"[26] The one who remained well and even prospered was Mother Teresa Comerford. She and Mother Frances Warde in Pittsburgh—who also flourished in the United States—were truly arguments for Darwinian survival of the fittest.

The religious women of the first wave, especially their leaders, had strength and vision as well as an abundance of confidence. They tended to be older (usually over twenty when they entered an order) than the young women who journeyed in the second wave.[27] And first-wave nuns often had important family connections, since they frequently came from the most respectable and wealthy Catholic families of Ireland. If not wealthy, they most certainly represented the rural middle class; as daughters of substantial farmers and shopkeepers, they could bring to religious communities sizeable dowries, generally between £200 and £600 depending on time and place.[28]

Although the sisters who went to the United States in the early years knew less about American life than those who came later, the first wave was well educated by nineteenth-century European standards. They knew more than the catechism, having studied literature, mathematics, history, and geography along with needlework, French, music, and drawing. Some had studied abroad, as had been the custom during penal times when Catholic education was prohibited in Ireland. Others were taught by private tutors or governesses, who frequently had been educated on the Continent; still others had attended pay schools in Ireland, once they were established. Whatever the particulars may have been, one fact held true: "the essential feature of female education throughout the nineteenth century was . . . its stratification along social lines."[29]

Mother Teresa Comerford in San Francisco and Mother Frances Warde in Pittsburgh, who were both thirty-three when they left Ireland for the United States, are cases in point. Mother Teresa, daughter of Nicholas Comerford and Margaret Hendrican, was born into an old Norman family at Coolgraney, Gowran, County Kilkenny, in 1821. She received her early education at home from tutors and governesses and later at Catholic academies in Kilkenny and Tulow. On the personal recommendation of the bishop of Ossory, she entered the Presentation convent in Kilkenny and became interested in the missionary movement.[30]

Mother Frances Warde, who was one of the first to reside in the House of Mercy in Dublin, was born at Bellbrook, Mountreath, County Laois, in 1810. She was the daughter of John Warde, a successful merchant, and Mary Maher, a member of one of Ireland's most distinguished Catholic families. Frances received her education at home from tutors and from her older sister, Sarah. In 1833 Sarah also entered the Mercy convent on Baggot Street and later became superior of St. Maries of the Isle in Cork, from where she sent scores of young Irish women to her sister's foundation in the United States.[31]

These women and others like them entered religious life for a variety of reasons. All of them believed they had been called by God to a life of service in the church, but there were other attractions as well. For women of respectable backgrounds who had no occupational alternatives to marriage and motherhood, the new religious orders (more active than contemplative) founded in nineteenth-century Ireland offered an exciting opportunity. They provided such women with an arena in which to use their education, develop their talents, and assert a measure of their independence. "Taking the veil, contrary to contemporary popular belief, meant the beginning not the end of a useful life."[32]

Not surprisingly, nineteenth-century Ireland witnessed a dramatic increase in women entering convents. From 122 nuns in 1800, the number rose to 1,552 in 1850 and to 8,031 in 1901.[33] In 1800 the ratio of nuns to the Irish population was about 1 per 32,000, but in 1900 it grew to approximately 1 per 400.[34] At the beginning of the nineteenth century, 11 convents existed in Ireland; at the end, there were 368, and most were located "south of an imaginary line from Dublin to Galway."[35] It is this wellspring that provided missionaries to faraway places.

But not all who journeyed out in the first wave had privileged backgrounds. Among every group of missionary nuns, there could be found one or two lay sisters; some were professed, and others were still in training. Lay sisters dated from the Middle Ages, when it was customary for wealthy women who entered the cloister to bring their maids with them. However, only the wealthy contributed large dowries, and only they were capable of reading the Latin prayers of the Divine Office. Hence only they were admitted to the "choir." Their maids, who took care of the laborious chores of the monastery, became "lay" sisters.[36]

In nineteenth-century Irish convents lay sisters were, in short, religious servants. For the most part, they came from working-class families who could provide only a small dowry or none at all. The Mercy Sisters, for example, required simply that a lay postulant have "a vocation, a good constitution, and an ordinary education." Lay religious were responsible for "life-maintaining" tasks; they cooked and cleaned, answered the door and gardened, fetched and carried, and did whatever else needed to be done to keep a well-ordered home.[37] Indeed, their work made it possible for choir sisters to teach, nurse, visit the sick, or carry out other activities encouraged by their Rules.

Work, however, was not the only distinction between choir and lay religious. The latter often took simple vows, even in religious orders that had solemn vows, and lay sisters were never expected to recite the Divine Office, even when it was said in English. They sometimes dressed differently from choir nuns (wearing aprons instead of trains, black habits instead of white ones, or small collars instead of large) and usually ate before or after them, not with them. In rank, lay sisters always followed the most junior choir nuns, and in convent elections, lay sisters could not vote or hold office.

Although lay religious were usually not as well educated as choir sisters, they were very often literate. In fact, they became more educated as the century progressed and Ireland's national school system developed. Nevertheless the distinctions in status between choir and lay sisters remained into the twentieth century, probably because servants continued to be indispensable. Religious communities were reluctant to hire lay women as servants—even if they were affordable—because they threatened convent privacy and discipline. At the same time, these communities considered it unjust to deny to lay sisters the opportunity of living as nuns.[38]

The lot of lay religious may have no appeal today, but there is little doubt that some women of working-class families saw in it an opportunity to better their lives. According to a nineteenth-century biography of Mother Catherine McAuley, she did not initially provide for lay sisters in her Institute of Mercy. But she was finally persuaded to do so by some industrious and pious women who had "neither fortune nor education" and were thus unable to seek "admission into any of the religious communities then in Ireland." These women were "not only willing but anxious to make themselves useful in any way that should be appointed for them" in the Mercy order.[39] They were not afraid of the long hours of physical labor that awaited them in convents; they had been introduced to hard work in their homes. Instead they were probably attracted to a community of educated and religious women, where they would receive regular meals, a full night's sleep, periods of recreation each day, and care when they became ill or old.[40]

Women of the small farming and working classes did not lead easy lives in nineteenth-century Ireland. Many of their chores were exceedingly "painstaking and back-breaking." A traveler in Galway in 1834 noticed women carrying sacks of potatoes weighing about 250 pounds. About twenty years later, a Galway driver remarked that women were "graight slaves in this counthry . . . they carry loads as would do for horses"; and as late as 1880, teenage girls in Mayo were seen doing "the work of cattle."[41] At night, when the day's chores were done, they would "card and spin wool or flax until . . . [they] would fall asleep over the wheel with fatigue." Women married to successful farmers and shopkeepers also worked hard, but they usually had servants to help them.[42]

Women's place in Irish society may not have been enviable before the famine, but it became even less so in the years following it. Women lost a good deal of the economic independence and autonomy that had accompanied their lives as farmers and spinners. As farmwork became less labor intensive and the textile industry contracted, women forfeited their main source of income and subsequently took on more household duties from which they received no financial compensation (and probably only limited personal satisfaction). Although cities continued to offer the possibility of domestic service, few semiskilled jobs or white-collar positions existed anywhere until late in the century. If single, educated women aspired to something more, they could become teachers or nuns; poor women or women with family responsibilities obviously could not.[43]

Marriage, which was symbolized by "the pooling of property," was not a romantic escape for young women disheartened or confused about the future. Daughters from farm families normally brought cash rather than land to "the match" and worked to earn the money. Farmers with many daughters did not feel obligated to dower more than one; it was simply too expensive. By 1880, a modest match in the west of Ireland—an area that suffered a series of crop failures and became the center of land-reform agitation—cost ten times more than a passage to America.[44] Thus, in a society dominated by farmers and lacking in employment opportunities for women, it was not surprising that daughters, out of habit or obligation, left the family farm in great numbers. "Born with their faces to the West," they made up the ranks of those religious women who journeyed out in the second wave.[45]

The Second Wave

The heavy influx of Irish immigrants to the United States did not end with the Great Famine. In fact, between 1851 and 1920, 3.3 million Irish settled in American locations. By 1885, single women came to dominate this emigration, and they tended to originate in those counties—only eight in all Ireland, and seven located in the west and south—that lost women in larger numbers than men. Most Irish women traveled alone and were met by a family member in cities on the other side, where they found jobs as domestic servants.[46] But there was also a smaller group of Irish women in motion, who almost never traveled by themselves; they became Catholic sisters in a fast-growing immigrant church. Unlike those who preceded them, they were not responding to personal invitations from Irish-born bishops and priests. Instead they were recruited by those nuns who had gone out as missionaries in the first wave.

Sisters who came early to the United States found the needs of the transplanted Irish as immense and diverse as the country itself. In New York City, for example, Mercy Sisters from Baggot Street, who founded a House of Mercy for homeless immigrant women, were nearly overwhelmed by the "hundreds of starving emigrants" who arrived there "every day." In their first year, the nuns located positions for more than 1,200 women and never sheltered fewer than 200. Yet Mother Agnes O'Connor confessed that they had to turn away "as many poor girls as would fill a poor house."[47]

Mother Baptist Russell, superior of the Mercy Sisters in San Francisco, found her community in similar circumstances—understaffed and overworked. Shortly after their arrival, the nuns became involved in a wide range of activities, as Sisters of Mercy were wont to do.[48] They opened schools, to be sure, but they also founded a House of Mercy for unemployed women and a Magdalen asylum for ex-prostitutes and unwed mothers. Their major occupation, however, involved caring for the sick; they nursed cholera victims in the 1855 epidemic, then accepted charge of the local public hospital and later built a Catholic one. They always served everyone, unlike the nuns in Ireland, whose ministry concentrated on native Catholics. One San Francisco sister remarked in a letter home: "To describe the multitudes that have found shelter under St. Mary's roof would be a difficult task. I do not know any country unrepresented. Of all religions, we have had members."[49]

Although Mother Baptist received some staffing assistance from Ireland, she probably felt like Pittsburgh's Mother Frances Warde, who could have "put [to work] at least 20 . . . in this City *and forty* in the Diocese."[50] Both of these energetic and ambitious nuns received Irish recruits through the efforts of friends and relatives, and both returned one time to Ireland seeking their own. Mother Baptist, who also came from a distinguished Catholic family, had recruiting help from her mother as well as from the Sisters of Mercy at Kinsale and elsewhere. In 1876 she went back to Ireland in search of postulants, made a round of Mercy convents, and brought back eleven—more women than in the original band of eight.[51]

Mother Frances Warde, who would eventually establish thirteen Mercy foundations in the United States, returned to Ireland only two years after her own journey out. Following this 1845 visit, she never needed to return, because her older sister, Sarah, who had become Mother Josephine, unfailingly responded to Mother Frances's special appeals for "very well educated young persons."[52] It is unclear exactly how many women Mother Josephine sent from Cork to the United States, but many tell the story that a county official once said of her: "That woman will not leave a bright girl in the County for a man to marry."[53]

Mother Josephine, who came from Dublin to Cork in 1837, was the superior of the Mercy nuns in Cork for nearly forty years. Her "favorite apostolate was to send young girls" to convents established by her sister in the United States. In fact, Mother Frances's biographer concluded that by 1879, when Mother Josephine died, the "two Warde sisters [had become] a kind of two-woman, two-continent collaboration in the expansion of the Sisters of Mercy in the West."[54]

Mother Teresa Comerford, who found herself in San Francisco with only one nun after the others returned to Ireland in 1856, proved equally resourceful. She first called for help from friends and relatives in Ireland and received it. Because of her difficult circumstances, the superior and the bursar of the Presentation convent in Kilkenny, along with two postulants, volunteered for the San Francisco mission. In 1861 her own sister, Sister M. Bernard, a young religious in the Presentation convent in Midleton, also responded to Mother Teresa's call.[55]

On two occasions Mother Teresa went back to Ireland in search of recruits. Her first visit was reported in the local newspaper, the *Kilkenny Journal.* The editorials that appeared on March 2 and 30, 1867, explained Mother Teresa's plight. She was the superior of a community of "many Irish ladies" who were responsible for over 1,100 schoolchildren. She had returned to her native land to "procure as many subjects as are requisite for carrying out the great objects to which she has devoted her life." The paper announced that she would be in Kilkenny for a fortnight and (presumably) available for interviewing possible candidates for the religious life. There was "no doubt that a zealous band of missioners" would accompany her to California. And eight "accomplished young ladies" did so, arriving in San Francisco in June 1867.[56]

Mother Teresa returned to Ireland again in 1879, not simply to recruit a group of volunteers but rather to establish a "Missionary Novitiate" that would prepare middle-class women for work in San Francisco and Berkeley. The Presentation nuns had by this time opened three nonpaying schools and needed religious to staff them. Few American women were attracted to this cloistered teaching order, and often those who were could not afford the customary dowries. In Ireland, where the Presentation Sisters were founded to teach poor children, the nuns' dowries were invested and used to support them during their lifetimes. Thus Mother Teresa hoped to solve a major problem in California by building a novitiate in Kilcock, County Kildare.[57]

She probably was aware of the increasing competition in the 1860s and 1870s for Irish women who had religious vocations. Not only were Irish nuns of the first wave in need of postulants, but so were religious communities in the United States that had originated in other European countries, particularly France. In fact, as their founders settled in and their responsibilities grew, they became desperately in need of zealous women who were educated and spoke English. A good example is the Sisters of the Incarnate Word and Blessed Sacrament, who were brought by Bishop Jean Marie Odin from Lyons, France, to Brownsville, Texas, in 1852. Thirteen years later, when Mother St. Claire Valentine traveled to Europe in search of volunteers, she returned with twelve women—eight from France and four from Ireland. The Irish recruits were members of the sodality at George's Hill, the large Presentation convent in the center of Dublin.[58]

During the 1870s, Mother Angela Gillespie of the Sisters of the Holy

Cross also looked to Ireland for a supply of women to join her order, a community of French nuns brought from Le Mans to Notre Dame, Indiana, in 1843 by Father Edward Sorin. For nearly three months in the spring and summer of 1873, "from early morning until ten at night," Mother Angela and her companions had "not a moment to call [their] own" as they searched for candidates. The nuns began their recruiting tour in Dublin with a visit to Cardinal Cullen. With his blessing, they accepted overnight accommodations from the Mercy Sisters on Baggot Street and then went to George's Hill, where they spoke to young women in the Presentation Sisters' school and sodality. Here and elsewhere, Irish sisters—whom Mother Angela described as "ladies of high birth and culture"—welcomed them in convents and schools at Kildare, Limerick, Thurles, Cashel, Clonmel, Carrick on Suir, Waterford, and Cork.[59]

Wherever they went, Mother Angela explained the heavy demands placed on the Holy Cross Sisters in the United States as a result of "the great Catholic emigration from Ireland." She wanted "to obtain efficient, holy, and heroic ladies to aid [them] in saving souls in America." Besides possessing a true vocation, interested women were "to be in good health, educated, and not over twenty-five years of age." The dowry was "of minor consideration—£50 being all that [was] strictly required." Even though Mother Angela found that the southern cities had been "thoroughly gleaned" by Dominican and Mercy nuns who had preceded her, she left Ireland with twenty aspirants "of good, plain education but no means, who wish[ed] to be nuns." The following year, she returned and recruited another twenty-five.[60]

The young women who joined the Holy Cross Sisters in Indiana would not have met Mother Teresa Comerford's criteria. At Kilcock, she did not want to recruit individuals of "no means"; she wanted "ladies of independent rank" whose abilities—as well as dowries—would support the California mission she had led almost from the beginning. In this enterprise Mother Teresa was assisted by her cousin Reverend Thomas Geoghegan, the parish priest at Kilcock. He built a "magnificent" convent, novitiate, and school that were financed out of inherited funds and donations made by wealthy parishioners. Their complex opened in December 1879 and was dedicated the following May.[61]

Mother Teresa and Father Geoghegan had every reason to believe this undertaking would succeed. They had received authorization from Pope Leo XIII to begin, and they had been encouraged along the way by the appropriate Irish and American bishops. By June 1880, 150 girls were enrolled in the school and six postulants had become novices. But, although the school has continued to the present, the novitiate did not endure. Mother Teresa, who found the Irish climate extraordinarily severe and became ill, asked permission to return to California, where she died in August 1881. The new archbishop of the San Francisco diocese, Patrick William Riordan, who did not want a novitiate in Ireland, refused to support the institution. Yet, before closing its doors, it sent fifteen Irish sisters (all were apparently dowered but one) to the Presentation convents in California during the 1880s.[62] This small group of nuns of "independent rank" hardly compared, however, to the much larger number of Irish women of "no means" who journeyed out in the second wave.

The Kilcock novitiate was not as original as it may appear. Its model was most likely All Hallows Missionary College, founded in Dublin in 1842 by Father John Hand, to train priests for the foreign missions—those places where Irish emigrants had settled and where they were feared in danger of losing their faith. California, along with New South Wales and Victoria in Australia, became "one of the most concentrated mission fields of the College." Archbishop Alemany, who brought Irish nuns to San Francisco in 1854, had visited All Hallows in 1850 in search of priests for his diocese. From then until the end of the century, the college was "the main supplier of its missionaries"; at one point, 90 percent of the priests in northern California and Nevada were from there. And those priests supported Mother Teresa Comerford in her recruitment initiatives.[63]

Mother Teresa was neither the first nor the last who wanted to create an All Hallows–type college for women. Mother Bridget Carroll, superior of Dublin's Presentation convent at George's Hill and good friend to Father Hand, had hoped in the 1840s to aid him in realizing his "grandiose vision" of building a seminary that would include nuns as well as priests. Hand's untimely death in 1846 prevented their dream from coming true.[64] In the 1850s and 1860s, Mother Josephine Warde, superior of Cork's Mercy convent and sister of Mother Frances Warde, also wanted to establish a women's college, similar to All Hallows, where aspirants to the religious life could be trained for missions in the United States. But she died in 1879, the same year that Mother Teresa Comerford's novitiate began in Kilcock.[65]

In 1884 the Sisters of Mercy in Callan, County Kilkenny, opened St. Brigid's Missionary School, a "second All Hallows" that continued until 1958. During these years St. Brigid's trained more than 1,900 young women for convents primarily in Australia, New Zealand, and the United States. Although its purpose was identical to that of All Hallows, in its financial structure St. Brigid's more closely resembled the Apostolic School of Mungret, near Limerick, founded by Jesuit William Ronan in 1880. It educated "poor Irish lads . . . for the Foreign Missions" at a cost of £25 a year per student. The school also accepted donations of £700 to create a "burse" that was used to support students of "no means." At St. Brigid's a burse held £600, and the yearly cost of maintaining an aspirant remained £22 well into the twentieth century. Unlike All Hallows, however, St. Brigid's never received financial support from the Society for the Propagation of the Faith.[66]

Mothers Michael Maher and Joseph Rice deserve credit for the foundation, operation, and longevity of this unique missionary school. Mother Michael, superior of the Mercy convent at Callan and a member of one of the country's most renowned Catholic families, decided in 1881 to establish St. Brigid's. She had for a long time been interested in the revival of the Catholic Church in Ireland and the expansion of its missionary movement, influenced as she was by her two prominent relatives, Cardinals Cullen of Dublin and Patrick Moran of Sydney, Australia, formerly bishop of Ossory.[67] It is undoubtedly true that these two nuns could not have undertaken such a project without the approval of their local bishop, Moran, who was Mother Michael's cousin and friend. It is likewise true that St. Brigid's Missionary School never would have succeeded without the resourcefulness and dedication of these women. When the school opened its doors in 1884, Bishop Moran left Ireland for a post in Australia. But that same year Mother Joseph was appointed "sister in charge" and remained so for nearly thirty years.[68]

The first group of young women to leave St. Brigid's went to Australia. In fact, according to an undated list of 1,204 aspirants trained at Callan and their subsequent destinations, the largest number (359) settled in Australia, New Zealand, and Tasmania; the second largest number (256) made their homes in the United States. Others went to Africa (165), Canada (44), India and Ceylon (54), France (49), South America (21), Central America (16), Belgium (20), Jamaica (12), and Java (4). Another fairly large group (204) stayed in the British Isles. Many of these religious emigrants became Sisters of Mercy, but many joined other religious orders, through invitation or by preference.[69]

The women who entered St. Brigid's came from nearly every part of Ireland, with a majority from towns in the south and west. Some could afford the annual fee of £22; others could not and thus occupied "free" places, for which there was no expense "for pension, nor for passage." These places were offered to women with teaching certificates or with experience as monitresses. Because the demand for teachers was so great both in the United States and Australia, and because struggling religious orders often were willing to pay the annual fee in order to receive aspirants who would in time teach in their schools, Mother Joseph assured the superior of the Mercy Convent in Athlone that "we could give a free place almost at any time to a *well* educated postulant, or rather aspirant."[70]

St. Brigid's young women were "aspirants," not postulants. They were at least fourteen years old, had completed their primary education, and desired to become nuns. However, they had not "entered" religious life, even though their daily routine resembled those who had. Because many religious communities abroad wanted postulants but could not find them in sufficient numbers in their own countries and did not want to import them directly from Ireland for fear "of having to send them back again in the event of failure," they turned to St. Brigid's. It was "a kind of preliminary novitiate," where vocations could be tested and educational deficiencies ameliorated.[71]

Those who had vocations gradually adapted to the regimen at St. Brigid's, where they learned the habits and rituals of convent life. All rose each day at 5:30 A.M. and retired each evening shortly after 9:00 P.M. The hours in between were filled with prayer, classes, study, chores, and recreation. As the aspirants chose to leave the world of their families, they were restricted to the confines of St. Brigid's; they could not, for example, write to outsiders or see visitors without the superior's permission. Encouraged "to act as ladies," they also received instruction in "personal neatness" and "table etiquette." In their formal classes, they did not repeat what they should have learned in the national schools; instead they concentrated on languages (French, Italian, and Latin), music (vocal, piano, and violin), drawing, and painting. They also took courses in the "best methods of teaching."[72]

Education gradually replaced *dowry* as the all-important word in the search for religious women of the second wave. Especially during the last decades of the nineteenth century, Catholic bishops and priests considered nuns who could teach in America's developing network of parochial schools as nearly priceless—certainly more valuable than any dowry. As economists would say, human capital was far preferable to monetary capital.

Bishop Eugene O'Connell of the Diocese of Grass Valley (later Sacramento) was clear on these points. In 1870, he wrote the president of All Hallows that he would not spend any more on priests because his diocese had a "far more urgent need . . . of teachers for our children . . . than of Priests to administer Sacraments."[73] This need became even greater in 1884 following the Third Plenary Council of Baltimore, at which the bishops voted to require within two years a school "near each church were [one] does not exist."[74] No wonder that an irritated sodality moderator at Harold's Cross in Dublin responded that she was "training *Religious* not schoolmistresses," when she received a frantic request from Chicago for teaching nuns, accompanied by "a liberal offer to pay all expenses."[75]

Children of Mary sodalities were a rich source of religious vocations. A Loreto Sister in Dublin wisely advised missionary nuns in Mauritius to "establish the Children of Mary among the boarders" and "many will enter the novitiate."[76] By the late nineteenth century, nearly all the schools in Ireland had sodalities, where girls were taught to express their piety through frequent confession and communion. They also took part in many other devotions—rosary, forty hours, benedictions, novenas, retreats, and so on—that revolutionized the Catholic Church in the years after the famine.[77]

Although boarding schools were the first to sponsor sodalities, "poor" schools and parishes with many working-class women who could not afford to continue their education also organized them. In Dublin the Presentation Sisters at George's Hill and the Sisters of Charity at Harold's Cross had the largest of these sodalities. At George's Hill, Sister M. Stanislaus Donohuc, moderator of the Children of Mary Sodality for thirty-five years, sent nearly sixty young women to the United States between 1862 and 1897. A majority entered the Sisters of the Incarnate Word and Blessed Sacrament in their Texas convents at Brownsville, Victoria, and Houston. Mary Dillon, a Child of Mary who journeyed to Victoria in 1867, returned to George's Hill at least twice as Mother Gabriel and brought many of her own "Children" back to Houston, where she was founder and superior of the convent from 1873 to 1895.[78]

The sodality at Our Lady's Hospice, Harold's Cross, was especially popular among young women who worked in factories nearby. The blue ribbons and silver medals presented annually to each member at a special ceremony, presided over by Archbishop William J. Walsh of Dublin (1885–1921) and reported in the *Irish Catholic,* served to attract neighborhood girls. But older teenagers, too poor to remain in school, also found a comfortable place in this sodality, largely because of its moderator. Sister Mary Eustace Eaton, who was thirty years old and a Sister of Charity for only three years when she took charge of the Children of Mary in 1868, was a convert, an Englishwoman, and had finished her education in a French convent school in Paris. For an unknown reason, she developed a staunch commitment to Dublin's "struggling girls." She was concerned about their religious instruction, to be sure, but she was equally bent upon helping them improve their lives.[79]

Sister Mary Eustace showed her interest in the sodalists' social lives by organizing gatherings on Sundays, the only day most of them did not work. There were breakfasts after Mass or at the close of retreats, followed by jam-tart parties with music and singing in the afternoons. She also began night classes for those who had difficulty reading or writing.[80] And when a third of her night-school pupils went out on strike at the Greenmount Spinning Company in September 1890, she supported them, contending that they were "wretchedly paid" and heavily fined for petty reasons. They returned to work only after the company's owner, Frederic W. Pim, promised to raise their wages and abolish many of the fines. Sister Mary Eustace boasted to Archbishop Walsh that "Pim has a higher opinion of 'our girls' than he ever had before."[81]

Most of the sodality members married and over the years brought their babies to Harold's Cross to be baptized. Those who did not marry and who expressed a desire to become nuns generally found situations in convents outside Ireland, where they did not need dowries. During her thirty-eight years as moderator, Sister Mary Eustace sent nearly four hundred women to the United States alone. Much of her time-consuming work of finding places and arranging passages for them became easier once Archbishop Walsh took a personal interest in the sodality and began publicly referring to it as another All Hallows.[82] During the summer months, she was besieged by recruiter-nuns looking for postulants and was forced to spend "no end of time . . . interviewing them." Exasperated by their numbers and their persistence, she wished "so many of these nuns were not allowed to travel about."[83]

Young women from the Harold's Cross sodality became Mercy, Presentation, Good Shepherd, and St. Joseph of Carondelet Sisters in the United States. But by far the largest number (more than a hundred by 1904) entered the Sisters of Charity of the Incarnate Word in San Antonio, Texas. Sister Mary Eustace liked this religious community above all others—and for good reason. By 1899, seven of her "Children" had become superiors in it. When Mother Mary Cleophas (Rosanna Hurst, Child of Mary, 1883) returned in May 1904 as a recruiter, the sodality gave her "a great welcome." And Sister Mary Eustace advised her "to start at once for the Provinces so as to be the first in the field before the country is deluged by other nuns." In August, when Mother Mary Cleophas left Dublin's North Wall embarkation pier for San Antonio, thirty-eight women accompanied her.[84]

Four years earlier Mother Mary John O'Shaughnessy, another Incarnate Word nun whom Sister Mary Eustace preferred, had brought out forty women "from different parts of Ireland" (though the majority came from Harold's Cross). Mother Mary John, who was born in Cahirciveen, County Kerry, was also a former Child of Mary. She would later be elected superior general of the Sisters of Charity of the Incarnate Word, and Mother Mary Cleophas would become superior of the order's St. Louis Province.[85]

By the 1890s, women who emigrated to the United States as nuns came without dowries, which had ceased to be required because the need for religious women was so great. Mother Joseph Butler, who had been recruited in 1885 from the Presentation convent in Bandon, County Cork, to the Dakotas, did not want women from wealthy homes. Although her order had begun "by taking in rich girls," she looked for "poor ones" who were willing to work hard. And she found several in the Sisters of Mercy's Industrial School in Kinsale on each of her four recruiting trips to Ireland between 1903 and 1913.[86]

Advertisements in newspapers occasionally stated what had already become general practice. In 1898 and 1899, for example, the Mercy Sisters in Hornellsville, New York, ran a series of ads saying they would "receive as novices respectable young girls of good education who feel called to the religious state. . . . no dowry will be required."[87] But more often than not the subject of dowry was never mentioned. Time and again during the early 1900s, the Galveston (Texas) Sisters of Charity of the Incarnate Word, well known in Tipperary for their care of orphans and the sick and aged, simply encouraged "young ladies desiring to become Sisters of Charity on the American mission" to apply. In the years after 1882, when Bishop Nicholas Gallagher of Galveston forbade bringing any non-English-speaking candidates from France to his diocese, almost all of the Incarnate Word's recruits came from the west of Ireland. In fact, beginning in 1894, a succession of mothers general—Mothers Benedict Kennedy, Mechtilde Ryan, and Columba D'Arcy—had grown up either in Tipperary town or county.[88]

Young women of "no means" in the west and south of Ireland were often well educated despite the lack of free secondary schools. The Presentation Order, founded by Honoria ("Nano") Nagle in Cork to instruct the poor, had been teaching girls and training monitresses in the schools of County Kerry, for example, since the 1830s. Forty years later, the nuns in the Presentation Convent National School in Castleisland taught subjects including the basics as well as geography, French, drawing, music, needlework, and bookkeeping.[89] Thus daughters of farmers and shopkeepers came out "fitted for the practical work of life." As the New York *Freeman's Journal* observed in 1884: "No better element has been mingled with the population of the United States than the daughters of poor Irish farmers, whose rich and only dowry was the training received in these schools."[90]

With the question of dowry removed and the demand increasing for nuns in American schools, hospitals, and orphanages, Irish women who wished to become religious could choose the type of work that best suited their abilities and personal preferences. Those who were educated usually joined teaching orders. Individuals who were not sometimes did, but more frequently they entered communities that cared for the sick, orphaned, and aged. And, because nearly every small farmer and workman had "dear and near friends in America," their daughters often chose religious orders where they too had family members and friends.[91]

Molly Mackey, who in many ways symbolizes the religious emigrants of the second wave (just as Mothers Frances Warde and Teresa Comerford do the first), chose to enter the Sisters of St. Joseph of Carondelet in Troy, New York, where an aunt or cousin, Sister John Baptist Mackey, preceded her. One of ten children, Molly grew up on a small farm in Templemore, County Tipperary, in a cottage with three rooms. She attended the Castleiney National School and when she was sixteen went to the United States with a couple of friends to become nuns.[92]

In letters home Molly told of her happiness and good health, having had four teeth filled "by a very good Dentist." She hoped her parents thought she had "chosen the better part"; she felt she had, especially after becoming Sister Agnes Frances on March 19, 1899. She said that "if people only knew what happiness is found in religion," convents could not "contain all those who would wish to enter."[93] After her father died, she urged her mother to send her youngest daughters to school regularly. For, if they did well, Sister Agnes Frances expected them to join her and "share [her] happiness."[94] Had she not died of tuberculosis in 1900, there is a good chance that one sister—if not both—would have followed her to Troy.

Before Sister Patricia Prendiville died in a Dominican convent in New Orleans in 1907, she managed to bring out two of six sisters. Nora Prendiville, who was one of eleven children, went to the Castleisland National School until she became a pupil at the Dominican boarding school at Cabra in Dublin. In 1889, at the age of twenty, she and five others journeyed to New Orleans, where a contingent of Dominicans had established a foundation in 1860.[95] Mother John Flanagan, the founder, had come to New Orleans at the invitation of Father Jeremiah Moynihan, a friend of her cousin, Father John Flanagan, a priest at a neighboring parish. In 1877 Mother John brought her two sisters to New Orleans; one became a Dominican, and the other lived near the convent and did the nuns' buying and odd jobs.[96]

The recruitment of young women by sisters who had emigrated earlier represents a previously untold form of chain and serial migration that was so prevalent among the millions who left all parts of Europe from the 1840s to 1914. Most of these emigrants followed established trails, blazed already by members of whatever group they belonged to—family, neighborhood, village, synagogue, or labor organization.[97] In the case of Irish nuns, younger ones of the second wave followed closely behind those of the first, often to American convents of the same religious orders. This chain of migration was, however, made even stronger by kinship, sodality, school, and parish links.

Chosen Paths and Common Mission

It was not by chance that several thousand Irish women emigrated to the United States as nuns (or to become nuns) during the nineteenth and early twentieth centuries. They came with a purpose and by invitation. Although different in many ways, religious emigrants of the first and second waves shared a common culture and mission. Proud of their Irish Catholic heritage, they were women of strong faith, dedicated to the work of the church in missionary territory and blessed at home for their willingness "to follow and work amongst Irish exiles for the pure love of God."[98]

Sisters of the first wave, especially their leaders, were generally older and more adventuresome and self-confident than those who came later. Invited personally by Irish bishops and priests, these nuns graciously tackled any assignment given to them. Except for those who were cloistered, their ministries were surprisingly varied. Besides teaching, they opened employment bureaus, houses for unwed mothers, and makeshift hospitals for epidemic victims, and they taught adult education courses for green immigrants. Daughters of respectable Catholic parents, these founders related easily to bishops and priests, who in turn treated them as cousins or daughters, since they frequently knew their families. Thus nuns of the first wave saw themselves in league with the hierarchy in expanding the Irish Catholic Church. When Mothers Frances Warde and Teresa Comerford opened new schools, for instance, they received the clergy's support for extending the church's influence.

The pioneering nuns of the first wave recruited younger, more malleable women who would in time become consolidators rather than builders. Following the American bishops' decision in 1884 to place most sisters in classrooms, emigrants of the second wave usually became schoolteachers or administrators and developed more formal relationships with the clergy, ones that tended to mirror those they knew in Ireland. Family connections with priests and bishops were for them less the motivator of their nascent vocations than the adult women of the new, activist Irish orders. Following the famine, their convents had formed "a network over the land" where young women observed an appealing, alternative way of life to marriage and childbearing.[99] But without dowries, they could become only lay nuns. In known instances of superiors petitioning bishops to allow them to make an exception and to accept into choir rank a "proposed postulant . . . without dower," the requests were denied.[100]

Growing up in large families of farmers, shopkeepers, or laborers, daughters understood that scarcity limited their life choices. They also knew that Irish society offered them little in the way of social or economic benefits and that emigration had become something of a tradition—at times even an obligation. In this context, religious life abroad presented a tantalizing possibility, especially to "young girls [who] had nothing to look forward to but a loveless marriage, hard work, poverty, a large family and often a husband who drank."[101] However, most viewed their vocations not only as an escape or an adventure, but also as an opportunity to enlarge the scope of their lives.

At the same time, the decision to become a nun in the United States gave anxious parents a way to "offload" one daughter (or more) and yet confer a degree of status on all. The daughter would have chosen "the better part"; and her mother, by sacrificing a child, would become "the mother of a nun." Then, as Mrs. Luke Latimer discovered, "everyone would be kind to her . . . and everyone would treat her with respect."[102] Although most parents would not deliberately have encouraged their daughters to enter foreign communities simply to be freed from providing for them, they must have welcomed these decisions all the same.

The second wave, like the first, traveled to the United States in groups. They were not, however, escorted by bishops or priests, and they usually had second-class accommodations rather than first-. Nuns of the first wave often went out in groups of five to seven; women of the second wave were more likely to travel in groups of ten to thirty, and larger parties were not unheard-of. In February 1898, Sister Mary Paul McHenry, a native of County Clare, brought out aboard the *Pennland* fifty-four recruits from Tipperary, Clare, Limerick, Kilkenny, and Laois to Troy, New York, and St. Louis, Missouri, where the Sisters of St. Joseph of Carondelet had their motherhouse.[103] These women spent the night before leaving Ireland in Queenstown (now Cobh) at the Hennessy Hotel, a popular lodging house for such groups. The proprietor, Richard Hennessy, catered to large parties by locating a ticket agency and a currency exchange on the ground floor, attending personally to their special needs, and finally escorting them to the correct quay. From there, they boarded a tender that ferried them to an ocean liner that took them to the United States.[104]

The weeks spent traveling were filled with such excitement and adventure that they resembled a slumber party more than a retreat. One woman wrote in a letter home that she and her companions had wanted to dance and "have a good night's enjoyment before leaving Ireland," but that "Mr. Hennessy ordered all to bed at an early hour."[105] Sister Mary Ailbe O'Kelly, who entered the Sisters of St. Joseph from County Tipperary in 1912, recalled years later that she and her friends had "had more fun on that boat"—so much fun that other passengers thought they had been "let loose out of an orphanage."[106]

The second wave did not experience much of the apprehension that sisters of the first wave felt on their "floating convents." Because so many family members and friends had emigrated and sent back accounts of their new lives, America had become in a very real sense "a home away from home"—certainly not foreign missionary territory like India or Africa. A young woman who traveled by train from New York to Silver City, New Mexico, in 1907, commented that people living in the Arizona desert appeared "up-to-date." She also reported that, once the sadness of leaving had passed, she and her companions had enjoyed their experiences. Indeed, they considered themselves fortunate and possibly the subject of envy: "It seems to be always true that 'he who goes is happier by far than those he leaves behind.' Our dear home friends might be very jealous if they saw us."[107]

Was there reason for those who were left behind to envy emigrants of the first and second waves? Were these women "successful"? In short, had they enlarged the scope of their lives through service to others in a country not their own? This is a case of immigration for opportunity's sake, but not economic opportunity in the usual sense, in that economic gain and material comfort were not the primary motivating factors, as they were for most emigrants who left Europe for America in the nineteenth and early twentieth centuries. The women who left Ireland as nuns (or to become nuns) first sought opportunities that were spiritual, psychological, and nonmaterial. Religious life did provide them security, but other options probably would have done so as well.

Did they find what they sought? Obviously, young women like Molly Mackey, who died of tuberculosis shortly after arriving (as many did), did not realize their aspirations; nor did those who discovered that religious life in the United States did not suit them and returned to Ireland. Some, largely in the first wave, went back as nuns—as did the Ursuline Sisters from Cork, who spent only three years in New York, and the Presentation Sisters from Midleton, who left San Francisco after two years. Others who were never professed, primarily in the second wave, returned as lay women. And some, like Kathleen Macken, who left the Sisters of St. Joseph of Carondelet before profession, remained in the United States. Since Macken had no one to return to in Ireland, the nuns found her temporary quarters in Wheeling, West Virginia.[108]

Irish emigrant women who lived out their lives as religious in the United States did not always achieve what they had hoped. Many who were not educated became lay sisters.[109] Distinctions between lay and choir nuns did not completely disappear; in some cases, as historian Margaret Susan Thompson has shown, the distinctions remained all too long, especially in orders with strong ties to the Old World.[110] In other instances, women chose to live as lay sisters, believing it was "a hundred times better to knit a pair of socks humbly for the glory of God than to write the finest poem or symphony for mere self-glorification."[111] Sister Philomena Mosbacher, a lay Sister of Mercy in Erie, Pennsylvania, determined at thirteen "never to go to any other school and to avoid all worldly knowledge." But some, who emigrated to improve their opportunities, learned after arriving that they were "to stand and wait" behind the nuns of choir rank. They clearly resented it.[112]

Sister Mary Eustochia Devine, a lay religious born in Smerwick near Ballyferriter in 1851, had a disappointment of another kind. Although she never learned to read and write, she knew how to milk cows and make butter. To escape this farmwork, she accepted an invitation from her brother, a priest in Omaha, Nebraska, to keep house at the rectory. She later joined the Sisters of Charity of the Blessed Virgin Mary in Dubuque, Iowa, hoping to become a "housekeeper in a big convent—maybe in Chicago where she had relatives." Instead she was assigned to the dairy at the motherhouse, where she spent fifty years.[113] Perhaps Sister Mary Eustochia should have remained a farm woman on the Dingle Peninsula. It seems she would not have agreed, because she was influential in bringing out nine family members (nieces and cousins) to join the order she had entered in 1880. Although no one can measure the personal success of another's life, by all external and conventional measures most of these women were "successful." Those who became teachers, nurses, and administrators achieved in the United States what they probably could not have achieved had they remained in Ireland. Because of their success, the emigrants who journeyed out to do as they did continued to arrive well into the twentieth century.

2 Walking Nuns:
Chicago's Irish Sisters of Mercy

Chicagoans, like Dubliners, called them "walking nuns," those first Sisters of Mercy who refused to remain behind convent walls. Upon arriving in Chicago in 1846, they took to heart the counsel of their Irish founder, Catherine McAuley, who encouraged them to remember the words of St. Paul and "go into the middle of a perverse world." She told them not to dilly-dally, nor to be afraid; for the poor, the illiterate, and the sick "need help today, not next week."[1] These instructions were unusual—revolutionary, in fact. Prior to the 1800s, nuns had seldom, if ever, been seen in Ireland's streets or alleys. Yet several decades later, the Sisters of Mercy had high visibility in Irish towns and villages as well as in many English, Australian, and American cities.

Known by contemporaries, but lost to history—that, sadly, is the circumstance in which Catholic sisterhoods tend to find themselves today. It is curious that such a compassionate and competent group of women have so small a place in the history of Chicago and the United States, especially considering how inclusive American history has become— it has admitted minorities and women of nearly every kind. Yet nuns continue to evoke little interest.[2] Early on they were ignored because they were women and also immigrants. But today the history of women

Originally published as "Walking Nuns: Irish Sisters of Mercy," in Ellen Skerrett, ed., *At the Crossroads: Old St. Patrick's and the Chicago Irish* (Chicago: Loyola Press, 1997), 39–51, 139–44.

and immigration are rich and full fields. Have religious communities of women been overlooked or possibly dismissed because they are Catholic? Despite the sophistication of American historians and the broad range of topics they research, many seem to believe that religious women were backward whereas secular women were forward-looking and progressive. Yet Catholic sisters frequently challenged widely held assumptions about a laissez-faire economy, blurred the public-private divide between men and women, and reached across religious and racial boundaries to address the needs of their neighbors. Thus, to overlook the efforts of nuns in a city like Chicago is to lose a significant part of its past. From early in the nineteenth century, according to a prominent Catholic layman and civic leader, sisters were "everywhere, active, and indefatigable" in ministering to the less fortunate and building social-service institutions that would provide for the health and well-being of generations.[3]

Not a Moment to Spare

On September 23, 1846, five Sisters of Mercy arrived in Chicago and established themselves as the first and, for the next ten years, the only community of nuns in the city. Mother Agatha (Margaret) O'Brien, born in County Carlow in 1822, was appointed superior. She and the other four traveled to Chicago in the company of Father Walter Quarter, brother of Bishop William Quarter, who had invited them, and Mother Frances Xavier Warde, the American founder who had led the Mercys to Pittsburgh from Ireland in 1843. After a brief stay, she returned to Pittsburgh, leaving the future of this frontier foundation in the capable hands of Mother Agatha.[4]

Although she was only twenty-four years old when she arrived in Chicago, Mother Agatha was someone to be reckoned with. She was one of seventeen children born to the wife of a barrelmaker. Educated by the Presentation nuns, she entered the Sisters of Mercy in Carlow in 1843 as a lay sister and worked in the convent kitchen. As discussed in Chapter 1, it was common in Ireland at this time for working-class girls who could not provide a dowry and who were usually not well-educated to become lay rather than choir nuns. Responsible for a full array of "life-maintaining" tasks, lay sisters cooked, cleaned, gardened, shopped, cared for the sick, and whatever else was necessary to provide for a well-run home. Although poor, Margaret O'Brien was educated and had abilities that distinguished her. Thus, when she received the Mercy habit and her religious name in Pittsburgh in 1844, she did so as a choir nun. The Irish-born Bishop Michael O'Connor, who had invited the sisters to Pittsburgh, recognized her potential and refused to be deprived of her services "because her father happened to be a poor man in Ireland." Later the bishop recalled that Mother Agatha was "capable of ruling a nation."[5]

When the Sisters of Mercy arrived in Chicago, it was a rude western outpost of fewer than 20,000 people. The nuns took up residence in what had been the bishop's house at Madison Street and Michigan Avenue. They remained at this location, where they opened St. Xavier's Academy for young women, until November 1847. They then moved to a "commodious edifice" adjacent to the cathedral at 131 Wabash Avenue and stayed there until fire destroyed it in 1871.[6] As their ranks increased, the Sisters of Mercy became the church's shock troops (Chicago's St. Vincent de Paul Society did not begin until 1857), extending a public arm to desperate immigrants who escaped Ireland's Great Famine. Despised by Anglo Protestants for their alien religion as well as their filth, ignorance, and strange ways, most of these uninvited newcomers secured public-works jobs on railroads and canals. They lived in makeshift, crowded shanties near their work, were frequently sick and disorderly, and thus generally were regarded as health menaces.

Not surprisingly, when a cholera epidemic struck during the summer of 1849 and spread along the Illinois and Michigan Canal, a large number of Irish died. Although the Sisters of Mercy were operating three schools, teaching Sunday school at St. Patrick's, running an employment bureau for working women, volunteering at a free dispensary opened by Rush Medical College, and holding night classes for illiterate adults, they began nursing cholera victims. It was part of their tradition. In Dublin's 1832 epidemic, Mother Catherine McAuley and her companions, along with the Irish Sisters of Charity, had enhanced their public image through their tireless care of strangers. As the Chicago outbreak subsided and the sisters' nursing assignments let up, they agreed to take charge of the city's first Catholic orphanage, "a haven for children who had lost their parents to the epidemic." Two years later, Mother Agatha accepted control of what became Mercy Hospital. She remarked in a letter that she was "fearful and uneasy because an [sic] Hospital is such an arduous undertaking, but if Heaven aids us all will be right."[7]

In Mother Agatha's letters of 1850–51, there is a continuing, almost numbing, refrain. She wrote repeatedly that she had "not one moment to spare," that "time is real precious here," that "we are very busy," that "my hands are full."[8] Besides the sisters' heavy teaching obligations and their diverse program of social services, they also had opened a branch house in Galena, Illinois, a dozen miles from Wisconsin and Iowa, in 1848. Although two nuns (both from the first band of five who had come from Pittsburgh) died in Galena, this active community of Chicago Mercys grew quickly. In 1851, Mother Agatha told her brother that there were forty-four Mercy Sisters in the Chicago diocese: "Irish, American, German and French . . . a mixture of many nations, but all one with respect to religion." Yet, according to data from the federal census, a large majority were Irish.[9]

Because so many young women chose to enter the Mercy community, Mother Agatha initiated new ministries. In late 1850 the Mercys began nursing at the Illinois General Hospital of the Lake. Despite winter winds and clogged streets, they walked every day from their convent on Wabash to the hospital, located at Michigan Avenue and Rush Street, and back again. Because they were sometimes forced to wait "an hour at a time" to cross the Lake Street Bridge, which was "only a collection of planks chained together," they searched for better ways to reach their destination. When management of the Lake hospital was transferred to them in February 1851, Sister Vincent McGirr (whose brother, Dr. John McGirr, was a member of the hospital staff) ánd three other nuns moved there. The number of patients in their care averaged from sixteen to twenty during their first year. In June 1852 the Sisters of Mercy received a new charter in their name, creating an early version of today's landmark institution, Mercy Hospital.[10]

That same year, Mother Agatha agreed to open another parish school. It was for the girls of St. Patrick's and was located on Adams Street, near where the new church would stand (and still stands). Although it is not known exactly when the Mercy Sisters began teaching Sunday school in Father Patrick J. McLaughlin's old church at Randolph and Desplaines streets, they probably did so shortly after their arrival in 1846. St. Patrick's was, after all, an 1846 offshoot of St. Mary's, where the sisters lived. Therefore, when regular classes commenced on Adams Street, these "walking nuns" trudged the distance from Madison and Wabash to Adams and Desplaines, crossing the troublesome Madison Street Bridge each day and in all kinds of weather. Yet, unlike most other respectable women, whose public activities were restricted, by the 1850s the Sisters of Mercy, who had begun to build an urban infrastructure that provided health care for the sick and injured, shelter for the homeless, and learning for children and young women (both Catholic and Protestant), moved freely through the city.[11]

Chicago's Mercy Sisters had many Protestant students, friends, and supporters. Writing to a nun in Pittsburgh, Mother Agatha remarked that she had "so much to do with Protestants." She pointed out that "almost all the children in the select school [St. Xavier's Academy] were Protestant, that Protestants visited them "constantly," and that they had "some very warm friends among them."[12] Thus, despite strong nativist sentiments expressed in the press against Irish Catholics, no Chicago newspapers publicly criticized these Irish nuns. Perhaps by 1852 most Protestants recognized the "vast and incalculable . . . good" these women had accomplished during their first six years. But in 1855 this goodwill was tested when an academy student, Mary Parker, sued the sisters. She claimed that she had been held at the school against her will. The incident was reported only in the *Democratic Press*, and it supported the Mercys, correctly suggesting that the young woman, who had a lover, "fell into a very common error of thinking that her liberties were abridged." When given the chance to leave school, Parker chose to stay and the case was dismissed.[13]

Unlike this legal incident, the cholera epidemic of 1854 proved devastating. Still the only nuns in Chicago, the Sisters of Mercy were actively planning during the early 1850s to expand their network of social-service institutions and thus alter the physical layout of the city. Because Mother Agatha had quarreled with Bishop James Van de Velde in 1849 over the sisters' right to own property (she won with the assistance of Bishop Michael O'Connor in Pittsburgh), she was determined to avoid future disagreements over deeds. Thus, in 1852 and in 1853, she discreetly purchased two pieces of land: a strip of prairie on the outskirts of Chicago (at Twenty-sixth Street and Calumet Avenue), and fifty acres of farmland south of Chicago (at Forty-seventh Street and Cottage Grove). On the prairie land adjacent to the city, Mother Agatha intended to open a second academy and a rest and retreat house for the sisters.[14]

Her plans were realized, but Mother Agatha lived to see only the beginnings of them. During the scorching-hot summer of 1854, cholera returned to Chicago with terrific force. By the end of June more than two hundred people had died. Families who could afford to escape fled to Milwaukee, but even some of them did not get out in time. Cholera was a horrible disease, largely because of the speed with which it killed—individuals who seemed healthy one day could be dead the next. Nevertheless, the determined and indefatigable Sisters of Mercy went everywhere, walking to where they were needed and "ministering with tender solicitude." They set aside all their other duties to nurse the sick and dying. Overwhelmed by the crisis, they also organized bands of courageous laywomen to assist them with their rounds of mercy.[15]

Following a full day of nursing on July 7, Mother Agatha became ill and died the next day. She was thirty-two years old. By July 11, three more nuns—all born in Ireland—also had become cholera victims. Later in the month, on July 31, Father McLaughlin, pastor of Saint Patrick's, died. He and the sisters were among the better known of the 1,424 people who succumbed that summer to the poorly understood killer disease. Shocked Chicagoans began to realize, however, that "cleanliness is conducive to health, and filth is productive of disease." As a direct result of this tragedy and repeated appeals for preventive sanitary measures, the city council authorized construction of an underground sewer system and required homeowners to install drains.[16]

When the Sisters of Mercy opened their second Chicago academy in December 1854, it bore the name of St. Agatha. In this way, they paid public tribute to their leading spirit, the young woman from County Carlow who had "succeeded by her zeal and wisdom" in laying a firm foundation for so many charitable and educational enterprises (both private and public) that would follow.[17] By responding generously to the distressed around her and trusting in Providence, she had unknowingly turned the convent on Wabash Avenue into something of a social settlement—the kind that many have come to identify with late-nineteenth-century Chicago. But Mother Agatha O'Brien had completed her life's work and made an imprint on Chicago's history and geography before either Jane Addams or Ellen Gates Starr, the founders of Hull-House, were born.

Setting the Pace

The McAuley-O'Brien legacy went a long way in directing the Irish women who led Chicago's Mercy Sisters during the late 1850s and Civil War years. The flexible, "can do" activism of Mothers Catherine McAuley and Agatha O'Brien worked well in a "can do" city bent on progress. Their energy and efforts to lift up their own contributed in no small way to the influence Irish Catholics would have in Chicago, an influence that from the beginning was "all out of proportion to their numbers." Irish Catholics not only grew up with the city, but their institutions became an essential part of its lifeblood. The sisters' bricks-and-mortar investments did more than shape the city's neighborhoods, particularly on the South Side. Their good works and steady efforts, which early on set them apart and set the pace, offered assurances to the uprooted that they belonged and gave many of them the means of upward mobility. And the Sisters of Mercy's groundbreaking achievements would be complemented by thousands of women-religious who followed their lead during the late nineteenth and early twentieth centuries.[18]

Mother Agatha's immediate successors were equally diligent and demonstrated an astute business sense, keeping their eyes on the future as well as the present. Mother Vincent McGirr, one of the pioneers who had come to Chicago in 1846 and later headed Mercy Hospital in 1851, opened a third academy for young women in 1857. Unlike St. Xavier and St. Agatha academies, St. Angela's was not a boarding school, but the tuition earned in each of these institutions helped support the Mercys' free schools and charities. Like the other two academies, St. Angela's offered "a refined and solid education" as well as "the constant care and attention of the Sisters." Although religion and theology were not officially listed among the course offerings, they formed "the core of the curriculum." All students received instruction in the "Christian principles of solid virtue and strict morality" that was part of a Mercy education.[19]

After opening St. Angela's, the Sisters of Mercy again spread themselves dangerously thin. In 1858, at the urging of Father John McMullen, they began the city's first Magdalen asylum, a shelter for unfortunate and abandoned women, in a rented house on the West Side near St. Patrick's Church. The Mercys staffed the asylum until the following year, when four Irish Sisters of the Good Shepherd (see Chapter 3) arrived from St. Louis and began their long history of service to Chicagoans. Relieved of this responsibility, Mother Francis Monholland (another Irish-born Mercy superior) sent a group of five nuns to Ottawa, Illinois, in 1859 to establish a new foundation. Then, in September 1861, she led her "soldiers of mercy" (all were Irish) to nurse the sick and wounded in the Civil War. Colonel James A. Mulligan, leader of Chicago's Irish Brigade and a future war hero, secured the sister-nurses on behalf of his largely Catholic regiment.[20]

The Mercys were the first but not the only Chicago-based nuns to go to the front. The Daughters of Charity, who had begun teaching at Holy Name parish in 1861, closed their school early in June 1862 to answer "a call for more help for the sick." Sister Anne Regina Jordan, born in Donegal in 1821, took Chicago's Daughters of Charity east, most likely to Satterlee Hospital in Philadelphia, where a large group of nuns from Emmitsburg, Maryland, had begun nursing that June. The Sisters of Mercy, for their part, spent six months working in a field hospital in Jefferson City, Missouri, and then continued their labors aboard the *Empress,* a hospital ship of the United States Sanitary Commission.[21]

The Mercys' wartime nursing did not end with their return to Chicago in May 1862. About two years later, they began visiting the sick and wounded prisoners at Camp Douglas, located on the city's South Side within view from the roof of St. Agatha Academy. Built as a training center for Union recruits, it was converted into a prison camp for Confederate soldiers early in 1862. Colonel Benjamin Sweet, who became camp commander in May 1864, placed his daughter at St. Xavier's Academy on Wabash. When he at first refused permission for the nuns to enter the camp, he was persuaded by Chicago's mayor—and perhaps his bright, persistent daughter—to allow them to do so. Years later, Ada C. Sweet recalled her many visits to Camp Douglas on weekends; the sisters, she said, often gave her "a great iced cake to carry to the Fifteenth Veteran Reserve Band." In return, on trips downtown, the band serenaded the nuns and their pupils.[22]

Long before the war's end, these "soldiers of mercy" had been transformed into "angels of mercy." Their "religious training and personal discipline, along with their practiced ability to treat soldiers with a compassion that remained devoid of sexual energy, won the respect of most people."[23] Thus, in April 1862, when Chicago's Protestant Female Nurse Association issued a call for nurses, it described the kind of women it needed in familiar terms: "they must be women of the most unimpeachable integrity, religious in spirit, thoroughly kind and gentle-hearted, possessed of the rare gift of common sense . . . self-reliant, entirely subordinate and obedient to the surgeon. . . . They must be women of cheerful and active temperament, industrious and energetic—in short, model women." Taking a cue from Superintendent of Nurses Dorothea Dix, whose anti-Catholic and anti-immigrant sentiments were well known, the Chicago association also required that "every nurse shall be at least thirty years of age." Many sister-nurses were younger.[24]

At the war's end, the Sisters of Mercy had been in Chicago for nearly twenty years. Their nursing, teaching, and charitable activities of various kinds had won for them an enviable place. As fearless and relentless caregivers on the fields of battle as well as on the city's streets, they had won for Irish Catholics and their church an increased tolerance and a new respect. Moreover, they had caused earnest Protestant women to take serious notice. The remarkable Mary Livermore, who with Jane Hoge organized Chicago's highly successful Great Northwestern Sanitary Fair in 1863, became acquainted with the Mercys and other nursing nuns during the Civil War. Decades later, she still held them in high regard. In a series of lectures titled *What Shall We Tell Our Daughters* (1883), she suggested that new communities of women "established on the basis of the Protestant religion . . . might be made very helpful to modern society." Livermore clearly recognized too how such organizations "would furnish occupation and give positions to large numbers of unmarried women, whose hearts go out to the world in charitable intent."[25]

Daughters Called to Service

Livermore was hardly the first, and certainly not the last, among prominent Protestant women to see Catholic sisterhoods as an attractive force for good in American society. Earlier in the nineteenth century, in 1851, Catharine Beecher had taken note of the achievements of pioneer nuns on the western frontier and pointed with envy to the Catholic Church, which had "posts of competence, usefulness and honor . . . for women of every rank and of every description of talents." And at the century's end, Addams and Starr consciously or unconsciously chose a successful ecclesiastical form on which to model their social settlement. To live as neighbors among poor migrants and work on their behalf would hardly have been considered new to Chicagoans who had witnessed or benefited from the labors of the Sisters of Mercy or other religious communities of women. By 1889, when Hull-House opened on Halsted Street, hundreds of Catholic sisters—the majority from Irish families—had already shown how good-hearted single women could live useful and gutsy lives.[26]

Strange as it may seem today, religious life, especially in active communities like the Sisters of Mercy, offered Catholic women an appealing alternative to the life choices then available to most American women: motherhood and spinsterhood. Nineteenth-century society and culture were also far less secular than today's. Americans, who were generally churchgoers and Bible readers, found their faith, morality, and identity rooted in religion. For women, particularly Catholic sisters and Protestant evangelicals, religion often stimulated "a life of usefulness" that "replaced stylish idleness or aimless busywork with purposeful activities."[27]

The best hope for benevolent daughters of Protestants was to become the wives of ministers or missionaries. As such, they could lead "lives devoted to soul-winning" and assume "a public, assertive form of usefulness." In choosing husbands, therefore, these young women also selected careers or challenging ways to lead lives of service. Before the Civil War, Emily Judson wrote to a friend about her decision to marry a missionary: "Did you ever feel as though all the things you were engaged in were so trivial, so aimless, that you fairly sickened of them and longed to do something more worthy of your origin and destiny?" She wanted to spend her "short life in the way which would make [her] most happy—in doing real, permanent good." Despite these intentions, however, children and home duties made it difficult for women like Emily Judson "to function in the capacity of assistant missionary."[28]

Such was not the case for the daughters of Catholics who decided to become nuns. Their "commitment was life long and was not distracted by family obligations," and during the nineteenth century, when opportunities to save souls and do good were limitless, the restrictions on women-religious were comparatively few. Until 1908 the Catholic Church officially recognized the United States as "mission territory," and the Irish women who immigrated as nuns saw themselves as missionaries in their own right. Settling in faraway places, they remained flexible, responding as best they could to local needs and crises. The heavy influx of famine refugees to American cities after 1847 also encouraged the first wave of Irish sisters to emphasize the public dimension of their vows. That Chicago's Mercy convent on Wabash Avenue became the center of so much social action was not surprising.[29]

The hectic pace and the singular competence with which these determined nuns engaged in benevolent enterprises and built respected urban institutions—ones largely free of male management—fueled the aspirations and idealism of other Chicago women who wanted to make a difference. Most of them were the daughters of immigrant and working-class families. No doubt some saw religious life as an escape or possibly an adventure, but many entered convents because they "expanded the narrow range of what was possible for women who were coming of age" 150 years ago. By accepting a religious vocation, these first- and second-generation daughters of Erin were not only choosing what their families and friends considered "the better part" (rather than getting married or staying single) but also enlarging their sphere and infusing it with tough challenges and good works.[30]

Living among and serving the poor, sick, and uneducated "demanded extraordinary stamina and dedication to the cause of religion." For most of the antebellum period, nuns lived and worked in convents and schools that were unattractive and often unhealthy. For Chicago's walking nuns, bitter cold and excessive heat heightened their discomfort and made their daily routines more taxing; bad weather also contributed to the terrible mortality among them. Large numbers of sisters died during epidemics; but many more, especially among the Irish, were lost to tuberculosis, the result of inferior living conditions and long hours of hard work. Sister Callista (Mary Ellen) Mangan, who was baptized at St. Patrick's in 1855 and subsequently became a Sister of Mercy, died of consumption twenty-eight years later. She was simply one of many.[31]

These hardships and early deaths did not lessen the attraction of convent life. Called to service by the growing number of Catholic poor and the threat of Protestant proselytism (especially among children), young women saw that religious life offered them a way to do necessary work and feel important. Defining themselves in terms other than those imposed by having husbands and children, Catholic sisters quietly challenged the "cult of true womanhood." In short, they acted "in the world to a greater degree than was permitted to most women or was pursued by most men" by voluntarily linking their "individual identity to a larger corporate identity." The Sisters of Mercy were not only free to walk the streets of Chicago without male escorts, they were also educated and self-supporting, held top administrative posts, and owned substantial amounts of property.[32]

Mother Agatha O'Brien, an Irish immigrant in her late twenties, must have offered a stunning example of how religious life could transform a bright young woman into an able person of status and authority. In the 1849 property dispute with Chicago's Bishop Van de Velde, for example, the twenty-six-year-old stood firm and refused to return a deed that she believed belonged to the Mercys. Three years later, through the legislative act that incorporated Mercy Hospital, she and the sisters elected to the board of trustees received sole corporate responsibility for the institution. Mother Agatha, who no longer needed the bishop's permission, could and did use the real estate as collateral to secure loans and mortgages to purchase more properties. Thus, she stands in stark contrast to Livermore and Hoge, who realized after their successful sanitary fair that, although they had money in the bank, "our earnings were not ours, but belonged to our husbands."[33]

Unlike many articulate Protestant women reformers who emerged in the post–Civil War years, the Sisters of Mercy and their successors claimed no public voice. They were products of their times and training—very much devout members of a patriarchal Irish church. Like other daughters of Erin, they "behaved aggressively and valued their economic prowess," but, despite "the web of support" they created for so many women of varied circumstances, they and their students generally "turned a cold shoulder to the organized women's rights movement." Its leaders were, of course, Protestant middle-class women of Anglo-Saxon stock who "carved out a political space that was in some ways a private turf . . . rather than a place of civic deliberation open to all." Protestant denominations also permitted divorce and more sexual freedom than did the Catholic Church.[34]

It seems that, for these reasons, the Sisters of Mercy and other women-religious, who in various ways set the pace for social reform in the nineteenth century, remain absent from so much of American history. It is a mistake to dismiss them too readily, however, because they sought little public notice, spoke infrequently to the press, or held a subservient place in the Catholic Church. Respect for and cooperation with bishops and priests did not always signify submission. As Mother Agatha O'Brien demonstrated, Catholic sisters frequently resisted patriarchy with as much resolve as a suffragist or feminist. They also showed the value of living as neighbors among working-class immigrants. Because of their example, followed later by more privileged settlement-house residents, "living in city neighborhoods alongside the poor became a distinct form of moral witness, social responsibility, and civic education." And, although nuns may have been "unlikely entrepreneurs," they were successful.[35] As St. Xavier University and Mercy Hospital indicate, the Sisters of Mercy creatively seized opportunities to invest in the city where they lived and in the people whom they served. They were, however, only the first of scores of women-religious who would define themselves and their goals through religious organizations and institutions that effectively shaped Chicago's culture and landscape.

3 Caring for Abandoned Women and Girls: The Sisters of the Good Shepherd, 1859–1911

The Sisters of the Good Shepherd, like the Sisters of Mercy, arrived in Chicago before the Civil War. By 1889, when Jane Addams and Ellen Gates Starr launched Hull-House on Halsted Street, the Good Shepherds were preparing to open their second charitable institution, the Chicago Industrial School for Girls. Thirty years earlier, four Irish-born nuns founded what would become the city's House of the Good Shepherd. The purpose of this Magdalen asylum, named "House of the Good Shepherd" when incorporated in March 1867, was to reform "abandoned women." Over time, the sisters extended their care from women accused of prostitution or disorderly conduct to delinquent and dependent girls and also performed works of mercy for others who sought their assistance.[1]

Although not well known outside Catholic circles, the record of the Sisters of the Good Shepherd should not be lost or completely overshadowed by the achievements of Protestant women, especially those in the settlement-house movement. The Good Shepherds, who today shelter battered women with children, built the House of the Good Shepherd to assist some of the most despised of Chicago's immigrant poor. In 1909, when the sisters celebrated a half-century of service, they took honest

Originally published as "Caring for Chicago's Women and Girls: The Sisters of the Good Shepherd, 1859–1911," *Journal of Urban History* 23 (March 1997), 260–94.

pride in what they had accomplished with so little notice, even among sympathetic observers. The Chicago Industrial School had survived a tumultuous beginning in the 1880s and continued to prosper on the city's South Side at Forty-ninth Street and Prairie Avenue, where nineteen nuns cared for about 210 girls. On Chicago's North Side, the older House of the Good Shepherd held a commanding position at the corner of Grace Street and Racine Avenue. There, forty-one sisters provided for more than 375 women.[2] Although indications of change were in the air, the routines and concerns of those who lived in these two Catholic charities remained firmly rooted in their nineteenth-century origins.

Beginnings

The Sisters of the Good Shepherd began their unique ministry in Chicago on May 20, 1859. Four Irish sisters arrived from their motherhouse in St. Louis and took up residence in a small frame house near St. Patrick's Church on the West Side. The Irish-born Father John McMullen, who acquired the house, had persuaded the Sisters of Mercy to open it as a shelter for "unfortunate females" he had met at the county jail. The Mercys agreed on condition that within a year they could hand over the Magdalen asylum to "specialists." The Good Shepherds, who took the usual vows of poverty, chastity, and obedience, also professed a fourth one, a vow of zeal. Through it they dedicated themselves specifically to the care of wayward, abandoned, and unfortunate women and girls. This vow removed artificial ethnic and spatial boundaries: the sisters could serve whoever sought their help and go wherever needed. The vow of zeal made them both caregivers and missionaries.[3]

The Sisters of Our Lady of the Good Shepherd were a semicloistered order with origins in seventeenth-century France. There, as in Ireland and later the United States, religious congregations proved especially attractive to young women who sought "a real vocation in life" apart from motherhood. Serious middle-class women with ability and ambition became nuns primarily to perform good works by helping people in need. Through the years, demand for the Good Shepherds' services increased. After establishing a central headquarters in Angers in 1835, the order internationalized and spread to several continents. By 1895, there were 185 Good Shepherd convents, most of them in Ireland, Britain, and the United States.[4]

Despite their French beginnings, Chicago's Sisters of the Good Shepherd were almost exclusively Irish and Irish American. A large majority had Irish parents. The four nuns who came to Chicago from St. Louis in 1859 were Irish-born. In 1910, thirty-three of the forty-one sisters at the

House of the Good Shepherd had Irish parents, four had one Irish parent, and ten had been born in Ireland; only one had both parents born in the United States. Across town at the Chicago Industrial Schools for Girls, fifteen of nineteen sisters had Irish parents; five of them had been born in Ireland. None had parents who both were born in the United States.[5]

It is common belief that Irish bishops and priests built the Catholic Church in American cities during the nineteenth century. In Chicago, for example, Irish bishops dominated the nineteenth- and early-twentieth-century church. From the first bishop, William Quarter, until the death of Archbishop James Quigley in 1915, "all bishops of Chicago were either Irish-born or of Irish parentage . . . [except] Bishop James Van de Velde, a Belgian who briefly presided over the diocese from 1849 to 1854." Parish priests of Irish heritage were less dominant, but in 1902 they headed 63 of 132 parishes in Chicago.[6] Only recently has it been recognized that the growth of the American Catholic Church relied heavily on the dedicated labors of thousands of nuns, many of whom were also Irish.[7]

It is impossible to know exactly how many Irish women came to the United States during the nineteenth century as sisters or intending to become sisters; it does seem safe to say a minimum of four or five thousand. It is certain that they all came in groups at the invitation of a bishop, priest, or nun, almost all of whom were also Irish. Not all Irish sisters were recruited as adults in Ireland. Many immigrated as children and subsequently entered religious congregations; others joined orders in France or elsewhere in Europe and later found themselves assigned to American missions. Still others, daughters of Irish immigrants, were born in the United States and attended parochial schools often staffed by Irish-born nuns. At some point these young women decided to enter religious congregations that they knew best—those of aunts and cousins, teachers, sodality sponsors, or favorite charities. Despite their different journeys to America and to religious life, these sisters shared an Irish, Catholic heritage.[8]

The first five Sisters of the Good Shepherd came to the United States in December 1842 at the invitation of Bishop Benedict Flaget. Only one was Irish. She was Sister Mary of St. Joseph Looney, who was born in County Tipperary and was the first English-speaking postulant accepted by the Good Shepherds at Angers. All of the pioneering group were young, between twenty-four and twenty-nine, and each had responded enthusiastically to the opportunity to become missionaries in America. Flaget, a refugee from the French Revolution and the first bishop of Kentucky, periodically traveled to France to recruit priests and nuns for a diocese that stretched from the Mississippi to the Alleghenies.[9]

In 1845, Bishop Flaget welcomed two more sisters from Angers. One, Mother Mary of St. Andrew Corsini O'Rourke, was a native of County Clare, Ireland. Four years later, when Bishop Peter Kenrick of St. Louis, Missouri, a Maynooth-educated Dubliner who had come to America in 1833 and become bishop ten years later, asked Mother St. Andrew to send a small contingent of nuns to his city, she did so. In St. Louis this "French" community of sisters grew under the leadership of another Irish woman, Mother Mary of St. Francis of Assisi Dwyer. Born in County Tipperary in 1817, she entered the Good Shepherds in London in 1843 and spent two years in training in Angers. In 1852 she became superior of the St. Louis convent, which was designated a "provincial house" three years later.[10]

The Sisters of the Good Shepherd ministered to "fallen" or "penitent" women who wished to redeem themselves. In St. Louis, as elsewhere, the nuns neither restricted their efforts to Catholics (although most whom they helped were) nor limited the length of time or the number of times a woman might seek refuge with them. During the early years of the sisters' ministry in the United States, women came to them voluntarily or were recommended by family members or priests. The majority were among the most scorned and desolate of Irish immigrants (and later their daughters) who fled to American cities in the wake of the Great Famine of the 1840s and 1850s. Because of them, the sisters knew well the tight link between poverty and prostitution—low wages and frequent unemployment offered few alternatives.[11]

In the United States, the Sisters of the Good Shepherd attracted women who wanted to enter religious life as a kind of "rescue worker." Most of them were Irish immigrants from working-class families, but they were not as destitute as the penitents and certainly not "defiled." The Good Shepherds never accepted anyone into the community who had been in their care. Thus recruits embraced their special vocations and created lives of useful service by aiding women less fortunate than themselves. Among them were Margaret and Jane Jackson, siblings born in County Tipperary and nieces of the provincial superior, Mother Mary of St. Francis Assisi. In 1859, Margaret, known then as Sister Mary of St. John the Baptist, led three Irish companions to Chicago. Her assistant, Sister Mary of St. Philomene (Mary Kavanaugh), who had emigrated from County Carlow when she was ten, would live her entire life in the Chicago community.[12]

On the eve of the Civil War, Chicago was less than thirty years old, still in many respects "a cow town knee deep in mud." But it was handsomely situated at the head of Lake Michigan, and a boomtown with promise and prospects to rival St. Louis. During the 1850s its population tripled, pulling people from the eastern United States and immigrants from Ireland, Germany, England, and Scandinavia. Some were skilled, but many were not. The Irish, largely unschooled and unskilled, took jobs where they could get them and made homes for themselves in an endless chain of low wooden shanties on the city's West Side.[13]

Chicago may have been new and oozing with vitality, but its Irish immigrants were desperately poor. Driven from their homes, debilitated by disease, and humiliated by the rags on their backs, they arrived in America without money or contacts, and often without shoes. In Chicago, jobs for men were "irregular, seasonal, dangerous, unhealthy, and often badly paid." Women had a harder time. The unemployed, widowed, and sick filled poorhouses and prisons. During the spring of 1859, the matron of the "city bridewell" reported that there were "between forty and fifty women in the prison" and that thirty-seven of them were Irish and Catholic.[14] It was largely for them that the Sisters of the Good Shepherd came to Chicago. Unlike New York City, where the indomitable Archbishop John Hughes initially refused to allow the nuns to open a Magdalen asylum, Bishop James Duggan welcomed them. He had studied for the priesthood in Ireland but was ordained in St. Louis in 1847; almost immediately he was assigned to its cathedral, and twelve years later he was installed as the fourth bishop of Chicago. Well acquainted with this "devoted sisterhood" and their "heroic charity," he recognized Chicago's need. During the spring and summer of 1859, Bishop Duggan encouraged Father McMullen's fund-raising efforts.[15]

Prior to his citywide appeal, Father McMullen had gone door-to-door to collect food and other necessities. Chicagoans responded generously, but the small house occupied by the nuns and their charges was embarrassingly crowded. The *Chicago Tribune* granted that "providing a place of residence for a class of unfortunates and erring women" was a "worthy" cause but criticized the "sectarian" nature of the charity—one "wholly under the care of a particular denomination." Nevertheless, Mayor John C. Haines and city father William B. Ogden, neither of them Catholic, each donated $100, matching Bishop Duggan's gift. Duggan also gave Mother St. John the Baptist a choice of sites on which to build, and she selected a lot north of downtown on the corner of Market and Hill streets (near today's Cabrini-Green public housing project).[16]

It is not clear why Mother St. John the Baptist chose to move the House of the Good Shepherd away from downtown. She may have been looking for a quieter, cleaner, and more secluded place. She would not have been alone. Between 1850 and 1870, a number of Chicago's churches separated themselves from the sweeping commercial development at the city center. In 1859, Bishop Duggan designated Holy Name Church, on the north side of the Chicago River, as the cathedral. Perhaps because the Magdalen asylum served the entire city and did not belong to any one parish, Mother St. John the Baptist hoped to strengthen its position in Chicago.[17]

These prospects went up in smoke the morning of August 15, 1859, when a fire completely destroyed the frame building under construction. Father McMullen suspected arson, having received complaints and threats from North Siders opposed to the location of the Magdalen asylum. Their objections—that depraved women did not deserve special care, and that such care should not be given in their neighborhood—resembled those registered against the asylum when it first opened its doors. Undeterred, Father McMullen organized festivals and bazaars to collect funds for a substantial brick building, and the Good Shepherds inconspicuously extended their reach by moving to a larger, temporary residence on Franklin Street. In January 1860, Bishop Duggan asked the diocese to contribute generously to "the world's victims and outcasts," whose abode was "maliciously destroyed."[18]

Although this unhappy episode disturbed the sisters and their friends, few such incidents occurred in Chicago. Compared to older cities of the Northeast, where convent raids and burnings happened with some regularity before the Civil War, Chicago remained largely free of open hostility. Because it was still a city of newcomers (natives as well as foreigners), Protestant British attitudes had not become entrenched. Tolerance and cooperation between Catholics and Protestants were not unusual. Prominent Yankees contributed to Catholic charities, and Protestant parents sent their daughters to Catholic academies. However, as the immigrant church grew in size, anti-Catholic and anti-Irish bigotry developed over the use of public money for private institutions, particularly schools and asylums. It manifested itself frequently in the growing use of words like "Romanism" and "sectarianism."[19]

Fear of the spread of Catholicism fueled such charges. As Catholic convents, schools, and charitable institutions took root in immigrant and working-class neighborhoods, devout Protestant women recognized what they were up against. The sheer volume and variety of the nuns' municipal undertakings defined them as able competitors. For example, the Good Shepherds had worked for almost four years among the most ostracized of Chicago's poor, and their reputation had grown by word of mouth and through fund-raising appeals and church-sponsored fairs. In 1863, a group of Protestant women, motivated by the sisters' success and an increase in the number of prostitutes during the early years of the Civil War, began the Chicago Erring Woman's Refuge for Reform.[20]

Public charitable institutions were rare in Chicago and Illinois prior to the war. Poor and needy adults and children went to either the state almshouse or the county jail. Private organizations were left "to fill the cavernous need." Chicago's earliest charitable institutions were Protestant and Catholic orphanages started during the 1849 cholera epidemic. From that beginning, religious denominations regularly cared for their own, establishing a model that would last into the twentieth century. Thus it was not surprising when Protestant women, following the lead of the Good Shepherds, opened *their* refuge during wartime.[21]

The economic boom of the Civil War dramatically changed Chicago. As industries expanded, the population grew from 109,260 in 1860 to 298,977 in 1870. Skilled workers earned better wages, but the unskilled and those on fixed salaries (teachers) or in low-status jobs (garment workers) did not. High inflation caused one well-to-do Chicagoan to comment that "the price of *everything* is so high. . . . The poor must do without many of the necessaries of life." By July 1864 an estimated four thousand women had turned to prostitution, earning for Chicago the title of "Wickedest City in America."[22]

To these "fallen" women, the Sisters of the Good Shepherd and their Protestant counterparts offered food, shelter, religious instruction, job training, and compassion. But the House of the Good Shepherd always cared for nearly twice as many as the Erring Woman's Refuge. From the outset, Irish-born females constituted the majority of those arrested for prostitution and vagrancy or committed by families and priests. In 1865 the Protestant institution housed thirty-one women and girls, compared to eighty-nine at the Magdalen asylum. In each of the preceding eight years, an average of seventy-three "daughters of misfortune" had found accommodation and "protection" with the Good Shepherds.[23]

The sisters, who looked at the world through a hierarchical lens, divided their inmates into two major groups. The penitents, delinquent women and girls, lived apart from dependent children and orphans. Delinquents sent by the court could leave when their sentences ended but could return if they chose. Some did come back, and a few never left. To those who found solace in an environment in which "order replaced disorder, routine offset bedlam, and civility supplanted abuse," the Sisters of the Good Shepherd offered two more options: Consecrates and Magdalens. Consecrates did not take vows, nor were they strictly bound by the cloister; instead, each year they "consecrated" themselves to Our Lady of Sorrows and entered a semireligious state that they could leave with relative ease. The Magdalens removed themselves forever from the outside world, professed solemn religious vows, and formed a separate contemplative order of nuns. Dressed in brown, they lived with white-robed Good Shepherds but were distinct from them. A community of six Magdalens began in Chicago in 1869.[24]

During the inflationary war years, the sisters and those who shared their roof lived hand to mouth. Their situation may have been further complicated in 1863 by an unexplained "problem" that resulted in the unexpected transfer of their young superior, Mother St. John the Baptist, to Philadelphia. Her replacement was the Montreal-born Mother Mary Nativity (Adéline) Noreau, who arrived in Chicago in August 1864 accompanied by Sister Mary St. Catherine of Siena Lavoie. They accepted the assignment from another French Canadian, Mother Mary of the Sacred Heart Tourville, who in 1862 had replaced Mother St. John the Baptist's aunt as provincial superior in St. Louis.[25]

The few remaining records do not tell us how this Irish household received the news of Mother Nativity's appointment. Whatever feelings or concerns the nuns may have had stayed private. Catholic sisters did not customarily act with an eye to the public; they assiduously shunned any form of self-revelation or self-promotion as they went about the business of pursuing good works and "saving souls." William J. Onahan, a prominent Chicago Catholic and generous friend of the Sisters of the Good Shepherd and other women-religious, correctly observed that they were "prohibited by the spirit and teaching of their religion from 'advertising' before the world their beneficent work." Yet the charitable and educational institutions they built are highly visible and speak to their intentions and aspirations.[26]

Mother Nativity proved herself a builder, despite the difficulties she confronted during her fifteen years as superior. In 1864, when she assumed office, the Magdalen asylum was already overcrowded and without any regular means of support. The brick structure on Market and Hill streets, which had seemed adequate a few years before, could barely accommodate those who wished to enter or were sent. By 1866, through the exercise of "much energy, domestic thrift, and never-failing charity," eighteen sisters had done what they could—primarily by sewing, laundering clothes, and gardening—to stretch their fledgling charity over a hundred residents.[27]

Not all of the nuns in the House of the Good Shepherd were, like Mother Nativity, white-robed and cloistered. Approximately one-fourth of them wore black and worked as lay sisters, or as religious servants. As explored in more detail in Chapter 1, their backgrounds differed from those of the "choir" nuns who governed convents or were teachers. Lay sisters usually came from poor families and had less education, although they were often literate. Among this small group of Good Shepherds included a few who were known as "tourière" or "outdoor" sisters. They did chores outside the cloister, such as shopping, delivering clean linens, carrying mail, and sometimes begging or "collecting." With a large basket on her arm, Sister Martha (Bridget) Shine, a native of County Cork, "mingled with the people of Chicago" from her arrival in May 1859 until her death in July 1880. Not only was she "a great favorite," according to one observer, she was also "the strength and shield of Mother Nativity."[28]

It was Sister Martha who frequented the offices of the Catholic laymen from whom Mother Nativity sought legal and financial services as well as expert advice. Most of these business and professional men had strong attachments to Chicago's Irish community, serving as "advisors" to the heads of Catholic charities and leading public campaigns for support. The House of the Good Shepherd's survival depended not only on the sisters and their friends among the clergy and neighborhood parishes but also on prominent citizens like Onahan, Thomas Brenan, and Charles C. Copeland.[29]

In the summer of 1866, Mother Nativity opened a small industrial school. Because it could accommodate only a handful of young people, she wanted to expand operations to an adjacent and vacant lot on Sedgwick Street, but she was unable to secure permission and financial assistance from the mercurial Bishop Duggan. While he was in France, the owner of the property indicated he had a buyer who wished to open a "Dutch garden" (saloon). Mother Nativity quickly obtained the necessary $500 from her provincial superior in St. Louis and received authorization from Father Denis Dunn, vicar general of the diocese, to purchase the lot. He had the deed drawn up in the bishop's absence. When Mother Nativity made the second payment, she discovered the bishop's name, not the sisters', on the deed. Once she learned that an unincorporated religious community could not own property, she successfully petitioned the Illinois State Legislature for incorporation in March 1867. It appears that this action introduced her to a young lawyer and recent convert, Charles Copeland.[30]

Bishop Duggan continued to refuse to transfer the deed of sale to the Good Shepherds. Mother Nativity insisted that "not one cent" of their savings should be used to pay for diocesan property. Failing to persuade the vicar general of her position, she asked Copeland to take her case directly to the increasingly arbitrary and deranged bishop. Copeland somehow convinced him that the purchase of the adjacent land and the deed transfer (which occurred in April 1867) were "indispensable for the good order of the House." A year later, however, Mother Nativity faced a new problem when she asked for the deed to the Market Street property on which the House of the Good Shepherd was located. She wished to mortgage it—it had been given to her predecessor—and to begin major construction on Sedgwick Street. But the bishop's desperately unstable condition made a settlement impossible.[31]

Mother Nativity and her advisors devised other ways to enlarge the House of the Good Shepherd and expand its services. In 1869, City Collector Onahan and City Treasurer Daniel O'Hara convinced the state legislature and the city council to divide the fines collected by the City of Chicago "from keepers, inmates and visitors of houses of prostitution" between the House of the Good Shepherd and the Erring Woman's Refuge. Although the amounts varied from one year to the next, the sisters relied on this assistance, which yielded nearly $9,000 during the first two years.[32] But by 1872 the payments became irregular, and by 1876 they stopped altogether. The House of the Good Shepherd and the Erring Woman's Refuge brought the city to court and successfully argued that their work had grown because they cared for women who would have otherwise become public charges. The city, however, made future payments only reluctantly and never fully.[33]

In April 1869, Onahan chaired a citywide committee of Catholics sponsoring "a fair to aid in the erection of suitable buildings of the Magdalen Asylum." Parishioners throughout Chicago donated goods and labor. The fair, held at Turner Hall the last week of June, received support from more than six thousand Catholics and Protestants and contributed almost $4,000 to Mother Nativity's building fund. In August, she and "good Mr. Brenan" mortgaged the Sedgwick Street lot. By the end of November, she had finally acquired the deed to the Market Street property from a new vicar general, Father Thomas Halligan, although he asked that she pay $5,000, "the small sum of its original cost," at the end of five years. She was not pleased but took her chances. In 1874—after all was lost, old and new buildings alike, in the Great Fire of 1871—Bishop Thomas Foley absolved this promise.[34]

An elaborate ceremony to lay the cornerstone of the new Magdalen asylum took place in August 1869. Despite the day's heat, an estimated eight thousand people attended what the *Chicago Tribune* described as "one of the grandest demonstrations of the year." The four-story, pressed-brick structure on Sedgwick Street cost $51,400 when it was completed in the fall of 1870. Mother Nativity reported the following year that $35,000 of this amount had been paid. Except for the $8,741 in city fines, all of the funds for Chicago's House of the Good Shepherd came from fairs, mortgages on property, private contributions that ranged from $5 to $500, and donated labor and materials. The sisters and their charges earned nearly $13,000 during 1869 and 1870, working as laundresses and seamstresses.[35]

The fire of 1871 destroyed everything. As late as December of that year, according to Mother Nativity, the ruins were "still smoking." No one in the Good Shepherd family died during the fire, but they suffered a loss valued at $118,000 and found themselves among the homeless. Fleeing the flames, they took refuge in St. Stephen's school. Mother Nativity then sent girls home to parents or relatives and older residents to the provincial house in St. Louis. Several nuns left Chicago for Good Shepherd convents in New Orleans and St. Paul. Those who remained were guests in the Convent of the Sacred Heart, one of the few Catholic institutions to escape destruction. Less than a month after the fire, ten Good Shepherd Sisters, twelve Magdalens, and eighteen penitents moved into a house at 218 Green Street. There they grieved for all they had lost, resolved to begin again, and took courage and comfort from their belief that "many dear souls were snatched from evil surroundings and placed on the narrow path of salvation" during their twelve years in Chicago.[36]

The House of the Good Shepherd was insured and received some compensation, though not enough to rebuild what had been destroyed. Once again, Mother Nativity was forced to depend on her wits, the labor of her household, the good will of Chicagoans, and friends in the United States, France, and Canada. Besides blankets, shoes, flannel, muslin, and sewing machines, the Chicago Relief and Aid Society gave the House of the Good Shepherd $16,025 during 1872 and another $11,000 in 1873. Good Shepherd convents elsewhere also sent several thousand dollars. The indefatigable Sister Martha collected $350 in the streets of Chicago during November 1871. These funds, along with other private donations of money and goods, allowed Mother Nativity to design and build a smaller, single-story house on the site of their blackened and frozen ruins during the winter of 1872. Because of the crisis, Mother Nativity suspended the rule of enclosure and, each day for about six weeks, walked a couple of miles in the cold with a companion sister to oversee construction of this makeshift institution.[37]

In March 1872 the sisters and their charges returned to the properties on Market and Sedgwick streets. They gradually resumed their normal activities and welcomed back those who had left Chicago after the fire. To accommodate their growing numbers, Mother Nativity added on rooms, creating a shelter that resembled a long rowhouse. However, she focused most of her attention and energies on the future. In early spring she traveled to St. Louis to discuss plans for a larger building of Gothic design in the form of a Maltese cross. In June she hired the architectural firm of Dixon and Hamilton, which estimated total construction costs at $125,000.[38]

Mother Nativity embarked on this bold enterprise without apparent fear. The tragedy of the fire seemed to strengthen her resolve and the sisters' belief that St. Joseph would provide what was essential. But the building project was not easy. Thirty-nine churches had burned and were rebuilding; labor and materials were at a premium. Watching their convent and asylum constructed in parts and living even more frugally during the process, the Good Shepherd household shared the sufferings of other dislocated Chicagoans. In September 1873, the sisters and the Magdalens moved into the main building, making it possible to enlarge the industrial school and penitent class. By 1878 the number of women living at the House of the Good Shepherd rose to just over three hundred, including eight African American penitents and thirty-three nuns. To provide for them, Mother Nativity borrowed money and added a wing to the main building. The sisters and the Magdalens expanded their laundry service, continued their sewing and embroidery work, and opened a public bakery. They did not, however, free themselves from debt.[39]

The House of the Good Shepherd received no public funds, other than small sums in police fines and $27,000 from the Relief and Aid Society mentioned above. Prominent Catholic laymen knew that other cities appropriated money for private charities and agreed with Onahan that Chicago should provide the Good Shepherd Sisters with aid equal to that spent in maintaining "those who would otherwise be supported in public institutions." It was not to be had, however, in a state becoming known as a welfare "cheapskate." In 1878, with Mother Nativity's encouragement and Bishop Foley's approval, these men again used their influence to raise money from Catholics and Protestants alike to benefit the House of the Good Shepherd.[40]

Aided by a committee of 100 women, Catholic businessmen and professionals sponsored a huge bazaar in the Exposition Building—the largest hall they could find—during the first week of November. Mayor Monroe Heath publicly endorsed the fund-raiser and served as honorary chair. The executive committee published 5,000 copies of an eight-page *Appeal* that explained the background of the House of the Good Shepherd and its needs: $30,000 to remove all debt. It asserted that Chicago owed the asylum "a measure of gratitude . . . and a liberal and munificent support so as to enable it to enlarge the scope of its usefulness." This grand affair removed a third of the Good Shepherds' debt and gave them a greater sense of their importance to Chicagoans.[41]

Despite the growth of private charitable institutions in the post–Civil War years, the Sisters of the Good Shepherd had secured for themselves a unique position. By the end of the century, orphanages with religious and ethnic affiliations would develop in this expansion along with more specialized Catholic institutions that cared for working girls, infants, and newsboys. But the Good Shepherds remained able and ardent specialists, doing what no other nuns or priests did.[42]

In March 1879, Mother Nativity died of pneumonia. Local newspapers carried extensive accounts of her illness, death, and funeral. This cloistered, Canadian-born nun had not only made friends among Chicago's Irish Catholics but had also earned the public's "respect, esteem, and love." The executive committee, which had worked closely with her in staging the fall bazaar, met to pay her homage. Old friends—Onahan, Brenan, and Copeland—were present, as were other notables, including State Assemblyman R. P. Derickson (a Presbyterian), City Attorney Richard S. Tuthill (an Episcopalian), and an array of city judges. They resolved to complete "the building and extension of the House of the Good Shepherd, as an appropriate monument" to her memory. At her funeral Mass, Father McMullen, who had recognized the need for a Magdalen asylum in the 1850s, eulogized Mother Nativity. Her commitment and leadership had resulted in a highly regarded ministry that regularly rescued significant numbers of destitute women and despondent girls, mostly of the working class.[43]

Controversies

The House of the Good Shepherd remained in Mother Nativity's building (although the street name changed from Market to Orleans) until 1907, when it moved to its current location at Grace and Racine (near Wrigley Field). Mother Nativity's replacement was her assistant, Mother Mary of St. Angelique Cleary, who was born to Irish parents in Milwaukee thirty-four years earlier. She remained superior for ten years. In 1889, Mother Mary of the Holy Cross McCabe succeeded her and served as superior until 1898. Little is known of either woman because almost no convent records remain from these uneasy years, and there is no 1890 manuscript census.[44]

After Mother Nativity's death, the Good Shepherds continued in an inconspicuous and efficient manner to perform traditional and routine assignments that were grounded in the corporal and spiritual works of mercy. They provided shelter as well as food and drink to the homeless, gave instruction to the ignorant, and comforted the afflicted. The women and girls who came to them through the courts or family members also received vocational training as seamstresses or domestics. Some of them had been prostitutes, and others were accused of vagrancy, disorderly conduct, or intoxication, but most had shown signs of "immorality" or lack of restraint by coming home late, using obscene language, or associating with individuals of questionable character. All were poor and unable to find work that paid more than a pittance; a majority of them were daughters of immigrants. In 1880, according to the census, 336 females lived on Orleans Street: 43 nuns, 22 Magdalens, and 271 inmates. Of the latter, 119 had Irish parents and 54 had German. Almost all the Good Shepherds—40 of them—had Irish parents, and 25 had been born in Ireland.[45]

Of similar background, these sisters understood the problems of the working poor and generally showed compassion to them, even to the sexually promiscuous. The mission of the House of the Good Shepherd was a delicate one: "bandaging the wounds of the erring sheep," enhancing their self-esteem, enabling them to support themselves "honestly in the world," and teaching them "with a view to their eternal salvation."[46] Most Catholic sisters tended to equate social reform with the corporal and spiritual works of mercy. The Good Shepherds, in particular, were engaged in "a crusade of charity" directed at women who were poor, homeless, despised, and often abused. Many Irish immigrants found solace from the distress and disappointments of everyday life through devotions to an understanding God who would reward them in heaven. Thus the sisters' goal was not to change society but to make the lot of the oppressed and demoralized more humane, offering "a stepping stone to salvation, not a stumbling block."[47]

Although the Sisters of the Good Shepherd did not challenge the economic system, they offered "no cheap pitying phrases either." In fact, they were very realistic and always practical. Irish nuns, who understood the workings of class in day-to-day life, did not encourage those in their care to "get ideas beyond their position in life." Because the sisters believed that "a life of labor [was] the allotted portion" of their inmates' future, they promoted training as domestics and seamstresses, the chief occupations open to immigrant women in the 1880s and 1890s. The nuns also taught reading, writing, and arithmetic along with lessons in industry, thrift, order, and cleanliness. Young women were encouraged "to be able to support themselves, but also their parents."[48]

Most inmates "of age" stayed at the House of the Good Shepherd for two years. Younger women and girls frequently remained until they were eighteen. Parents or guardians who could pay a fixed sum each month did so, but the object was to take "all who present[ed] themselves; to refuse none, however poor they may be." At the end of the rehabilitation period, many went home to family or friends; some stayed on. The sisters sought employment for those who wished it. No one was forced out, and no one was refused readmittance. Knowing the difficulties that confronted stigmatized women (especially if older), the Good Shepherds often encouraged them "to remain . . . where they [were] assured of the grace of a happy death." Only when a penitent could return to a supportive family and "find no obstacle to her perseverance in virtue" did the nuns take joy in her leaving.[49]

When a woman or girl left the House of the Good Shepherd, she received whatever she had come with. If she had been at the asylum for a considerable time, her services were acknowledged "with a suitable outfit and a little sum of money." In Chicago, there was no formal "wage fund" (money paid to inmates but held until they departed) before 1918, when Archbishop George W. Mundelein agreed to contribute half of the estimated cost ($500 a month; $6,000 per year) of each inmate's support. Those who returned to visit or stay were welcomed, and the Good Shepherds tried "to do all in [their] power not to lose sight" of their women and girls, in order to "aid them in being faithful." The sisters strictly honored the privacy of those who had been with them, understanding its importance to their reputations.[50]

The Sisters of the Good Shepherd saw their inmates not as single women but as members of families. They insisted that younger women "show respect to their parents, and great devotion to their families." During the nineteenth century, women and girls often entered Magdalen asylums voluntarily, choosing them over the poorhouse or acting at the insistence of desperate relatives and parents. And the nuns showed concern for family members and their problems, big and small. They did not, for instance, keep "a poor workman" waiting when he came to visit his daughter because they knew he had probably "deprive[d] himself of his dinner." Thus families frequently looked upon a place like the House of the Good Shepherd as more of a boarding school than a reformatory. In the sisters' care, their troubled daughters would be safe and disciplined while they received vocational training for work and religious instruction for life.[51]

Work and self-reliance, not marriage and dependence, were the watchwords of these Irish nuns. They were not in the business of preparing good wives. Although it became fairly common during the 1880s for former

inmates of the Erring Woman's Refuge to hold weddings at that institution, no such ceremonies took place at the House of the Good Shepherd.
Irish single women were expected to work. Their labor "remained vital
to the family economy and often made the difference between survival
and destitution." Unmarried women contributed regularly to the household income; they also sent money to parents in Ireland to help maintain
farms, pay for a Holy Communion dress, or bring siblings to America. The
Good Shepherds thought that strong, determined females who worked
would not lose their souls.[52]

Because the sisters believed that respect and redemption accompanied honest work, Mother Nativity had opened an industrial school in
Chicago in 1866. It was small but nonetheless innovative, since industrial schools would not become popular in the United States for another
decade. They were, however, present and government-funded in England,
Scotland, Ireland, and Canada by the 1860s. Mary Carpenter, an English
reformer, had pioneered this kind of education for neglected and delinquent young people, touting the "direct moral influence" of industrial
work. In Ireland these schools were initially placed under lay direction,
but eventually women-religious became their administrators. As Catholic sisters were more numerous, more efficiently organized, more committed, and worked more cheaply than laywomen, the state welcomed
the change.[53]

When the Sisters of the Good Shepherd expanded to Ireland from
France in 1847, they established themselves in Limerick. There they
operated a large industrial school, St. George's School for Girls. The nuns
also opened institutions in Belfast, Cork, New Ross, and Waterford; and
industrial schools were always part of the asylums, not separate. The programs and routines in each location were similar and highly structured:
schooling, work and training in useful domestic skills, and religious
instruction to instill habits of devotion and piety. As in most "total"
institutions of the late nineteenth century, the emphasis on discipline,
order, and good behavior reflected the values of middle-class society.[54]

What was taught in Ireland was subsequently taught in America,
where the predominantly Irish and English-speaking Good Shepherds
founded numerous houses. The nuns may have been medieval in religious dress and some customs, but their centralized and internationally
established order had many of the markings of a modern corporation. The
sisters traveled back and forth as needed, moved often with little notice,
and usually asked few questions. In city after city, they performed compe-
tently and effectively, adapting to local conditions as demanded but generally relying on time-honored ways and a common set of procedures.

In Chicago during the 1880s, these proven practices came into conflict with a Protestant culture that espoused American ideas of the separation of church and state. Nevertheless, Carpenter's work in Europe stimulated interest in industrial education in the United States. After her 1874–75 visit, seventeen states quickly established more than thirty-six industrial schools. Illinois was not among them, and it probably would have lagged behind longer had it not been for the Illinois Women's Centennial Association, which in 1877 opened what it believed was the state's "first" industrial school for girls.[55]

The new school had no shortage of inmates, but it lacked funding. The organizers faced a second problem as well. They had no legal authority to retain the girls. Thus a committee of three, which included Judge James Bradwell, his associate, and his wife Myra, drafted a bill that became law in July 1879. It saved the Illinois Industrial School by requiring the county to pay $10 a month to maintain each dependent girl under eighteen. Mrs. Bradwell, then president of the Soldiers' Aid Society, persuaded its board to donate use of the Old Soldiers' Home in Evanston to the school, where it remained for thirty-five years in its "original, unsuitable" condition.[56]

When the industrial school bill was before the legislature, Onahan and City Attorney Richard S. Tuthill went to Springfield to "secure such amendments . . . necessary to include the House of the Good Shepherd." In the end, the act did not specifically mention either the Illinois Industrial School or the House of the Good Shepherd. Instead, the words "any" and "all" were used to describe current and future schools for dependent children. The act also included an admonition to avoid sectarianism "as far as practicable" yet provide for "the moral and religious instruction" of inmates. These cautionary phrases were not as confusing as they now appear. Nineteenth-century Protestants and Catholics alike concerned themselves with matters of redemption. For instance, philanthropist Louise deKoven Bowen, a close friend of Jane Addams, asked prosperous Chicagoans: "What is it going to profit us if our children lose their souls?" And Protestant institutions frequently had chapels and offered religious instruction. Yet, because people from several denominations sat on their governing boards, they were not thought to be sectarian. But Catholic institutions were always considered such.[57]

After some difficulty, but with the support of Chicago's archbishop, the Sisters of the Good Shepherd secured a charter and incorporated as the Chicago Industrial School for Girls in November 1885. The school operated as part of the House of the Good Shepherd, where it had functioned unofficially and without public funds since 1866. But once the sisters began receiving county money, trouble ensued. The Illinois Board of State Commissioners of Public Charities warned in 1886 that the industrial school act was "far from satisfactory" because it permitted private institutions to operate at county expense. The commissioners claimed that "the state should retain control of the entire system" and also disapproved of what had become accepted practice—placing dependent and delinquent children in institutions of their own religion. However, in 1886–87, an attempt to create a new state industrial school for girls failed. The *Chicago Tribune* characterized the proposal as a "useless extravagance" and commented favorably on the "economical" management of the private industrial schools.[58]

The state charities commissioners were not convinced and refused to pay any bills from the Chicago Industrial School. Cook County lawyers argued that the state constitution forbade the use of public money "in aid of any church or sectarian purpose." At the same time, the board's 1888 biennial report noted that the Illinois Industrial School, officially a nonsectarian institution, held chapel exercises "twice each day, prayer meetings twice each week, and Sunday school and church services every Sabbath." Such different viewpoints could be resolved only in court. In the summer of 1887, the Chicago Industrial School sued Cook County for $19,583 spent maintaining girls sent by the court between April 1, 1886, and June 3, 1887. By February 1888, Judge Tuthill, an Episcopalian and friend of the Good Shepherds, had risen from city attorney to judge on the Cook County Circuit Court. He ruled in their favor. The county appealed to the Illinois Supreme Court.[59]

Seven months later, the supreme court reversed Judge Tuthill's decision. The county won what its attorney, E. R. Bliss, considered the leading issue of the case: "whether the county could . . . pay money to officers of an admittedly sectarian institution"—that is, one "under the control of the Roman Catholic Church." The court ruled such payment unconstitutional because it would support a school "controlled by a church, and in aid of a sectarian purpose." During the trial, Bliss also argued that the Chicago Industrial School did not exist apart from the House of the Good Shepherd but was "a paper organization." He accused Mother Angelique Cleary of placing public money into a common operating fund, implying that the sisters had been devious. But the supreme court stated clearly that they were "animated by the purest motives" and did "their work faithfully and well." In short, they were conducting business as was customary in their other American and Irish schools.[60]

Nevertheless, the Chicago Industrial School had lost its case, and it appeared that it would not be able to continue. All that remained, according to the *Chicago Tribune*, was "to see how wide a swath the decision cuts." What would happen to the Illinois Industrial School, where "children are instructed in the way common to all the Protestant evangelical churches?" Although the county had won, its victory was Pyrrhic. Because it lacked adequate facilities, it continued to support both institutions. In September 1889, the Sisters of the Good Shepherd moved their school across town to Forty-ninth Street and Prairie Avenue and placed it under secular management. The Chicago Industrial School was no longer "a paper organization," and it now had a lay board of directors made up of Catholic men and women.[61]

The Chicago Industrial School for Girls remained at its new location until 1911, when it became the Illinois Technical School for Colored Girls. Until then, the large brick building—"new and in excellent condition"—accommodated two hundred dependent girls, offering them "all the branches of an English education," along with "industrial pursuits" and religious instruction. About twenty nuns and the older girls performed the housekeeping, gardening, and maintenance work. A county inspector commented that they had "no use for a man in this institution" and that even the engineer who "attends to the steam heating apparatus" was a woman. As self-sufficient as they were, the Good Shepherds and the school's directors remained uneasy that their public support might be withdrawn. But in 1899 the "opponents of industrial schools, private interests, and sectarianism" suffered a major defeat. That year the Illinois Juvenile Court Act, the first in the United States, declared that the court should place children "as far as practicable in the care and custody of some individual holding the same religious beliefs as the parents."[62]

The credit for turning common practice into law went to Timothy Hurley, president of the Catholic Visitation and Aid Society. When incorporated in September 1889, the society established a Child Bureau to "claim Catholic children" from county institutions. Once rescued, the society found temporary homes for them in Catholic charities. The House of the Good Shepherd and the Chicago Industrial School received many women and girls in this fashion. But, until passage of the Juvenile Court Act, Hurley and his supporters feared that their work might at any time be ruled illegal.[63]

Hurley and Chicago's Catholics welcomed the Juvenile Court Act as a happy resolution to what they had long believed was an unfair, even hostile, juvenile justice system. The legislation and the appointments of Tuthill as judge of the new court and Hurley as chief probation officer must have pleased the Sisters of the Good Shepherd. In 1900 they received their first delinquents from the juvenile court, and three years later the

House of the Good Shepherd and the Erring Woman's Refuge became official "shelters" of Cook County's penal organization. The charge of sectarianism had been lifted and doubts about the sisters' charitable work were removed. Yet, with its new status, the House of the Good Shepherd seemed more of a reformatory than a refuge.[64]

The legal controversy surrounding the Chicago Industrial School had focused public attention on the Good Shepherd Sisters and their institutions, and not all of it was good. In a second incident, in 1890, they were somewhat more fortunate. Criticisms registered against them by the Illinois Woman's Alliance received comparatively few headlines and little press coverage. And the alliance itself, which had come together in 1888 and achieved many positive reforms, had dissolved into factions of "petty differences and personal spites" by 1894.[65]

The alliance, made up of delegates from nearly every woman's organization in Chicago, was founded and led by two socialist trade unionists, Elizabeth Morgan and Corinne Brown. Its main purpose was to assist working women and their children by building schools and public baths, enforcing compulsory education laws and factory inspection ordinances, and ending child labor. It also campaigned for fairer treatment of prostitutes by police, insisting that women should not be convicted of prostitution "unless the men involved were willing to come forward and bear witness against them." Following a visit to the Erring Woman's Refuge, one member asked publicly why society "has not deemed it necessary to build a refuge to reform men who have betrayed these girls?"[66]

Evidence suggests that the alliance approved of the general work of the Erring Woman's Refuge and the House of the Good Shepherd. But the alliance disliked "all forms of private charity" and strongly disapproved of using public money to support a private, sectarian institution. In June 1889, amid charges of sectarianism against the Sisters of the Good Shepherd, the alliance resolved "to agitate for the establishment of an industrial school for dependent children to be supported by the State." During the summer, alliance representatives inspected the House of the Good Shepherd. They found its management "everything to be desired" and expressed appreciation for the "open-hearted and frank explanation of every detail [they] inquired into." Nevertheless, the alliance passed a second resolution: "the State is false to itself when it delegates its functions to a private sectarian institution, though such institute be of the highest possible character."[67]

The most severe criticism against the House of the Good Shepherd came in December 1890. Alliance leader Fannie Kavanaugh suggested that some inmates were held against their will and thus "deprived of their liberty." In return, the sisters received "the $10 monthly allowance for their board" from the county. The Good Shepherd Sisters were "much annoyed" by these accusations. Their advisor, Thomas Brenan, told the press that county funds went to the Chicago Industrial School—now at a separate location—and not to the House of the Good Shepherd. He said too that women who chose to remain at the House of the Good Shepherd were "at liberty to leave whenever they choose." Mother Holy Cross McCabe also spoke publicly. She admitted that she had occasionally persuaded inmates to remain longer but, having served their sentences, they were free to leave. The alliance presented no evidence to the contrary.[68]

Both the Sisters of the Good Shepherd and the Illinois Woman's Alliance had the interests of poor women at heart, but their views of what was best for them were diametrically opposed. Cultures had, indeed, clashed. Some members of the alliance asked retired judge Richard Prendergast, who had befriended both groups, about the nuns' practices. Not wishing to become involved, he simply responded by asking: was it not "better for the girls to remain at the house [of the Good Shepherd] than to return to the streets?" Mrs. Kavanaugh said Judge Prendergast had evaded the real issue—"the right to personal liberty."[69]

From the sisters' view, this was not the *real* issue. They believed, like Judge Prendergast, that many of the women and girls in their care would not be "free" in the streets of Chicago. Although most Irish immigrants settled in urban areas, they knew that cities could as easily enslave as liberate. From years of experience, the sisters were well aware of what life on the outside offered women with few job skills and little formal education. They understood why many poor women were drawn into prostitution—and that fact further explains why the nuns so carefully and deliberately protected their inmates' privacy. The tag of "immorality," though unfair, was persistent. The Good Shepherds were not naive. They knew that their program of reclamation was efficacious, particularly for those who chose to stay or those who returned to good families. They knew too that it did not always provide an easy route to a free and full life in American society.[70]

The Sisters of the Good Shepherd came to believe that the alliance's public attack was the price they had to pay for their "measure of success." During 1891, the House of the Good Shepherd cared for 491 women and girls; by year's end, 161 had returned to families or friends and 57 were placed "at service in families." But the sisters were badly in need of more space and better heating and bathing facilities. In March 1892, Mother Holy Cross borrowed $15,000 and bought ten acres of wooded property

on Grace and Racine streets. Brenan, then an associate in real estate with
John F. Cremin, located the land and handled the purchase.[71]

By the century's end, sectarian threats had ceased. The 1899 Juvenile Court Act had effectively quashed them. Yet, even before, the Good
Shepherd Sisters had begun to plan for the future. They did so with a high
degree of confidence and some comprehension of how they had contributed to the creation of "redemptive places" in Chicago. In that spirit, on
December 21, 1896, the House of the Good Shepherd opened its doors
to the public for the first time in its history. During a "Donation Party,"
more than two thousand Chicagoans toured an institution that many
of them had heard about but never seen. Mother Holy Cross headed a
receiving line that included influential Catholic and Protestant women:
Jane Addams, Sarah Hackett Stevenson, Julia Holmes Smith, Eliza Allen
Starr, and the wives of William A. Amberg and John and Michael Cudahy.
In honor of the occasion, a *Chicago Tribune* headline proclaimed: "Their
Work Is for Woman's Good."[72]

A New Age

The Sisters of the Good Shepherd were well positioned to enter a new age.
Although not without financial worries, they had put the House of the
Good Shepherd and the Chicago Industrial School for Girls on the city's
map of charitable institutions. Chicagoans recognized the devotion and
care these sisters gave to troubled females and their families. And long
before Protestant reformers considered it essential to live among those
they sought to help, Catholic sisters had made the practice customary.
Like the Sisters of Mercy and other active communities of women-religious who were guided in their work by the corporal and spiritual works
of mercy, the Good Shepherds knew they could not love or serve their
neighbor from a distance.[73]

Yet, in the twentieth century, these sisters would find it more difficult to keep their edge. Paradoxically, their very success at nineteenth-
century-style charity work prevented them from experimenting with
different ways of treating the unfortunate in modern times. By 1907, the
Good Shepherds had sold their property on Orleans and Hill streets and
moved themselves and their residents to a "well-equipped" and "stately"
building, four stories high and aired by lake breezes, at Grace and Racine.
But by then, arguments against large institutions—many of which seem
to have resulted from the achievement of Catholic sisters in expanding
their network of charitable work—were becoming familiar. In general,
critics found them "destructive of initiative and individuality." Instead

they favored placing dependent children in families, arguing that institutions were "necessary evils" that should be replaced "by simpler and more natural instrumentalities." Pioneering social workers had also begun to question the wisdom of removing delinquents from their families and communities for long periods of time.[74]

Even before the era of the professional social worker, Chicago's settlement-house movement challenged the Sisters of the Good Shepherd and their place in history. In the 1890s, middle-class, college-educated women at Hull-House, who in many ways imitated the living arrangements of Catholic sisters, offered a new approach to the problems of industrialization and poverty. Reformer William Stead compared Hull-House to "a Catholic sisterhood" but observed that the nuns seemed to "generate more enthusiasm" for their work. Yet he found Jane Addams and her coworkers more tolerant, more successful at avoiding "denominational narrowness." They did not confine themselves "to the straight and narrow channels of [any single] conception of orthodoxy."[75] With a firm belief in social progress and democracy, Addams became less conventionally religious and more secular over time. Settlers and sisters may have opened their hearts and homes to Chicago's poor, but their worldviews were hardly the same. The Protestant social gospel and its humanitarianism differed radically from the Catholic theology that governed convent life and its service.[76]

The Good Shepherds were concerned primarily with their own salvation and that of the women and girls in their care. Their relationship to God, defined in large part through good deeds and works of mercy, was more important to them than public citizenship or social justice. Responsible for administering and financing two large charitable institutions, they focused most of their everyday efforts on the needs of those nearby and on events that demanded an immediate response. Just when more Chicago women (mostly middle-class and Protestant) were entering public life and expanding their social and political networks to work for a more livable city, the sisters retreated. By 1911, when they were well established and their work was widely recognized, their provincial superior advised them, for example, "never to leave the convent except through necessity." Mary McDowell, who headed the University of Chicago Settlement, believed it was important to venture out and discover the broad causes of poverty. She and her colleagues thought it was "not enough to convert a soul"—society or "the environment" also needed conversion. Mainstream Catholic theology, which governed the actions of Catholic sisters, had not yet embraced that idea.[77]

The Sisters of the Good Shepherd did not act independently. They were part of the American Catholic Church and subordinate to its patri-archal authority. From working-class backgrounds themselves, their lives were defined and controlled by middle- and upper-class Irish American Catholics who were socially conservative. Bishops, clergy, and male bene-factors commanded the sisters' attention and influenced their work. Their institutions and their peculiar place on the church's pedestal depended greatly on the spiritual and financial support of such men. Convent cus-toms and training that emphasized selflessness and silence also worked against them. Thus, despite their immigrant origins and their firsthand knowledge of the ravages of urban poverty, the Good Shepherd Sisters did not openly challenge the status quo.[78]

They did not actively participate in urban public life either. The church hierarchy, which strictly limited nuns' involvement outside the convent after 1900, simply did not permit it. A 1917 revision of the code of canon law further strengthened this development. Thus, when Chica-go's mayor appointed a Vice Commission in 1910 to study the causes of prostitution in the city, three Catholic priests were made official mem-bers. But no sisters sat with them or appeared before them. Nor did they publicly support the mothers' pension law passed in Illinois in 1911. And they were not present that year at the Chicago Child Welfare Exhibit and Conference hosted by Jane Addams. Preoccupied with matters of relief, rehabilitation, and redemption, the Sisters of the Good Shepherd failed to demand reforms of an economic system that victimized the women and girls they knew so well. Yet, for over fifty years and under enor-mous pressure, these same sisters responded generously and capably to thousands of Chicagoans who appeared at their door and succeeded in building permanent urban institutions that were assuredly "redemptive places."[79]

Sister Cleophas (Rosanna) Hurst, born in Dublin in 1865, was the first of many from Our Lady's Hospice, Harold's Cross, to enter the Sisters of Charity of the Incarnate Word in San Antonio, Texas. She became a registered nurse and later a member of the order's governing boards. Courtesy of the Sisters of Charity of the Incarnate Word, San Antonio, Texas.

The original Sisters of Mercy convent on Baggot Street, Dublin. Catherine McAuley opened it in 1827 and founded the Sisters of Mercy there in 1831. From it, small groups of sisters began other foundations in Irish towns as well as in English, Australian, and American cities, including Chicago, during the nineteenth century. Collection of author.

St. Brigid's Missionary School in Callan, County Kilkenny, Ireland (*on left*). Opened by the Sisters of Mercy in 1884, the school trained nearly two thousand young women "desirous of becoming Nuns" before closing in 1958–59. Most found new homes in Australia, New Zealand, and the United States. Courtesy of the Sisters of Mercy, Callan, County Kilkenny.

Young recruits aboard the *Pennland* in February 1898 sailed to America in the company of Sister Paul McHenry, a native of County Clare. They entered the Sisters of St. Joseph of Carondelet. Courtesy of the Sisters of St. Joseph of Carondelet, St. Louis, Missouri.

The Hennessy Hotel in Queenstown, now Cobh, was popular with young recruits for America. The owner, Richard Hennessy, was "strict but caring." According to a young woman who spent the night there in summer 1924, he "ordered all to bed at an early hour." Collection of author.

Kate and Nora Prendiville from Castleisland, County Kerry, became Sisters Austin and Patricia (*seated*) in two communities: the Sisters of St. Joseph of Peace in Nottingham, England, and the Dublin Dominicans in New Orleans. Nora later returned to Ireland and recruited thirteen young women, including her own sister, Maggie. Another sister, Nell, later followed. Collection of author.

The Mercy Sisters' convent in Carlow, Ireland. From it, young Margaret O'Brien traveled as a postulant to Pittsburgh, where she received the Mercy habit and the religious name of Sister Agatha. In 1846 she came to Chicago as superior of the first group of Mercys. Collection of author.

Mother Agatha O'Brien (1822–54), who was always eager to become involved in new ventures, died in the 1854 cholera epidemic and is buried in Calvary Cemetery, Evanston. Courtesy of the Sisters of Mercy, Chicago.

Chicago's Mercy Sisters lived at St. Xavier's Academy (*left*), near St. Mary's Cathedral (*right*), at Wabash and Madison until the 1871 fire. Courtesy of the Sisters of Mercy, Chicago.

In 1850 the Sisters of Mercy added nursing to their repertoire of services to the public, when they began caring for the sick and injured at the Illinois General Hospital of the Lake. Three years later, they dedicated the original Mercy Hospital. Courtesy of the Sisters of Mercy, Chicago.

The second Mercy Hospital (brick building) and the third (the taller building under construction), which opened on January 4, 1968. Chicago's first and oldest hospital became new again. A long line of Mercy Sisters is responsible for this achievement. (The photo was taken in September 1966.) Courtesy of the Sisters of Mercy, Chicago.

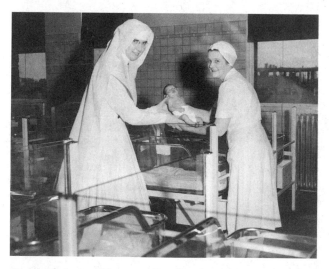

Sister Christine (Eleanora) Frieders, nursing supervisor of maternity services at Mercy Hospital from 1946 to 1962, with a colleague and newborn in the maternity ward in 1954. Courtesy of the Sisters of Mercy, Chicago.

This 1940s first-grade classroom at St. Gabriel's, east of the Union Stock Yards, resembled other Mercy classrooms. A hundred years after their arrival, the Sisters of Mercy operated a network of schools at all levels throughout Chicago. Courtesy of the Sisters of Mercy, Chicago.

The House of the Good Shepherd, at the corner of Grace and Racine, housed the Sisters of the Good Shepherd and their residents beginning in 1907. Today they remain at this location but in a smaller, more modern facility. Courtesy of the Sisters of the Good Shepherd, Chicago.

In the sewing room of the House of the Good Shepherd, young women received training as seamstresses, one of the chief occupations open to working-class women in turn-of-the-century Chicago (c. 1908). Courtesy of the Sisters of the Good Shepherd, Chicago.

Girls under the age of sixteen did not work in the laundry at the House of the Good Shepherd. They instead did handwork such as embroidery (c. 1910). Courtesy of the Archdiocese of Chicago's Joseph Cardinal Bernardin Archives and Records Center.

The Good Shepherds, along with the women and girls who lived with them, daily visited the magnificent chapel in the House of the Good Shepherd. Courtesy of the Sisters of the Good Shepherd, Chicago.

The Illinois Technical School for Colored Girls, owned and staffed by the Good Shepherd Sisters from 1911 to 1953, was situated on an acre and a half at 4910 Prairie Avenue on Chicago's South Side. Courtesy of the Sisters of the Good Shepherd, Chicago.

Outside a first-floor classroom, students received their textbooks. They wore uniforms of French blue blouses with red ties and navy skirts (c. 1930s). Courtesy of the Archdiocese of Chicago's Joseph Cardinal Bernardin Archives and Records Center.

Mother Mary of Perpetual Help (Anna) Hunter called her youngest student-violinists to attention in the spring of 1939. "Mother Help" was a friend to many. Courtesy of the Archdiocese of Chicago's Joseph Cardinal Bernardin Archives and Records Center.

Extensive sidewalks in "the Yard" of the Illinois Technical School gave
students a place to enjoy a favorite pastime, roller skating (April 1939).
Courtesy of the Archdiocese of Chicago's Joseph Cardinal Bernardin
Archives and Records Center.

When inclement weather forced boarders to spend their
recreations inside, as in March 1945, they took out their
sewing or art projects. Here several girls at the Illinois
Technical School made Easter greeting cards. Courtesy of
the Archdiocese of Chicago's Joseph Cardinal Bernardin
Archives and Records Center.

Mother Mary Nativity (Teresa) Hautzinger taught at the Illinois Technical School from 1925 to 1953. She is posed here with one of her classes during the 1940s. Courtesy of the Sisters of the Good Shepherd, St. Louis, Missouri.

Katharine Drexel (1858–1955) as a young woman of about sixteen. In 1891 she founded the Sisters of the Blessed Sacrament for Indians and Colored People, to be "home missionaries." Unlike the semi-cloistered Good Shepherd Sisters, the Blessed Sacrament Sisters were active and outgoing. Courtesy of the Sisters of the Blessed Sacrament, Bensalem, Pennsylvania.

Louise Drexel Morrell and Mother Katharine Drexel, sisters and friends, enjoyed an afternoon at the Bensalem motherhouse in the mid-1920s. Courtesy of the Sisters of the Blessed Sacrament, Bensalem.

In 1913, a year after their arrival on Chicago's South Side, the Sisters of the Blessed Sacrament opened St. Monica School in the former Eighth Regiment Armory at 37th and Wabash. Courtesy of the Sisters of the Blessed Sacrament, Bensalem.

A young Sister Paul of the Cross (Katy) Kiniry, who became the first principal of St. Monica's. She was the daughter of Irish immigrants and a former seamstress. Courtesy of the Sisters of the Blessed Sacrament, Bensalem.

On Easter 1914, an assembly of parishioners, priests, and sisters gathered in front of St. Monica's with children who had recently made their First Holy Communion. Courtesy of the Sisters of the Blessed Sacrament, Bensalem.

About 150 students attended St. Elizabeth High School in 1934. Staffed by the Blessed Sacrament Sisters, the school was located in the old Swift Club building at 4100 South Michigan Avenue. Sister Guadalupe (Helen) Hartman was librarian. Courtesy of the Sisters of the Blessed Sacrament, Bensalem.

The Sisters of the Blessed Sacrament were enthusiastic home visitors as well as teachers. Mr. and Mrs. John P. Triplet of St. Anselm's welcomed Sister Frances Therese (Anna) Kallay into their home at Christmas in 1937. They practiced saying the rosary. Courtesy of the *Catholic New World*, Chicago.

Sister Paulita (Maureen) O'Donovan (*left, background*), born in Dublin in 1914, taught first grade at St. Elizabeth's from 1936 to 1940. In 1938 her class received two visiting priests, Fathers Francis Wade (*seated*) and Vincent Smith, both of the Society of the Divine Word. Courtesy of the *Catholic New World*, Chicago.

In spring 1943, students at St. Anselm's grammar school (also staffed by the Sisters of the Blessed Sacrament) turned out *en masse* to see the jeep they had paid for with war stamps. Courtesy of the *Catholic New World,* Chicago.

The Sisters of the Holy Family of Nazareth, largely of Polish descent, were also home missionaries. They worked at St. Joseph's Mission on the West Side near Holy Family parish and Hull-House. Mother Melitona Mach, principal, is at far right; Father Arnold J. Garvy, SJ, who headed the mission, is in front row, center. (Photo is c. 1933–34.) Courtesy of the Sisters of the Holy Family of Nazareth, Des Plaines, Illinois.

4 The Good Shepherds and the Illinois Technical School for Colored Girls, 1911–53

In Chicago, where hundreds of thousands of European immigrants settled during the nineteenth century, the Catholic Church became identified most notably with the Irish and also with Germans, Italians, and Poles, but almost never with African Americans. They made up a much smaller segment of the city's population, and most of them were Protestant. Very few black women and girls found refuge or aid in the House of the Good Shepherd or the Chicago Industrial School for Girls. It was not until the mid-twentieth century that Catholics in any number became concerned with the plight of African Americans. And, when they did, nuns led the way and grabbed much of the nation's attention. Such was the case in 1965, when six Daughters of Charity from Marillac House on the West Side were arrested in a public demonstration at State and Madison streets in Chicago's Loop.

Although spared jail, these sisters refused to back down in their support of black Chicagoans. Sister Mary William Sullivan, director of Marillac House, stated why: "Sisters have been walking in hospital and school corridors for years . . . and I'm just Irish enough and Chicago enough not to want all that walking to go to waste!"[1] She may well have had

Originally published as "Illinois Technical School for Colored Girls: A Catholic Institution on Chicago's South Side, 1911–1953," *Journal of Illinois History* 4 (Summer 2001): 103–22.

the Sisters of the Good Shepherd in mind. Irish to the core and builders of century-old charitable and educational institutions in Chicago, they had enlarged their ministry in 1911 by opening the Illinois Technical School for Colored Girls. They did it on the city's South Side, at Forty-ninth Street and Prairie Avenue, where black migrants from the South had begun to make their homes. The nuns' initiative, which was met with strong protests from their white neighbors, was not encouraged by officials in the Catholic Church.

The history of Chicago's South Side black community is far from fully written. Although it is clear that few white people remained in neighborhoods "'taken over' by Negroes" during the Great Migration, very little is known about those who stayed. Catholic sisters formed the largest group of white Chicagoans who did. More than sixty of them were living in the "Black Metropolis" before World War II.[2] For much of the twentieth century—well before the advent of the activist "new nuns" of the 1960s—these unconventional women challenged the white supremacy of their society and church by building schools and linking their lives to black families in Chicago's "Black Belt." The Illinois Technical School, owned and operated by the tenacious Good Shepherd Sisters, is a prime example of such efforts.

As the previous chapter shows, the Good Shepherds were hardly strangers to Chicago in 1911. They arrived from St. Louis in 1859 and spent most of the next fifty-two years on the North Side at the House of the Good Shepherd. Thirty years later, they opened the Chicago Industrial School for Girls on the South Side between Prairie and Indiana avenues on Forty-ninth Street. Each year, from then until 1911, approximately twenty nuns cared for about two hundred dependent girls, mostly first- or second-generation whites and a few mulattos. Nearly all were from poor Catholic families, but the Good Shepherds offered "a home and proper training" to anyone, "irrespective of race, creed, or color."[3]

The Chicago Industrial School for Girls occupied a prominent place among the city's charitable institutions. With regular financial assistance from Cook County as well as enthusiastic backing from a lay board of managers composed of prominent Catholic men and women, the Good Shepherds and their residents flourished in a multistoried brick building situated on an acre and a half of land.[4] Inside, the dormitories were light, well ventilated, and clean; the food was substantial and varied. In classrooms, students received the usual grammar-school and religious instruction. Except for the youngest, they also took classes in millinery, embroidery, lace making, and fine sewing. In a laundry "equipped with the most modern machinery," the older girls worked to contribute to their support. Along with the nuns, they did housekeeping, gardening, and everyday maintenance. They were singularly self-sufficient.[5]

The overall success of the Chicago Industrial School, however, did not prevent Archbishop James E. Quigley from relocating it—that is, the girls but not the sisters. In 1911 he moved the institution to the grounds of St. Mary's Training School near Des Plaines, Illinois. A boys' school was already there, and Quigley intended to create a large, coeducational institution where siblings would live close to one another. The Sisters of the Good Shepherd and the school's lay board understood the reasoning behind the archbishop's action, but they resented his failure to notify them when he decided "to take charge of the girls." Left empty-handed, the nuns devised a plan of their own. When the archbishop approached them with an offer to buy their vacant building, they refused to sell it. They instead converted their old school into a new one, a school for dependent black girls between the ages of six and sixteen. The Illinois Technical School for Colored Girls, which began abruptly as an orphanage in 1911, gradually evolved into a boarding school. During the 1920s, the Sisters of the Good Shepherd accepted girls "of parents of medium or small income or of homes broken by death or divorce" as boarders.[6]

Not in Our Backyard

With the South Side's expanding population of southern black migrants, the Good Shepherds' school undoubtedly met a public need. It also posed a sizable threat. In 1911 the Black Belt had not yet reached Forty-ninth and Prairie. The nuns' impressive property was adjacent to the upscale white residential areas of Hyde Park and Kenwood, where racial skirmishes over housing and hostility against African Americans had been growing. In 1908, Hyde Parkers had organized the Hyde Park Improvement Protective Club to respond to what it called a "Negro invasion." The following year, with more than three hundred members and support from a local newspaper, the club promised to blacklist real estate agents who sold homes to African Americans and to boycott merchants who provided them with goods and services. It also promoted segregated public schools in the neighborhood and separate playgrounds in nearby Washington Park. Not surprisingly, club members disapproved of the sisters' plan.[7]

From the beginning, the Good Shepherds wanted to admit black girls *and* "keep the privilege of caring for white children." But that proved impossible. Even those in the vanguard of reform "tended to accept conventional assumptions about black cultural inferiority and the dangers of racial integration."[8] The color line had already been drawn in the minds both of state agents who inspected industrial schools that received public funds and Cook County Juvenile Court judges who determined the disposition of dependents or delinquents. Before the nuns obtained a charter for their school, Charles Virden, the state official who supervised the Division of Visitation of Children and who had been one of the first to encourage them to open a school for black girls, "questioned the clause in the [draft] charter 'for colored and white.'" He did not like it and counseled the sisters to restrict their school to African Americans and obtain a charter "under [the] title 'Illinois Technical School for Colored Girls' to provide for dependent children."[9]

Merritt W. Pinckney, presiding judge of the Cook County Juvenile Court from 1908 until 1916, supported Virden. Pinckney, whom the *Chicago Defender* described as a "Well Known Jurist, Renowned for Years for His Fairness to All Races," was a strong defender of the court and a faithful friend to the Chicago reformers who created it. He would later draft the Aid to Mothers Law in 1913 and usher in the Juvenile Psychopathic Institute as an official department of the court in 1914. Nevertheless, he also advocated the racial separation of dependent and delinquent children. In 1912, in a speech sponsored by the Cook County Board of Visitors, he expressed concern that black children in the North were neglected. To give them "a square deal" or "an even break" when placed in institutions, Pinckney argued that "colored children should be with colored children." The *Defender* disagreed. It contended that "distinctions based on color and race are un-American" and that a square deal meant "an impartial administration of public offices and public institutions without regard to race or color."[10]

The Good Shepherd Sisters felt the weight of conflicting pressures. After losing the Chicago Industrial School for Girls, they chose to continue on the South Side by responding to what state officials and judges of the juvenile court saw as an urgent need. Yet those professionals, upon whom the sisters relied for advice as well as financial support, believed that the best way to handle "the problem of caring for the colored children . . . who must be provided for in equal measure" was to house them separately. Once the nuns agreed to do so, they then faced opposition from "some of our best reputed citizens—our former friends and supporters— nay, even some of our reverend clergy." To their great surprise, Charles A. Mair, a respected Catholic businessman who had served as president of the Chicago Industrial School's Board of Directors for more than a decade, resigned. He told Mother Mary of St. Julitta Fitzpatrick that he did not want to be "identified with [their] new work" of educating black children other than what he might "do in the way of material assistance." And he offered her his "most sincere sympathy in her troubles."[11]

Board reaction to the sisters' new mission was mixed, but Mair was not alone in opposing it. Samuel C. Scotten, another longtime member, "emphatically declined" to serve because he "greatly disfavored the work." Others, like attorney Patrick J. O'Keeffe, who lived in the neighborhood (at Forty-ninth Street and Michigan Avenue) and belonged to the Hyde Park Improvement Protective Club, were initially ambivalent. A trusted friend and "always interested" in the nuns' work, O'Keeffe was anxious about the influx of African Americans to the South Side and had "many misgivings as to the success of the colored work." But, in the end, he sided with the sisters and remained "most devoted to the Good Shepherd Cause." He demonstrated his commitment by sending them "all communications he received [from the Hyde Park Improvement Protective Club] which might be of interest." Thus, throughout the ordeal, O'Keeffe, state officials, and juvenile court judges kept these semicloistered nuns "in touch with the public sentiment," hostile as it was.[12]

Judge Edward Osgood Brown, also a board member, supported creation of the Illinois Technical School. A law graduate of Harvard University and a convert to Catholicism, Brown took pride in his Massachusetts and abolitionist roots. He moved to Chicago in 1872 to practice law; in 1903 he was elected to the Circuit Court of Cook County and in the following year was appointed to the appellate court. He described himself as a "Radical Democrat," participated nationally in the single-tax movement, and showed an active interest in racial matters. In 1904, at Brown's home on the city's North Side, Celia Parker Woolley and others made plans for Chicago's Frederick Douglass Center, and in 1910, Brown became the first president of the Chicago branch of the National Association for the Advancement of Colored People (NAACP). Five years later, he and his wife, Helen Eagle Brown, traveled to Booker T. Washington's Tuskegee Institute as guests of Chicago philanthropist Julius Rosenwald. Deeply impressed by Washington and the Tuskegee students, Brown's commitment to racial justice was further strengthened. In an address at an NAACP annual conference in Chicago, he stated emphatically "that the color of a man's skin shall not subject him to insult, oppression and injustice in a country boasting of its democracy, its liberty and the political equality of its citizens." Although no record remains of Brown's opinion of the Hyde Park Improvement Protective Club, he must surely have disapproved.[13]

In the late summer of 1911, club representatives met privately with Archbishop Quigley. They asked him to terminate the Good Shepherds' plan for a school for black girls. But Quigley, assuming the sisters would admit only Catholics, explained that "it would be a very long time" before they would have "any number of colored children, and that consequently the school would be a failure." As a result, he did nothing to stop it. That autumn, members of the Hyde Park Improvement Protective Club appealed to Governor Charles S. Deneen, who also failed to act on their request.[14]

Accelerating racial hostility on the South Side, coupled with the recalcitrance of some board members, threatened to jeopardize the Illinois Technical School's survival. Mother Julitta feared that if she did not quickly form a corporation, the school would fail to obtain the necessary charter. To complicate the matter, she had already begun receiving children from the Cook County Juvenile Court. Thus, with the approval of Virden, who continued to reassure and support her, several Good Shepherd Sisters became the incorporators. In this way, they avoided further delay and the difficult task of asking "strangers to become subject to the ill-feeling that was rife against the school."[15]

By January 1, 1912, the freshly chartered Illinois Technical School was up and running. The sisters began their new enterprise by caring for twenty-five girls whom Judge Pinckney had placed with them. As the number of destitute children rapidly increased during the winter months, the Sisters of the Good Shepherd were cheered by their presence and behavior. They were "bright, docile little girls," who "accommodated themselves readily to their new surroundings, and manifested a spirit of gratitude and affection . . . which made efforts in their regard a pleasant duty." Equally encouraging to the sisters was "the grateful appreciation of their parents"—for the "antagonism" emanating from the Hyde Park Improvement Protective Club had not yet ended.[16]

Despite the unusual nature of the Illinois Technical School—one created by white Catholic nuns for destitute black children, who were largely non-Catholic, in an upscale neighborhood—the hostile actions and accusations of the Hyde Park Improvement Protective Club received little coverage in the city's newspapers (black or white, Protestant or Catholic). But in March 1912, the club's antics could no longer be ignored. Following an evening meeting on March 15, the *Chicago Tribune* described a "stormy" session at which club members protested the Good Shepherds' plan to make their school into "a refuge for dependent and neglected negro girls." On that night, however, the sisters and their young girls were no longer the sole objects of the club's contempt, which was also focused on "an aged minister" who spoke courageously on the school's behalf. John T. Jenifer, a retired minister of the African Methodist Episcopal Church who was born a slave in Maryland, stood up for "what he considered the rights of the negro" as well as the Illinois Technical School.[17]

African Americans respected Jenifer for having built the new Quinn Chapel at Twenty-fourth Street and Wabash Avenue in the early 1890s. As he stood before the Hyde Park Improvement Protective Club in 1912, he mentioned that he knew something about property rights but said he considered the rights of liberty and citizenship "more sacred." He firmly opposed a resolution asking state authorities to rescind the Illinois Technical School's charter; Jenifer declared that the institution was "indispensable" and one "of which the citizens of this city should be proud and not ashamed." He then pleaded his case: "It is far better that these dependent negro girls be taken care of than be left to drift into evil and become a menace." When he finished, a resentful audience "clamored for recognition," many speaking at once "of [the] depreciation of property that would follow the invasion of Hyde Park by negroes." But more was at stake. H. T. Davis, a forceful president who feared that the South Side's racial boundaries would be upset, shouted: "Would you be willing to sit down and eat with negroes? Do you want to be on a social equality with them[?]"[18] The resolution passed unanimously, except for Jenifer's dissenting voice.

Despite its best efforts, the Hyde Park Improvement Protective Club ultimately failed to convince the State to rescind the Illinois Technical School's charter. The Illinois Board of Administration, which considered the club's position at Governor Deneen's request, called upon Virden "to state what he knew of the matter." According to the sisters' account, he described their "excellent work done for the white children" who had previously resided in the Chicago Industrial School for Girls. Virden responded to the club's charges that the school was "conducted by Colored people" by indicating that the Sisters of the Good Shepherd were "about the whitest people he ever saw." To complaints about a high brick wall "covered with barbed wire," he stated that the property was "surrounded by a wooden fence about five or six feet high."[19]

The Illinois Board of Administration also appointed Thomas O'Connor, one of its members, to visit the school. Following his inspection, he assured the nuns that "the charter could not be withdrawn on the plea of its being a school for Colored Children." Accordingly, on April 14, 1912, Mother Julitta received a special-delivery letter from Virden, saying that he had spoken to Governor Deneen and Secretary of State James A. Rose. Both supported the Good Shepherds' new work. He encouraged Mother Julitta to "keep up [her] courage" and promised to be with her "to the finish." And he was. But he probably did not realize the contribution

these sisters made in challenging the way whites and blacks understood
segregated space in their neighborhoods and institutions.[20]

Second Homes for African Americans

Virden and his colleagues knew that the Illinois Technical School for
Colored Girls was unique. Although orphanages or "second homes" were
familiar sites in nineteenth- and early-twentieth-century urban neighborhoods, few such institutions existed for African American children,
Protestant or Catholic. According to historian Timothy A. Hacsi, 972
orphan asylums were operating in the United States in 1910. The majority of them, established to meet the child-welfare needs of immigrant
communities, were "local institutions, managed by private groups and
serving a specific clientele." And few of the children who lived in them
were true orphans. Most were half-orphans, who had one living parent
and had lost the other through death. A minority had two living parents,
who had fallen on unusually hard times. Many children stayed, therefore,
for relatively short periods and were reunited with their families.[21]

Asylum managers generally attempted to create homelike atmo-
spheres in which they provided shelter, food, education, and religious
training. But Catholic institutions also offered protection "from a society that was basically Protestant and anti-Catholic in nature." And they
were "especially willing to help families reunite," since Catholic charities
were generally "less judgmental . . . [and] less quick to condemn" than
Protestant ones. That stemmed in large part from the attitudes of Catholic sisters who were responsible for the day-to-day affairs of orphanages.
The Sisters of the Good Shepherd (and many other religious communities) had deep roots in the working class and knew that in reaching out
to the poor they were touching their own.[22]

Like American society, the vast majority of "second homes" were
segregated by race. That was true in the nineteenth century and remained
so as late as the 1930s. Orphanages that initially accepted a few black
or mulatto children tended to exclude them as their numbers increased.
For example, the Chicago Child Care Society and the Chicago Nursery
and Half-Orphan Asylum admitted African American children in the late
nineteenth century but began excluding them in the 1920s. Historian
Kenneth Cmiel has noted that as late as 1953, "*no* private Protestant
children's home in the city accepted black children." The Illinois Technical School welcomed black girls throughout that period, but it received
little recognition in the Catholic or black press for doing so. In fact, once
the battles over the charter had ended, the *Chicago Defender* criticized

the Catholic Church—the sisters were not specifically mentioned—for drawing the color line at Forty-ninth and Prairie.[23]

Concerns about religious persuasion as well as racial segregation prompted the *Defender*'s complaints. It argued that it was "unjust to have their orphan and dependent girls of the Protestant faith 'jim crowed' into a Catholic school, which was given thousands of dollars by the County for the care of these girls." Yet, at the same time, the *Defender* praised the Good Shepherds' advocate, Judge Pinckney, as a "RACE FRIEND"—one who "Defies the World." It did so because he had assisted the Amanda Smith Orphan Home in suburban Harvey in obtaining a state charter and public funds. Now, "our girls," the *Defender* remarked, would be sent to "an institution organized, maintained and controlled by our people." Not only was it all black, it was also Protestant.[24]

The Cook County Juvenile Court sent some black Protestant girls to the Amanda Smith Orphan Home in Harvey, but not all. The fourteen-year-old institution, twenty miles south of Chicago's Black Belt, never sheltered more than thirty or forty children at one time. Amanda Berry Smith, a former slave who became a renowned evangelist in the African Methodist Episcopal Church, officially opened the orphanage in 1899, when she was in her early sixties. She had completed a successful career as a missionary in New York, England, India, and Africa, and in 1893 she published *Amanda Smith's Own Story*. Proceeds from her autobiography and her newspaper, the *Helper*, along with personal savings and donations from friends (black and white), enabled her to purchase the Harvey property and operate the home.[25]

Even before her death in 1915, however, it was "a constant struggle" to keep the home afloat. The lack of ongoing public funding eventually resulted in conditions that were "almost intolerable." Yet, according to Virden, because there was an overwhelming need for an institution "for Protestant colored girls committed by the courts," it was chartered in 1913 as "The Amanda Smith Industrial School for Girls." Like the Illinois Technical School, it also received $15 per month from the county for every child sent to it. Boys who had previously lived at the orphan home found new quarters at the Louise Training School for Colored Boys, also chartered in 1913 in the Englewood neighborhood.[26]

Elizabeth McDonald, founder of the Louise Training School, was also a missionary of the African Methodist Episcopal Church. She did not travel abroad but concentrated her efforts on rescuing women and young girls from Chicago's criminal and sinful surroundings. In 1900 she showed the depth of her commitment by volunteering as a probation officer for the Cook County Juvenile Court. In 1905, she and her husband decided to take a small number of destitute children into their South Side home (at Sixty-first and Ada streets) and, two years later, to open the Louise Juvenile Home. With donations from black and white supporters (Judge Pinckney included), McDonald soon purchased a larger residence down the street, in which rent from the top floor helped support the orphanage below. In 1912 she reported that she had provided care to ninety children (with a daily count averaging between twenty and thirty) but was $1,400 in debt. Although the court regularly sent black children to the orphanage, it was ineligible to receive public funding. Thus, to ensure its survival, it was chartered as an industrial school for boys during the summer of 1913.[27]

Even with public assistance, the charitable enterprises of Smith and McDonald failed to endure. Although rechartered and given state aid in 1913, neither institution ever enjoyed a firm foundation. In 1915, Virden predicted that "unless radical changes could be brought about," the Smith School would close and the girls would be "removed to the only one which could receive them, the Illinois Technical School for Colored Girls." In an attempt to save the Smith School, Pinckney and Virden helped organize a new governing board, adding white men and women. Several women's clubs, both black and white, sponsored various fund-raising events.[28]

Still, complaints about bad management, deteriorating buildings, and poor staffing continued. In 1918 the Amanda Smith Industrial School burned to the ground; in 1920 the Louise Training School initially suspended its operations on Ada Street for a year and then finally closed when McDonald moved to California for health reasons. In reality, these schools simply confirmed what progressive reformers and social workers had already come to believe: institutional care was obsolete. By 1920, there was little doubt that "most dependent black children would *not* be cared for in institutions." Large ones, in particular, were considered "impersonal, rigid, [and] dehumanizing" and, hence, not worth saving. Foster care became the new system favored by the progressives.[29] Yet, after the Smith and McDonald schools closed, the Illinois Technical School continued to operate.

Orphanages for nonwhite children tended to be small, but not the Illinois Technical School for Colored Girls. It was a large institution that was "usually filled to capacity." In 1926, according to a contemporary account, it met "a great need" by caring daily for between 110 and 120 girls, about two-thirds of whom were not Catholic. By 1930, the school's estimated annual budget of nearly $30,000 was the largest amount spent "by private institutions serving Negroes (not including hospitals)" in Chicago. The Good Shepherd Sisters continued to accept children from the Cook County Juvenile Court, and they also admitted many more orphans, half-orphans, and children with both parents who came from outside the judicial system. In 1921, for example, in addition to the thirty-six girls sent by the court, there were ninety boarders.

The Sisters of the Good Shepherd were not unaware of the mounting attacks on institutional care and the growing preference for foster care. In response, they transformed the Illinois Technical School from an orphanage into a boarding school. By redesigning the purpose and form of their mission to black families, they were once again able to survive and build on their distinct advantage—the employment of a willing, trained, and dedicated corps of women-religious, who received little or no pay. Throughout the interwar decades, approximately eighteen nuns continued to live and work year-round at their boarding school on Chicago's South Side.[30]

Despite criticisms of being rigid and impersonal, places like the Illinois Technical School, not unlike the nuns who operated them, were surprisingly flexible and personal. Adapting to local needs and conditions, Catholic sisters built an array of institutions that were unmatched by any other single group of American women. Their orphanages, hospitals, and schools succeeded largely because they served local needs. That was especially true of those owned by the Good Shepherds, who had resided among some of Chicago's poorest since the mid-nineteenth century and become intimately involved in their lives. Since many of them had also grown up in immigrant homes, they knew firsthand how poverty ravaged family life. Once asylums became outmoded, the sisters altered the nature of their care and accepted the daughters of "working parents of small income, of mothers who face life alone, and widowers." Perhaps in 1911, when the nuns agreed to follow the advice of state and judicial officials and take *only* black children, they should have been less compromising. But had they turned their backs on such an obvious need, African American families would have been deprived of forty years of service.[31]

School Days

Although the Sisters of the Good Shepherd may have been generous to a fault in accepting needy children, they did not run a freewheeling school. As women who chose to live in community, they believed that routines and rules ensured the common good and furthered shared goals. They were less interested in individual rights and personal freedoms. Certainly, from the viewpoint of middle-class observers, life at the Illinois Technical School was monotonous and regimented. But it was not easy for working-class parents who were forced by unemployment, illness, or the death of a spouse to give up the everyday care of their children. Most took great consolation in knowing that their daughters were in a stable environment where they could be educated and live among individuals who could be trusted.[32]

Schools as well as jobs motivated many black migrants to leave the rural South for the industrial North during World War I. In response to an advertisement in the *Chicago Defender,* one father expressed his concerns: "I have some children I lost my wife just a year ago and I would like to get a place where I could prop[er]ly educate them." Whether he eventually made his way to Chicago's South Side is not known. But if he did, he might well have knocked on the door of the Illinois Technical School a few days after arriving and left a daughter with the Good Shepherds until he found employment, an apartment, and even a new wife. What he may have expected to be only a few weeks or months easily could have stretched into a couple of years, because newcomers were frequently sidetracked and disappointed by the discrimination and hostility that they met in the "land of hope."[33]

In later years, when fewer youngsters found second homes in orphanages, working parents still relied on local institutions for support and still sought out educational opportunities for their children. Boarding schools, where available, offered both. They were "safe places" that provided solid instruction, according to Mary Louise Mims. A graduate of the Illinois Technical School herself, she subsequently chose to enroll her daughter, Marguerite (Margo) Anderson, there in 1939, where she remained until graduation in 1947. Margo remembers feeling that she would have been freer and had more fun in a public school, yet she believes today that she received a better education from the sisters, a stronger set of values, and a deeper appreciation of classical music. She laughingly admits that she also learned how to sew and crochet.[34]

Girls at the Illinois Technical School spent most of each weekday in the classroom, engaged in formal or informal study. Like students in the city's other Catholic schools, they first learned the fundamentals of reading, spelling, grammar, and arithmetic. They later studied geography, history, civics, English literature, health, and penmanship. They also had classes in religion, either Christian doctrine or Bible history, in every grade. The Sisters of the Good Shepherd attempted to create a harmonious program that took "into account the whole child, her physical care, her education, social and spiritual well-being, and artistic training." Thus dance, music, sewing, and cooking embellished the standard fare.[35]

The younger children danced (tap or ballet) and sang in after-school hours, while most of the older girls had music lessons (piano and violin) or practice, including choir. By the 1930s, there were pianos in every classroom and several more in the parlors and auditorium; violins were also plentiful. But the Good Shepherds always stressed work and self-sufficiency. As a result, seventh and eighth graders learned the basics of cooking as well as the intricacies of sewing, so that in time they might take care of themselves or contribute to their families' incomes. Whoever stayed in the sisters' charge for any length of time knew how to sew. Beginners started by stitching flat pieces and ended by making graduation dresses. And everyone had daily chores—serving at meals, washing dishes, sweeping rooms and stairways. All, except the youngest, helped with the laundry, which the nuns and a few lay employees did on the premises in an outmoded steam laundry. Nevertheless, clothes and bedding were reportedly "clean and in perfect order."[36]

During the 1930s and 1940s, the school gave more time and attention to play. The Good Shepherd Sisters had come to believe that along "with studies and daily tasks," play made for "a balanced program of wholesome activity." Thus, equipment and excursions that seemed "meager" in 1925 were a good deal less spare a decade later. Although the boarders continued to perform routine chores, which were considered essential in building character and keeping the institution in good order, the opportunities to play and socialize increased.[37]

The Illinois Technical School, which occupied a full block of land between Prairie and Indiana avenues, had a large, enclosed field called "the Yard." The girls used it for outdoor games and sports on days without snow or rain. During the 1930s and 1940s, the chaplain from nearby Corpus Christi parish coached a softball team, and the sidewalks surrounding the field were "put to good use by enthusiastic and skilled roller skaters." Students took turns on the swings, maypole, and parallel bars. In inclement weather, their activities were confined to a large playroom. In 1939 the school had its own Girl Scout troop, Number 342, for boarders more than twelve years old. It held weekly meetings to which the scouts proudly wore their uniforms. They learned handicrafts and songs, went on hikes and picnics in Washington Park and at the zoo, and took trips to the Museum of Science and Industry. Boarders received visitors on Sundays and occasionally went home (or to a relative's), as they did on holidays and during summers. On special days, all of them enjoyed the carnivals at Corpus Christi parish, annual picnics sponsored by the Chicago Automobile Club or Catholic Charities, the popular Bud Billiken parades, and outings (beginning in the 1940s) to Riverview Park.[38]

It is unclear how much the students learned about black history and culture, but they definitely were conscious of their race and heritage. In 1915, four years after the school opened, the children won prizes for their needlework at the Chicago Coliseum during an exposition celebrating the fiftieth anniversary of the Emancipation Proclamation. During the 1919 race riot, which "raged with particular fury" in their vicinity, the police captain detailed a special officer to guard the premises at night. A sister later described the riot as "a disgrace to our city" and one that left the older girls confused and wondering if "our people . . . are now set back fifty years in progress."[39]

During normal times and within the confines of their school home, the students should not have doubted their value or worth. At least once each day, they passed a large engraving of Christ the Good Shepherd, "a kindly Man with a colored and white child at His knee." Underneath the engraving was the legend "He died for both." The Good Shepherd Sisters, who sometimes referred to "their children" as "ebony lambs," boasted of their pupils' progress, as indicated by letters to nuns living elsewhere. On most Saturday afternoons throughout the 1930s and 1940s, they arranged for groups of boarders to attend live performances by renowned black performers at the Regal Theatre, only a few blocks away.[40]

In 1953 the sisters sold their building and grounds to the Archdiocese of Chicago for one dollar. It, in turn, gave the property to the Franciscans at Corpus Christi parish so they could expand their school and open a day nursery for neighborhood children. The Good Shepherds chose to stay on the South Side in 1911, but forty-two years later they chose to leave. Times had changed, and so had their neighborhood.[41]

During the interwar years, the Illinois Technical School had become part of the city's Black Belt, and the nuns believed that "the special need" to which their institution had been dedicated had "now passed." Because African Americans had more educational opportunities, school enrollment had fallen to half of what it had been in previous decades. The sisters also feared that "in another year or so" they "might be asked to withdraw" because the school was increasingly viewed as segregated. In 1952, the principal of the Illinois Technical School for Colored Girls said that a priest had taken their "letter head and drawn a line through 'for Colored Girls'" and returned it. The Good Shepherds had never opposed admitting white girls, but from where would they come? The enrollment of white students in any school in their neighborhood was highly unlikely. Finally, the nuns noted the rise in local crime. Purse snatching and drug use had become "customary," and "frequent experiences with intruders [were] alarming."[42]

All of those issues—declining enrollment, segregated versus integrated student bodies, and neighborhood crime—would continue to challenge Catholic sisters and their institutions on Chicago's South Side for decades. Although their efforts have never been widely acknowledged, they demonstrate a generosity of spirit and strength of will unique among white women, Catholic or non-Catholic. As women-religious who chose to link their lives to those of African Americans, their vocation provided them with an "alternative identity" that clearly distinguished them from other women and brought them respect for what they represented as well as for what they offered. Their religious dress also gave them agency often denied to other white women and reduced the salience of color among black children and their families.[43]

Catholic sisters who taught African American children before the modern civil rights movement were not revolutionaries, nor did they publicly advocate political solutions to social problems, seek media attention, or even request adequate remuneration. Their work, not their words, expressed their values. As classroom teachers, routinely taken for granted, their interests and ambitions centered more on their students than on themselves. Yet their numbers in Chicago and elsewhere, the level of their commitment, and the rate of their success make them significant figures in the history of twentieth-century urban America.

5 *Missionary Sisters in Black Belt Neighborhoods*

Crowds of impoverished eastern European immigrants, the severe living and working conditions they confronted, and the generous response of a corps of settlement workers: these are, as previously noted, the typically remembered images of foreigners arriving in Chicago a century ago. But nowhere in this collage of faces are those of missionary sisters, who began their work in the city's South and West Side Black Belts early in the twentieth century. Female and white, they differed from their settlement counterparts—middle-class and Protestant—in that they were working-class (often immigrants) themselves, and Catholic. By the 1950s, close to one hundred missionary sisters resided in African American neighborhoods. Yet, because they lived and worked in locales that were not frequented by most white Chicagoans, the efforts of these nuns remained largely unknown.

All that began to change in the 1960s when Catholic sisters became more visibly involved in the civil rights campaign for racial justice. In July 1963, newspaper and television cameras captured images of seven Franciscan Sisters picketing in front of Lewis Towers on North Michigan Avenue to protest the discriminatory policies of the Illinois Club for Catholic Women. In March 1965, the national media carried dramatic photographs of "new nuns" walking with Martin Luther King Jr. from

Originally published as "Ministering Hope to Chicago," *Chicago History* 31 (Fall 2002): 4–23.

Selma, Alabama, to Montgomery. And in June and August 1965, Chicagoans saw and read frequent news stories about the Daughters of Charity from Marillac House, who were arrested, fined, and subsequently found guilty of blocking traffic in a downtown demonstration against school superintendent Ben Willis and his policy of "double shifts" in overcrowded buildings. The presence of sisters in the streets as visible witnesses to the Christian principles of justice and charity took almost everyone by surprise. But their "ministry of presence" had begun decades earlier, with little notice, in the classrooms of local parish schools.[1]

In the Beginning

It is difficult, if not impossible, to pinpoint precise moments of major change. Nevertheless, in 1891, American Catholics took a determined first step on the long, hard road to securing justice for all. During that nadir of race relations in the United States, a white Philadelphian and heiress in her early thirties, Katharine Drexel (canonized in 2000), founded the Sisters of the Blessed Sacrament for Indians and Colored People. Following the Civil War, church officials had shown scant interest in the welfare of African Americans, paying only lip service to suggestions of assisting them. Catholic bishops and clergy simply assumed that blacks were Protestant and therefore rejected any notion that the American Catholic Church as a whole had a responsibility to them. Drexel did not share that attitude. Instead she decided to commit her life and fortune to America's most oppressed by demonstrating that they too were God's people and deserving of support and care.[2]

The Sisters of the Blessed Sacrament commenced operations one year after a small group of women in Washington, D.C., established the Daughters of the American Revolution (DAR). Drexel could readily have been a founding member of the DAR; her maternal ancestors were living in Pennsylvania before the American Revolution and, according to family tradition, one was a Continental soldier. But she chose a radically different path that minimized rather than emphasized class and blood lines. She and her community of women-religious attempted to follow a New Testament directive to "show no partiality" in the practice of their faith, except to favor those most in need.[3]

In 1894, Walter Elliott, a prominent white priest in New York City, discovered to his dismay that Drexel's determination in this regard would not be altered. After she refused his request for $500 for a special project, Elliott wrote to a friend that "she said in effect 'no poor white trash need apply.' Only black and red are the team they [Drexel and her sisters] will back." Drexel's commitment to assisting African Americans and Native Americans remained firm until her death in 1955. Besides devoting her life, she spent her entire $20 million inheritance (a sum roughly equivalent to $268 million today) on their behalf. Hers was an unusual and radical response, even in contemporary terms.[4]

Although much of Drexel's work was discredited or ignored by white Catholics, her efforts did not go unnoticed by the American Catholic Church's first black priest, Father Augustus Tolton, pastor of St. Monica's in Chicago. Shortly after his arrival in 1889, he began an aggressive fundraising campaign to build a church for black Catholics at Dearborn and Thirty-sixth streets. Tolton almost at once asked Drexel for a "helping hand." In another appeal in 1891, he apologized for "vexing" her but again explained his overwhelming need. If Drexel felt vexed, her response did not indicate it. She sent an initial $100 and over time contributed approximately $30,000 before Tolton died in 1897. He appreciated her generosity, remarking that she stood alone "in the whole history of the Church in America" as the only person who had offered her "treasury for the sole benefit of the Colored and Indians." At the end of the nineteenth century, except for Drexel, the record of the Catholic Church was hardly impressive on matters of race.[5]

Fifteen years after Tolton's death, Drexel responded again to an appeal from the pastor of St. Monica's, then Father John Morris, an Irish American. This time she sent teachers rather than funds to Chicago. On a muggy day in August 1912, six Blessed Sacrament Sisters, who were accompanied by Drexel (or Mother Katharine as she was known and addressed), arrived by train. Their goal was to open a parish school. That they did: first in the convent at 3669 South Wabash Avenue, and later in the former Eighth Regiment Armory at Thirty-seventh Street and Wabash Avenue. The nuns' arrival marked a "turning point in the history of the Negro in the Archdiocese," which until then had made no concerted effort to educate black children, the majority of whom were not Catholic.[6]

Both convent and armory were located in the city's expanding Black Belt on the South Side, where more than 75 percent of the growing African American population lived. In 1912, a sizable number of white people still had homes between Twelfth and Thirty-ninth streets, Wentworth Avenue, and Lake Michigan, but ten years later, few of them remained. Almost no white women lived there except for the Blessed Sacrament Sisters. Their schools were intended for black children, but segregation was never a policy; whites were not excluded, but almost none ever came. Because Mother Katharine used her inheritance to cover the sisters' living expenses, children who attended the school paid no tuition in the first years and only a small amount later. Enrollment grew from 150 students in 1912 to nearly 1,000 in 1925. During that time, the number of sisters at St. Monica's increased from six to sixteen.[7]

In opening parish schools in Chicago and elsewhere, the Sisters of the Blessed Sacrament were responding to the long-standing demands of black Catholics who wanted a Catholic education for their children. Participants in the African American Catholic congresses, which held national meetings between 1889 and 1893, recognized this need. Attendees at the first congress in Washington, D.C., pledged "to aid in establishing, wherever we are to be found, Catholic schools, embracing the primary and higher branches of knowledge." At the third gathering in Philadelphia, in 1892, they praised "the magnificent generosity" and "devoted labors" of Mother Katherine and the nuns who were preparing to teach black children.[8]

The Sisters of the Blessed Sacrament, although white, had not grown up surrounded by family privilege.[9] Unlike Drexel, who was probably the most powerful woman in the American Catholic Church, most members of her religious community came from East Coast working-class Irish homes. Although Protestants looked upon Irish Catholics as "alien," Mother Katharine did not. Having grown up in the embrace of Irish servants, tutors, priests, and nuns, she knew the capacity of Irish women for goodness, generosity, and zeal. Most of those who entered Drexel's community had an education common to working-class women of the time; none had attended college, but some had high school diplomas. Mother Katharine did not neglect their preparation as teachers, however. She invited faculty from local colleges to offer courses at the motherhouse, and she sent a number of sisters to Drexel University (founded by her uncle) and to the University of Pennsylvania. On them she confidently rested the success of her grand design: a congregation of white women dedicated to the "service and sacrifice" of people of color, Catholic or not.[10]

Drexel left little to chance. She made sure that these missionary-teachers understood what this important but unpopular calling might require. Hence she asked each young woman, before admitting her to the community, to complete a questionnaire. Two questions directly asked the candidate whether she would "object to tending and washing Indian and colored children" or nursing them when they were sick "even with contagious diseases." Those who did not demur were usually admitted. Mother Katharine intended their benevolence to be hands-on and practical. She repeatedly warned that "if there is any prejudice in the mind we must uproot it, or it will pull us down."[11]

In Chicago, Sister Paul of the Cross served as superior of the small group of nuns who launched the Sisters of the Blessed Sacrament's long history on the South Side. (Several members are still at St. Elizabeth's.) Formerly Katy Kiniry, Sister Paul of the Cross had grown up the daughter of Irish immigrant parents in Sewickley, Pennsylvania, where she worked as a seamstress until joining the order in 1891 at age twenty. When Kiniry wrote Mother Katharine of her desire to enter the convent, she explained: "We are poor and I am obliged to sew for a living at $4.50 per week." Because she gave her earnings to her parents to support their large family, she had little or no money to bring with her to the community. Yet, despite the immediate hardship her departure would cause at home, she wrote that she felt called to "the duties of a Missionary Sister" as a way of offering her life "to the service of others." In 1899, Sister Paul of the Cross was among the first nuns sent to St. Francis de Sales in Rock Castle, Virginia, where she taught domestic science, among other subjects. She remained there until asked to open a new mission in Chicago in 1912. She was forty-one years old when she arrived at St. Monica's.[12]

In their first years, the Sisters of the Blessed Sacrament did not question the power of education to overcome bigotry or of Christianity to unite the races. They also shunned publicity and generally avoided politics. From unpleasant experiences, they knew that their efforts to educate black children were less likely to provoke hostility from whites if they eluded public notice. The nuns were also very much aware that most African Americans voted Republican. In Chicago, for example, the *Chicago Defender*, considered "the voice of a voiceless people," was also the voice of its staunch Republican owner and editor, Robert S. Abbott, a fervent Protestant. Only upon his retirement in the late 1930s did the *Defender* begin to support the Democratic Party.[13]

Most Blessed Sacrament Sisters were bred-in-the-bones Democrats. Although they set aside their old identities as working-class Irish women once they became "brides of Christ," the majority remained Democratic sympathizers and voters. Had they resided in immigrant neighborhoods, as did many other women-religious and settlement workers, their politics would not have been divisive. And although no documents reflect their feelings about Abbott, the sisters probably did not consider him friendly. In 1913, a year after they arrived in Chicago, the *Defender* criticized them and Father Morris, St. Monica's pastor, for opening a "Jim Crow" school. Abbott's militant newspaper, which opposed separate schools, used a banner headline to urge parents to remove their children. The nuns were surprised by the attack, as were some families in the black community, who rallied around the nuns. Sister Paul of the Cross wrote to Mother Katharine that "the 'Jim Crow' article in the paper seems to have helped" the school. "Yesterday," she continued, "we enrolled two more pupils, and some of our children's people, to whom I was talking, are indignant."[14]

At Hull-House, on the near West Side, no such conflicts with the *Defender* occurred. But few blacks lived nearby. The neighborhood was populated mostly by Catholics and Jews, so Hull-House residents, who were culturally Protestant, were prudent not to have appeared religious. That stance would not have been beneficial, however, in African Americans neighborhoods. Most blacks were Protestant, and well into the twentieth century they (members and nonmembers alike) regarded their churches as essential, powerful institutions. In fact, it was Christianity—belief in Christ as the Savior of all people—that provided common ground for many black families and Catholic sisters.[15]

In an era of scientific racism, Drexel's religious community did not subscribe to widely held beliefs that African Americans were innately inferior. Nor did the Sisters of the Blessed Sacrament think that a separate school for black children was harmful or discriminatory. Like most of their white contemporaries, they thought little about racial integration and more about personal improvement and broader opportunities. Thus the sisters focused their energies mainly on classroom instruction, which they regarded as the gateway to both. St. Monica's missionary-teachers believed that their school was an attack on Jim Crow, and they wholeheartedly agreed with the sentiments of a 1917 cartoon in the *Chicago Defender*. It affirmed that education would remove prejudice and "open the door of hope beyond which is success."[16]

For two decades, the Sisters of the Blessed Sacrament staffed the only parish schools in Chicago's Black Belt.[17] Then, in 1933, six Franciscan Sisters from Dubuque, Iowa, arrived at Corpus Christi parish at Forty-ninth Street and South Parkway (now Dr. Martin Luther King Jr. Drive). These nuns were, for the most part, German and German American. Unlike the Blessed Sacrament Sisters, who usually came from eastern cities and immigrant families of about six to eight children, the Dubuque Franciscans were raised on Iowa farms or occasionally in small towns and frequently had between ten and twelve siblings. Philippine Wieneke, the fourth of eleven children born to German immigrants, is a case in point. She grew up on a farm outside Cedar Rapids, Iowa, and attended rural public schools before entering the Franciscans in 1881 at age fifteen. In 1920, Wieneke, then Sister Dominica, became mother general of the entire congregation. When she stepped down in 1932, she surprised all by volunteering to lead the first band of Franciscans to Chicago's South

Side. These nuns went to Corpus Christi at the invitation of the pastor, Father Nicholas Christoffel, a Franciscan friar. In a letter to Dubuque, he had described the enterprise "as large and promising," the people as "poor," and the day-to-day work as "missionary."[18]

The Franciscan priests and sisters who worked together at Corpus Christi also shared a missionary outpost in Chowtsun, China. Chowtsun and Chicago had little in common, but from 1884, when the American bishops created the Commission for Catholic Missions among the Colored People and Indians, the prospect of conversion connected the Chinese to African Americans and Native Americans in the minds of most Catholics and their missionaries. Because blacks generally were not Catholics, they resembled in official church eyes the unconverted Chinese or Native Americans more than the Catholic immigrants from Ireland, Poland, Italy, or Mexico. During the interwar period, the words *race* and *ethnicity* were without fixed meanings and often overlapped, but for Catholics *converted* and *unconverted* were clearly opposites. All non-Catholics, whatever their cultural differences, were separate and apart. Thus they commanded, and at times received, the special attention of Catholic missionaries. In the case of the Dubuque Franciscans, the sisters who went to Chicago or to Chowtsun *volunteered* for the assignments. In all other instances, community superiors assigned them to a particular place without giving them an opportunity to choose.[19]

Black Catholics in Chicago, like many immigrant Catholics, had their own parishes. The policy of the Catholic Church in northern cities had been to segregate blacks just as it had previously segregated "ethnics" into "national" parishes. After thousands of southern blacks migrated north during World War I, the racial climate grew increasingly hostile. Thus what was once seen as a "pastorally appropriate" policy before the war became a "racially desirable" one later on. Although it became apparent that the barriers against African Americans were racial rather than simply ethnic, some Catholics believed that segregation into separate schools and churches strengthened black Catholic identity and did not promote discrimination. They saw previously white South Side parishes develop into vibrant places when black Catholics claimed them as their own. During the interwar years, Chicago's three African American parishes—St. Elizabeth's (1924, incorporating the earlier St. Monica's), St. Anselm's (1932), and Corpus Christi (1933)—functioned as national parishes in most ways. They were, however, considered missionary enterprises, and white priests and nuns staffed them. As a result, the Blessed Sacrament and Franciscan sisters who taught in the schools viewed themselves not only as teachers, but as missionaries too.[20]

From the 1910s until World War II, the majority of missionary-teachers entered religious life with an eighth-grade education. Only a few had completed high school, still a luxury that many immigrant and some native-born girls could not afford, especially during the Great Depression. Almost all had work experience: factory or clerical jobs for the Blessed Sacrament Sisters and farm chores for the Franciscans. Less educated than settlement workers, these nuns nevertheless knew from the traditions and practices of their religious communities how it important it was to reside among those they hoped to help. As neighbors, they could better understand the needs of Chicago's black families and identify more closely with them across racial and class lines. Although white, the sisters' backgrounds—compared to those of settlement workers—more nearly resembled those of African Americans. A German nun highlighted this fact. Remarking on the missionary-teachers' determination to improve themselves professionally by acquiring state certification and college degrees, she said "we can lift ourselves up and lift up blacks at the same time."[21]

On Chicago's West Side, in the Hull-House neighborhood, where there was a much smaller African American population, the Sisters of the Holy Family of Nazareth opened St. Joseph's Mission School at Loomis and Thirteenth streets in 1933. St. Joseph's was a part, but a separate part, of the large Jesuit parish of Holy Family, then made up mostly of Italians. In the 1890s, the Irish and German parishioners who had built the impressive Gothic church on Roosevelt Road had not welcomed the Italians, and the Italians in turn refused to accept black migrants in the 1930s. As a result of continuing neighborhood conflicts, the Jesuit pastor, Father Raymond B. Walsh, established a separate mission under the leadership of Father Arnold J. Garvy, an elderly but dedicated Jesuit who had been baptized at Holy Family in 1868. Father Walsh also appealed successfully to Mother Regina Wentowska "to find a corp[s] of at least three or four [nuns] to open up a school for colored children in this parish." Not until the late 1950s would African Americans be accepted into the main school of Holy Family parish.[22]

Unlike the missionary sisters on the South Side, the Sisters of the Holy Family were largely Polish and Polish American. Founded in 1875 by a Polish noblewoman in Rome, this order of nuns considered itself an international organization and prided itself on its willingness to go wherever needed in the interests of the Catholic Church. A handful of sisters had come to Chicago in 1885 to teach the children of Polish immigrants in St. Josaphat parish at Belden and Southport avenues. There the nuns worked primarily as teachers (and later as nurses) among Polish

Catholics, but they did not restrict their services to Poles. Even though
St. Joseph Mission was to be housed in a decrepit building and serve children who were black and extremely poor, the Sisters of the Holy Family
gladly accepted the new work and considered it "a high honor," according to the minutes of a 1932 meeting of the provincial council. Mother
Melitona Mach, a forty-six-year-old native Chicagoan with more than a
decade of teaching experience, became St. Joseph's first school principal
and convent superior in 1933.[23]

Acceptance of a religious vocation in the Catholic Church and belief
in the transforming power of literacy motivated these working-class
women of Polish, German, and Irish backgrounds to live and work for
years—often entire lifetimes—in black neighborhoods on the city's West
and South sides. Chicago's settlement workers often disavowed any claim
that their work was religiously inspired, arguing that missionaries (Protestant or Catholic) were too prone to proselytizing. Settlement workers
chose instead to separate themselves from such efforts and gradually
became more secular and scientific. In the process, though, they also
became more removed from the religious cultures and day-to-day needs
of the city's most underprivileged—a group that repeatedly placed their
faith in prayer and education to rise above their oppressed past.[24]

Missionary sisters believed that they had been called by God to a
life of special service in the church. Many of them, however, found other
attractions as well. Some young women, who had never been far from
their family farms, saw adventure in a life lived out of a single piece of
luggage; others left behind troubled homes or monotonous jobs with no
regrets. Most working-class women, whose circumstances were constrained and who had few of the educational advantages of middle-class
settlement workers, joined congregations of teaching and nursing sisters
to take advantage of the opportunity for self-improvement and service.

Throughout the nineteenth century and well into the twentieth,
active religious communities offered scores of young Catholics an exciting alternative to the choices available to most American women. Convent life provided a sure path of social mobility for those who wanted
both an education and a career, and Catholics traditionally accorded special status to nuns (higher than the laity though well below the ordained
clergy). Besides improving their own lives, these women desired to better the lives of others. One of the most compelling reasons for taking
the veil was to engage in an enterprise of good works, one that was not
only pleasing to God but also socially beneficial and widely respected.
Thus joining a religious community meant the beginning, not the end,
of a useful and admired life.[25]

The motives of the comparatively few sisters who chose to link their lives to African Americans in poor urban neighborhoods were fueled primarily by the power of religion. Missionary-teachers at home demonstrated an idealism and generosity of spirit that is more commonly associated with zealous missionaries who traveled to foreign lands. In choosing to enter the Sisters of the Blessed Sacrament, for example, a number of potential candidates expressed a strong desire to give themselves "entirely to the service of God." Still, the mundane efforts of home missionaries received almost no support or notice from the clergy and hierarchy of the Catholic Church. It was clear from the beginning that there was little status to be gained in following the lead of Katharine Drexel.[26]

Despite the publicity the Sisters of the Blessed Sacrament received at the order's founding in 1891, the community never numbered more than about five hundred women, and many of them were recruited in Ireland. One young woman who entered from Lismore in County Waterford in 1913 stated that an aunt, who had once lived in America, vehemently objected to her joining a convent in the United States and "working for the Blacks." A young Philadelphian remarked in a letter to Mother Katharine in 1915 that her mother "had not yet given in, and I am only afraid she will not, even at the last." During the 1920s, both of these women lived on the South Side of Chicago and taught at St. Elizabeth's. Sister Norma Drexler, a Franciscan who grew up in Dyersville, Iowa, wanted "to offer herself completely" to God. Years later, she remembered that her mother was "worried to death" when she volunteered in 1933 for the Corpus Christi mission. She taught at that location for twenty years.[27]

Ministering Hope

What did "home" missionary work include? For Catholic sisters, racial uplift and evangelization meant education. Above all else they were educators, and their primary work was in the schools. Because they had personally benefited from classroom instruction, they never doubted its rewards—nor did most African American migrants. For parents who wanted a better life for their children, neighborhood Catholic schools could not be ignored. According to contemporaries, students received a "more thorough education in a quieter atmosphere" than they could have acquired in Chicago's public schools, which began operating in shifts during the interwar years. Also, most white public-school teachers felt abandoned in overcrowded ghetto schools, where "the myth of black inferiority flourished." Missionary-teachers, who chose to teach in black schools, were different. They believed that ignorance was the result of circumstance rather than race and worked to mold black youngsters into responsible and capable young adults. In general, sisters provided good teaching in a stable, orderly environment; and they emphasized values learned in their working-class homes and schools—hard work, thrift, honesty, reliability, and cleanliness. Not surprisingly, they did not overtly challenge segregated society. Instead they created solid citizens and ministered hope within it.[28]

Parish schools were faith-based operations, although many who enrolled in them were unchurched or non-Catholic. The sisters, who shared the assumptions of pre–Vatican II Catholics, believed there was no salvation outside the church. Therefore, besides teaching lessons in reading, writing, and arithmetic, they instructed their pupils in the tenets of the Catholic faith and its liturgical rituals. As a result, many students (and often parents) became Catholics and participated fully in the sacramental life of their parishes. One girl, who was baptized with her family, said she liked "the ritual of acceptance into the Church" and loved "the quiet and peace there, the smell of incense and the glow of candles. . . . It all seemed very godly." She found in the parish church "everything [her] house was not: quiet, polished, respectful, and orderly." Father Joseph Eckert, a Society of Divine Word priest who was known as the "Great Evangelizer" for his success in bringing whole families into the church, served as pastor of three black parishes during nearly twenty years on the South Side. He prided himself on his activist approach in recruiting converts, especially among the unchurched. Yet he recognized the school as the most important parish institution and knew good teaching produced more results than good preaching.[29]

In 1932, when Father Eckert became pastor of St. Anselm's at Sixty-first Street and Michigan Avenue, he asked Katharine Drexel to provide "a nice staff of fine teachers." He remarked that St. Elizabeth's, where he had previously been pastor, was "in fine running order" because of the "efficient teaching done by the Sisters [of the Blessed Sacrament]." Several times during the 1930s, he appealed to Mother Katharine to send more nuns so that St. Anselm's would not need to hire lay teachers. Cost was not the problem, as Drexel generally paid the lay teachers' salaries when she could not send sisters. Rather, Eckert insisted that parents wanted their children in nuns' classrooms. Sister Janvier Williams, a 1948 graduate of St. Elizabeth's High School and a retired teacher, believes he was correct. The sisters "were hard on us, but they made us learn." That, she said, is why "so many [of us] were successful when we graduated."[30]

Missionary-teachers spent few hours inside their convents. They divided most days between the school and the neighborhood. The Blessed

Sacrament Sisters actively engaged in "home visiting" and routinely made rounds among the sick in Provident Hospital. Whereas the Franciscans and the Sisters of the Holy Family visited homes only in unusual circumstances, the Sisters of the Blessed Sacrament did so daily in the early years and later twice weekly. They went after school to the homes of students, occasionally walking them there but usually dropping in unannounced. A former student, Gwen Smith, remembered that she was afraid the nuns would disapprove of her mother's smoking. Therefore, whenever they appeared on her block—"they walked everywhere, always in twos"—she would run home and warn her mother that "the nuns are coming" so she could hide her cigarettes. During visits, the sisters discussed school problems, family troubles, and other difficulties. Because they knew what it meant to be poor, the nuns "never seemed surprised by what they saw or heard," according to Smith and her sister. And they often returned with food, clothes, or medicine. Although the Franciscans did not regularly visit homes, broadcast journalist Warner Saunders, who attended Corpus Christi schools between 1941 and 1953, recalled numerous field trips to parks, museums, and libraries. And one of his teachers enrolled him in a program at the Art Institute of Chicago because he showed a "proclivity toward art."[31]

On the eve of World War II, the first and only group of African American missionary-teachers arrived in Chicago. In September 1941, five Oblate Sisters of Providence settled in Morgan Park and opened Holy Name of Mary School to 110 children. Mother Mary Claude Hudlin, a forty-five-year-old native of St. Louis and former public school teacher, led this pioneering band of black sisters from Baltimore. A month later, the *Chicago Defender* announced their arrival with the headline "5 Race Nuns Placed in a Parish Here" and printed each one's name. A Catholic missionary magazine observed in January 1942 that the Oblates had "taken their place beside the Blessed Sacrament Sisters and the Franciscan Sisters and the Sisters of the Holy Family of Nazareth" in an "'all-out' effort" to bring Chicago's African Americans into the church. Their determination continued until July 2002, when the final four Oblates closed the school's doors—the result of low enrollments and budget deficits.[32]

The Oblate Sisters of Providence, founded in 1829, began educating and evangelizing African Americans nearly sixty years before the Sisters of the Blessed Sacrament commenced their work. Yet not until the middle of the twentieth century did religious communities of white women welcome blacks. Before then, African Americans who wished to become Catholic sisters were encouraged to join the Oblates or the Sisters of the Holy Family, whose motherhouse was in New Orleans. Over time, however, white women-religious grew to recognize that exclusion and segregation were forms of discrimination and sinful. Sister Lucy Williams, a Corpus Christi graduate, joined the Dubuque Franciscans in 1953; she was the first African American to do so. She admitted to living through some difficult days but remained in religious life because "the community changed." In the beginning, Sister Lucy said, a number of sisters considered her a "problem." Now they think of her as a "gift." Over the years, she has helped them to better understand the damaging effects of racism, a virus that poisons the soul.[33]

A New Day at Holy Angels

By the 1940s, there were sure signs that the missionary relationship between blacks and whites in the Archdiocese of Chicago was on the wane. The shift to interracialism was evident in the activities of the Catholic Youth Organization (1930), the programs of Friendship House (1942), and the educational efforts of the Catholic Interracial Council of Chicago (1947).[34] Yet in the day-to-day affairs of local parish schools, there was little indication that a movement away from segregation and toward integration was under way. On the tails of World War II, Cardinal Samuel A. Stritch "outlined a very definite mission plan" when he opened Holy Angels, a South Side parish on Oakwood Boulevard, to African Americans. He appointed a "zealous young [white] priest" as pastor, along with several energetic assistants, and replaced four Chicago-based Sisters of Mercy with twelve School Sisters of St. Francis from Milwaukee. He explained the new enterprise to them as "indeed mission work." Sister Hortensia Stickelmaier, the first principal of Holy Angels, left a Catholic mission in Yazoo, Mississippi, to go to Chicago in 1946.[35]

The second migration of African Americans, which began during World War II, dramatically affected Chicago's South Side. The neighborhood around Holy Angels became almost entirely black and enrollment in the school dropped, leaving only about a hundred white children. An "edict of a crusty old pastor," Father Maurice J. McKenna, who died in the summer of 1945, had prevented these newcomers from becoming students or parishioners. That changed quickly under the new administration, one that understood the school's significance in reaching black families. Priests and nuns personally invited parents to send their children to Holy Angels. In the first year, 600 youngsters responded; twenty years later, when Sister Hortensia left Holy Angels, the enrollment had climbed to 1,300. By then, there were more than twenty Franciscan Sisters teaching in the school; four of them were African American.[36]

Catholic converts at Holy Angels during this period numbered in the thousands—enough to fill several South Side churches. The sisters' full-court press brought new life to the school, and Father Joseph G. Richards's energetic program of religious instruction proved equally important. An assistant at Holy Angels until he became pastor in 1957, Richards had learned from Father Eckert, Chicago's successful Catholic evangelizer, how to be an activist and how to use the school in recruiting converts. When parents came to Holy Angels to register their children, they also agreed to attend religious instruction twice a week and Mass on Sunday. Neither children nor parents were required to become Catholic (although 60 to 75 percent did). They were forced, however, to take seriously the school's religious dimension. Each year at registration, parents or guardians met individually with a sister and also a priest. The conferences resulted in a partial parish census, which prompted Catholics and non-Catholics alike to believe that they had a stake in Holy Angels.[37]

Religious instruction was free, but the school was not. In the late 1940s, each child paid a dollar a month (siblings less) and purchased uniforms (about eight dollars) as well as several textbooks. The students attended Mass together on Wednesdays and then again on Sundays with parents present. In the classrooms, the School Sisters of St. Francis emphasized the basics while following a regular routine and maintaining order. More often then not, they re-created learning environments similar to those they had known as youngsters in ethnic parishes in Milwaukee or Chicago. Since Holy Angels' families invested money and time in this enterprise, parent-teacher relations were normally close and cooperative. With few major disciplinary problems and almost no dismissals, most pupils stayed in school and learned.[38]

Some families were Catholic, but a large majority were not active in any church. In the South, where the education of blacks was casual at best, few parents of Holy Angels' students had advanced beyond the eighth grade. Almost all of them were poor despite the hours they worked, and most lived in congested apartments that proliferated on the South Side in the postwar years, when Chicago's black population nearly doubled. The Catholic sisters who lived in this neighborhood were, for the most part, daughters or granddaughters of immigrants (German, Irish, Polish, Czech, Slovak, or Dutch) and intimately familiar with the hardships of trying to make ends meet. What they learned as neighboring nuns were the additional problems imposed by prejudice, "the only obstacle" to opportunity, according to a Sister of the Blessed Sacrament in a nearby school. It is clear that missionary-teachers saw African Americans as different or "other"—social and religious institutions had taught them that—but they understood better than most whites the burdens of black-ness. From their perspective, one of the best ways to overcome them and increase the chance of success was a religious education. Impressive numbers of black families agreed. It explains why they paid a premium to send their children to Holy Angels and promised to attend Sunday Mass and religious instruction.[39]

Throughout the 1950s, the Franciscans struggled to place a nun in every classroom. Parents wanted their children in a "sister's room," and Cardinal Stritch believed that a mission school should be staffed by as many as possible. Because the school proved attractive and the School Sisters of St. Francis found it difficult to turn any child away, they worked long and demanding hours. Most taught between forty-five and fifty-five students, and several had more than sixty. The nuns also had various recess, cafeteria, and after-school assignments. Although resources at Holy Angels were not plentiful, the school had a fair supply of maps, charts, globes, and other instructional material—some of it purchased, much of it donated. All of it enabled the sisters to emphasize reading, writing, geography, history, and math. And, in the 1960s, Sister Hortensia and Father Richards began literacy classes for adults, which were co-spon-sored by DePaul University and taught mostly by graduate students.[40]

As Holy Angels evolved from a mission to a parish in the 1950s and 1960s, the quest for literacy remained a defining factor. It was a traditional value, one shared by Catholic sisters and African Americans and one that had radical implications. Henry Louis Gates Jr. correctly observed that "it was no accident that the first great victory in the legal battle over segregation was fought on the grounds of education—of equal access to literacy." Nor was it an accident in 1965, when six nuns were arrested in a civil rights demonstration in Chicago's Loop, that they were protest-ing the city's segregated public schools. In fact, Father George Clements, who in 1969 would become Holy Angels' first black pastor, had invited the sisters to join the protest.[41]

With Clements as pastor, Holy Angels received national attention for "its no frills education and students' academic achievements." A native Chicagoan, Clements grew up on the South Side and attended Corpus Christi school, where he had the Dubuque Franciscans as teachers. In 1945 he entered the archdiocese's seminary prep school and four years later the seminary; in 1957 he was ordained. The nuns who taught him "left a deep impression," and he believed that they were "responsible for [his] vocation to the Priesthood." He served as an assistant pastor at St. Ambrose and St. Dorothy's before his appointment to Holy Angels. By then "an outspoken proponent of black power," he was frequently described in the press as "militant." Yet he succeeded in producing one of the largest, most successful, and "most conservative" Catholic schools in the nation.[42]

Father Clements wanted sisters in as many classrooms as possible. At a time when women-religious were given more choices in how to dress and where to work, he wanted the nuns at Holy Angels to wear habits and commit themselves to teaching in the inner city. The students continued to wear uniforms and pay tuition, and their parents continued to enroll in religious instruction classes and attend Sunday Mass. Sister Helen Strueder, who went to Holy Angels in 1960 and today serves as principal, said Father Clements was more traditional than conservative. From his experience at Corpus Christi, he believed that nuns were good educators and "faith filled." And, from talking to parents, he understood how much they "wanted women of faith to teach their children." In the end, it was the commitment of dedicated sisters who made it possible for Clements to create, with limited funds, a model school where "no one ever apologizes for being black or Catholic." By stressing the importance of literacy and religion, he built upon the "tried and proven" policies and practices of the School Sisters of St. Francis. He also struck off in new ways.[43]

In 1970, Father Clements hired Father Paul Smith, a black priest from Louisiana and former high school teacher, to become principal of Holy Angels. His educational philosophy, like that of the activist Clements, was "unabashedly traditional," and Smith's presence clearly indicated that the school would develop self-esteem and character in boys as well as girls. Although Father Clements received most of the headlines, the interracial team of Father Smith and Sister Helen (then assistant principal) led the school for twenty-three years. She remembers the former principal, who died in 1996, as a quiet but capable administrator. And she believes that in the heyday of the Black Power movement, it was important "to see a good and gentle black man in charge."[44]

Father Smith instilled black pride among the students as surely as did singing the black national anthem and saluting the black liberation flag (along with the American flag) each day. In a school where "the King's English" was required, corporal punishment was sometimes used, and the school year extended over the summer months, pupils learned to feel proud when they excelled in the classroom. Regularly tested and grouped according to ability, they could move up a level or two as they progressed. "That's how one's self-esteem is enhanced," remarked Sister Helen, "through learning and competence."[45]

Underneath what was often described as Holy Angels' "radical methods" were traditional policies and practices. Sister Hortensia and Father Richards insisted on many of them in the 1940s and 1950s. Although striking changes occurred in the late 1960s, much remained the same at Holy Angels, observed Sister Helen, who has served as teacher and administrator for more than forty years. Above all, the belief in the value of a religious education held firm. No one ever doubted its power to improve individual lives, produce responsible citizens, and advance the common good.[46]

In the End

In the end, white missionary-teachers were transformed by the world they set out to change. By linking their lives to those of African Americans, the sisters came to a better understanding of their neighbors and the insidious reach of racism in America. Despite cultural and racial differences, the nuns' generosity of spirit, willingness to sacrifice, eagerness to serve, and openness to God's grace demonstrated year after year their enduring belief in the transforming potential of education and in the efficacy of Christian ideals. In 1905, Katharine Drexel wrote a missionary priest that, after "fourteen years' experience working for non-Catholics amongst these Colored People," she was "sure they will make good Catholics [and good citizens] if some one will take up the work of instructing them."[47]

A number of women-religious in Chicago did just that. Although they may appear to have embraced the status quo in devoting their lives to the mundane rigors of teaching in elementary schools, they did not. They were instead radical agents of social change, who offered generations of children and young adults a way around low expectations, ignorance, and poverty. And they did so at a time when people in power showed little regard for the needs and rights of African Americans. Missionary-teachers may have been less visible than activist nuns who participated in local neighborhood organizations and marched in civil rights demonstrations, but those who came first struck a no less mighty blow to injustice and inequality. What is evident is that over time they forged a common identity connected, as they were to one another, by a religious calling and commitment to serve all God's people.

6 No Color Line at Loretto Academy

One of the most enduring images of the modern civil-rights movement is that of Catholic sisters in protest, marching in full habit down Dallas County roads from Selma to Montgomery, Alabama, in March 1965. Changing America forever, the movement "rose like a multistage rocket on the Fourth of July" and reverberated everywhere. Forty years later, dramatic images of the movement's boycotts, sit-ins, Freedom Rides, and rallies remain clearly etched in the memories of those who participated. Others, who experienced these events vicariously through their nightly news programs or daily newspapers, find that they too carry in their minds many of the same memorable places and faces of those revolutionary years. The protesting sisters resonate particularly; their photographs flashed across television screens and appeared on the front pages of the major dailies. As Ralph McGill of the *Atlanta Constitution* observed, they "inspired the committed and shamed the timorous."[1]

The women-religious who marched at Selma remained anonymous in media accounts. Nevertheless, their enthusiastic faith provided powerful testimony to the spirituality of the civil-rights movement, giving it added momentum toward what civil-rights leader Martin Luther King Jr. called "unstoppability." In subsequent decades, despite the publication of several fine books that demonstrate the importance of religion in the history of race relations, nuns remain absent from the story. Schools and convents are routinely mentioned as part of the parish complex (along

Originally published as "No Color Line at Loretto Academy: Catholic Sisters and African Americans on Chicago's South Side," *Journal of Women's History* 14 (Spring 2002): 8–33.

with the church, rectory, and occasional gymnasium), but rarely does anyone look inside. Yet Catholic sisters were teaching black students and helping black families long before the Selma march, the Montgomery bus boycott, or the *Brown v. Board of Education* desegregation decision.[2]

After World War II, urban Catholics often found themselves in the center of rapid, thoroughgoing shifts in racial demography. Because many neighborhood parochial schools were owned and staffed by Catholic sisters, they are fruitful places to study how gender interacted with education, race, and religion in particular cities. What happened inside these local landmarks is not known, most likely because they were largely the domain of women. Historians of the city have tended to assume that "the male experience was *the* urban experience" and have relegated "women to the role of outsider, to the status of 'other.'"[3] But the nuns who operated Catholic schools in mid-twentieth-century American cities were quintessentially "insiders" amid great change.

Only a few scholars have integrated Catholic women into the urban experience. In *The Origins of the Urban Crisis,* for example, Thomas J. Sugrue took seriously a group of Catholic housewives in Detroit who "played a crucial role in threatening those who transgressed racial boundaries." He described how "passersby were taken aback by picket lines of white mothers and babies" who, in working-class neighborhoods, often "formed the vanguard" of their defense. Left at home while their husbands went off to work, they looked upon the streets where they lived as friendly and reassuring places that belonged primarily to them. Afraid that black outsiders might jeopardize the safety and stability of their families and communities, these Catholic housewives willingly used confrontation and harsh rhetoric to keep their streets white.[4]

Another group of white Catholic women, also daughters of working-class families in the urban North, chose a completely opposite course of action. As fervent as those who defended their neighborhoods against black encroachment, these women opened their schools to African Americans who sought a religiously based educational environment. In Chicago, the Sisters of Loretto met the challenge of racial change years before widespread acknowledgment of an urban crisis existed and years before the Second Vatican Council and the Selma march occurred—the seminal events credited with placing Catholic clergy and laity in the thick of the civil-rights movement. But we need to know how these women-religious confronted the problems incident to the changing racial composition of their schools from the 1940s through the 1960s.

What follows is a complicated, bittersweet story about the workings of gender, race, religion, and education at the local level. It offers a penetrating look at what happened in a typical Catholic high school, owned by a religious community of sisters, in a changing neighborhood on Chicago's South Side in the decades after World War II. Although Chicago is assuredly not all the world, it is a major northern Catholic city that, except for New York, attracted more black migrants during the twentieth century than any other place in the United States. Its schools reveal untold stories whose significance is hardly unique to Chicago. Historian John Dittmer's study of civil rights in Mississippi demonstrated that the struggle's success depended on "local people" doing the right thing far removed from television cameras.[5] The Loretto Sisters were such people.

In 1906 the Ladies of Loretto opened Loretto Academy at the corner of Sixty-fifth and Blackstone in Woodlawn. They stayed in that South Side neighborhood until 1972, long after it had changed racially from predominantly white to black. In fact, in August 1960, Mother Denise Adams, a native Chicagoan and member of the Lorettos' Administrative Council, remarked that her community was "called upon by God to teach." But, she continued, "God didn't say we needed to teach only white girls." Their commitment would not have been expressed so clearly a decade earlier when only a few black, middle-class students were "Loretto girls."[6]

Loretto's Open-Door Policy

At the close of World War II, the Ladies of Loretto had been teaching for forty years in Woodlawn. Just south of Hyde Park and the University of Chicago, the neighborhood was then mostly white and middle-class. With the resumption of the Great Migration of African Americans after the war, Woodlawn changed irrevocably, as did most of Chicago's South Side. Racial change presented the Lorettos with a daunting challenge. Their academy was not a parish school, nor did it belong to the Archdiocese of Chicago. The sisters both owned and staffed the school; therefore, they shared many of the property concerns of their South Side neighbors. Despite these anxieties, the nuns altered their perceptions of themselves and their apostolate. They refused to base admission to their high school on racial quotas, chose to stay in Woodlawn, and aimed to graduate black girls to assume their rightful place alongside previous generations of proud Loretto girls.[7]

The sisters' prestige, along with their property, was at stake. Smaller and less well known than the Sisters of Mercy, the Ladies of Loretto shared with them a reputation for excellent teaching. Both had strong ties to Ireland and were founded by independent women who believed nuns had work to do outside the cloister. Two centuries older than the

Mercys, the Lorettos—or the Institute of the Blessed Virgin Mary, as the order is formally known—were established in 1609. English founder Mary Ward was committed to educating young women who, she said, could "do much" if instructed in "piety, Christian morals, and the liberal arts."[8]

Belief in the value of education was the legacy the Lorettos embraced and carried with them to Canada (Toronto) in 1847 and to the Archdiocese of Chicago (Joliet) in 1880. They took the same convictions to St. Bernard's parish school in Chicago's Englewood neighborhood in 1892 and to Loretto Academy in Woodlawn fourteen years later. When the academy opened its doors in 1906 to 110 day students and boarders, it fulfilled a decade of yearning by the sisters for a high school of their own in Chicago. Although they had no money, the endorsement of a Carmelite priest and Archbishop James E. Quigley allowed them to borrow $40,000 to purchase property at Sixty-fifth and Blackstone. With two more loans, the Lorettos built their impressive school/convent complex.[9]

Despite these debts, the eight nuns who welcomed the first pupils to Loretto Academy were confident about the future. The Carmelite Fathers, who had encouraged them in this new venture, staffed St. Cyril's College for young men—later Mt. Carmel High School—only blocks away, which in the sisters' view made the neighborhood ripe for their enterprise. Once established, they knew what their mission was: to provide girls with "the advantage of higher education in secular branches, combined with moral and religious training." Within two years, the Lorettos offered a full program of classical study and instruction in music and art.[10]

Over the years enrollment increased, but Loretto Academy was never large. During the 1920s, about two hundred young women attended the school; by the mid-1940s, it enrolled 450 female students. Tuition and special fees, along with second mortgages and additional loans, financed the school's operations, its enlargement in 1927, and the sisters' scanty salaries. Although they managed to pay their bills, they were never free of debt, even in their prosperous days. Because Loretto Academy was not part of a parish complex, the nuns did not benefit from parish contributions. Only in the 1960s did they receive any direct financial support from the Archdiocese of Chicago.[11]

Before the 1950s, the single largest problem the Ladies of Loretto faced was lack of money. That challenge, however, was perennial and something to which the sisters had become accustomed. During the interwar years, not only did Loretto Academy manage to stay afloat, it also thrived. Situated on "spacious landscaped grounds" near the Illinois Central and across from Mt. Carmel, the academy's student population peaked during World War II. Mostly from second-generation Irish, English, and German homes, these young women belonged to Catholic parishes in Woodlawn and the adjacent neighborhoods of South Shore and Hyde Park. "Loretto girls" were generally hardworking and ambitious; they did well scholastically and musically. Many became active in the city's Catholic action programs, particularly an influential organization called CISCA (Chicago Inter-Student Catholic Action). And upon graduation, a substantial number entered the Loretto community and became nuns.[12]

What happened to Loretto Academy in the aftermath of World War II resulted, for the most part, from its location in Woodlawn. A densely populated neighborhood of less than two square miles, it became the port of entry for black migrants from the South during the 1940s and 1950s. Woodlawn's main thoroughfare, Sixty-third Street, had served as the entrance to the 1893 World's Fair. From it had developed an efficient transportation hub. At a single point (Sixty-third and Dorchester), a three-story crossing formed: on top, the elevated railroad; on ground level, streetcar tracks; and, in the middle, the Illinois Central. It was the Illinois Central—especially the "City of New Orleans" train—that carried hundreds of thousands of uprooted African Americans from Mississippi, Louisiana, and Tennessee to Chicago's Woodlawn during "one of the largest and most rapid internal movements of people in history."[13]

The demographic change that began "almost imperceptibly" as a trickle at the beginning of World War II turned into a torrent at its end. Pushed off of farms in the South by the invention of the mechanical cotton picker, more than 300,000 southern blacks gravitated to Chicago in the 1950s, hoping for a better life—one free of economic deprivation and racial discrimination. By 1960, Chicago had over half a million more African Americans than it had in 1940. Woodlawn, 13 percent black in 1930, became 39 percent black in 1950. The transition accelerated, so that the neighborhood's total population became nearly 90 percent black by 1960. Many newcomers settled in leftover apartments and hotels, built to accommodate visitors to the 1893 World's Fair, that were hastily converted into kitchenettes and sleeping rooms.[14]

Confronted with this enormous population shift, the people of Woodlawn were on their own. In 1956, Roi Ottley, a black journalist for the *Chicago Tribune*, noted "one astonishing aspect" of the migration: "neither city, state, or federal governments ever established a policy to deal with this mass movement."[15] Nor, in fact, did the Archdiocese of Chicago. Not until 1960, at an obligatory conference for diocesan clergy on "The Catholic Church and the Negro in the Archdiocese of Chicago," did Cardinal Albert G. Meyer finally present his mandate to rid the church of "any possible taint of racial discrimination or racial segregation."[16]

The Ladies of Loretto developed a policy on school admissions five years earlier. They did not reach it easily, but by October 1955 they had one. Elected to the community's highest office just months before, Mother General Constance MacMahon, the first American-born woman to lead the North American Lorettos, asserted in a letter: "Do not use any ratio to determine the number of students for September registration. Whatever screening be used, let not the color of the student be considered."[17] This brief statement ended a debate that had reverberated within the convent and school for several years. It would, in turn, usher in a period of swift change in the academy's racial composition and in the sisters' view of themselves and their work.

The beginning of the "color-line" debate at Loretto Academy appears to have begun in 1949. That fall the principal, Mother Colette Srill, accepted "without hesitation" the school's first black students, two "beautiful girls" from middle-class families. Although there was "some reaction, not strenuous but some," she chose to ignore it and heard no more about it. It is possible that debate may have started earlier, but no documents suggest it. Then, in August 1953, an article in the archdiocesan newspaper—nearly a year before the Supreme Court decision in *Brown v. Board of Education*, two years before Mother Constance's ruling, and seven years before Cardinal Meyer's statement—announced that Loretto Academy would accept "Negro as well as white students" in a "pioneering" effort to "[break] down racial prejudice."[18]

The announcement reflected a need and a willingness to act. "Social justice," it claimed, had "passed from the realm of classroom theory to actual practice." Besides announcing the acceptance of both black and white students, the statement also revealed a desire to welcome young women from a range of socioeconomic backgrounds as well as those of average talent. Loretto Academy, the article noted, "embraces all classes and has planned a program that will satisfy those of superior intellectual ability and encourage those of lesser ability." Loretto educators, inspired by a long tradition of teaching young women, promised "to form the whole woman" through a well-rounded curriculum that included "the Christian principles necessary for sound Catholic living." This bold plan of action and determination came from the hand of Mother Edwardine (Mary Gene) Partridge, principal from 1950 to 1957. According to a colleague forty-five years later, Mother Edwardine "changed everything."[19]

Remembered by former students as a "strong person" who was "ahead of her time," Mother Edwardine was a Loretto graduate herself.[20] Born on Chicago's South Side in 1917, she went to the Lorettos' schools (elementary and high school) in Englewood. During the early 1930s she was involved in Catholic action programs; became a friend to a girl of mixed race; and learned attitudes of fairness from her mother, the oldest of seven in an Irish-Catholic family and a woman who was "most unprovincial in her views." According to Mother Edwardine, it was God's grace, inspiration from Mary Ward's life, and the papal encyclicals on social justice that influenced her. They enabled her to make Loretto Academy a "different kind of place" during the 1950s. A priest from a nearby all-black parish described it as "the [high] school that was most open to the changing neighborhood."[21]

Not everyone agreed with Mother Edwardine. The sisters who opposed her had their reasons. Above all, they feared the loss of their prize investment and their reputation. Loretto Academy was a school that legions of nuns had built, and it had become a source of pride to graduates and their families. Mother Callista McGuire, superior of Loretto convent in 1955, wrote to the Toronto motherhouse that same year, saying, "The white girls here are meeting the interracial situation in our school in an admirable way, but their parents, older brothers and sisters are not able as yet to take the breakdown." She described "the breakdown": "the order is terrible, the standards are low, the girls are unmannerly, unkempt, undisciplined, noisy." In her opinion, Loretto Academy did not have "the same type of girl as in the days of yore." Although Mother Callista was most likely influenced by stereotypes, she correctly predicted that, if there were no quota or if the proportion of "colored girls is increased," Loretto would "lose some of the white girls already registered." This was a serious consideration for a school whose only source of funding was tuition. Fearing loss of financial support and prestige, she wanted to keep the academy "interracial" and favored a black-white ratio of "2/5—3/5."[22]

A few of the older sisters considered Mother Edwardine, then thirty-eight, too young to be principal. Mother Callista suggested that she might be "changed from Woodlawn"; she questioned if she were experienced enough to shoulder "probably the biggest problem that the Institute anywhere has ever had." Yet she admitted that Mother Edwardine "speaks and writes so convincingly and so intelligently that I wonder if I should disagree with her." Mother Callista then asked the superior general "to make the final decision" on an admissions policy for Loretto Academy.[23] In October 1955, she did—there would be no color line or quotas.

The Question of Quotas

The question of quotas was not an easy one, then or years later. In the early 1950s, when the Lorettos grappled with it, there were few places to turn to for expert advice. Discussions of the "tipping point," studies of communities "in transition," and debates over the benefits of the "benign quota" would soon be common, but they had not yet occurred. Thus Mother Constance's decision, favored by Mother Edwardine and her supporters, was difficult. How did it happen? Not all of the reasons for Loretto's open-door policy are clear, but several are. Most significant of these were the sisters' belief in the theology of Christ's "Mystical Body," their formation as Catholics in activist organizations, and the example of their founder, Mary Ward.

These factors, filtered through a lens of personal experience and responsibility, influenced leaders in both Toronto and Chicago. Mother Constance, the Lorettos' first American superior general, was born in Elmira, New York. In 1918, at age twenty-four, she entered religious life with a degree in education from Elmira College. Two years later she began a long teaching career in Sault Ste. Marie, Michigan, a place rife with discrimination against Native Americans. She was elected head of her community in summer 1955, and shortly thereafter she visited Loretto Academy to discuss "the weighty question of the *Negro and Woodlawn.*" Having served on the General Council in Toronto since 1943, Mother Constance was obviously well aware of the situation's seriousness.[24]

In March 1954, Mother Victorine O'Meara, superior general until July 1955, had visited Chicago and met with Cardinal Samuel Stritch. He was "personally grateful that the colored girls were being accepted" at Loretto Academy, for they were "almost completely excluded" everywhere else. But in response to Mother Victorine's idea of selling one of their two South Side high schools (Woodlawn or Englewood), he replied: "Who would buy it? You never hear of anyone buying a private school." Unconvinced, Mother Victorine consulted Cardinal James McGuigan of Toronto when she returned home. He urged her to "get money for Woodlawn and Englewood and go elsewhere." Had she remained in office, she might have sold both to the expanding public school system. It needed more physical space for the booming African American population and eventually did buy the Englewood facility in 1966.[25]

Mother Constance chose a different course, however. When she met with the sisters in Woodlawn in August 1955, she did not mention selling either property. Instead she gave a "beautiful talk on the Mystical Body of Christ." The bottom line of her message was clear; the Lorettos would not sell, but stay. She urged "anyone who was afraid to live in the neighborhood" to see her and receive another assignment. According to the convent annals, "no changes occurred." After a second visit in March 1957, Mother Constance noted that "the doctrine of Christ's

Mystical Body is being lived" at Loretto Academy. Without doubt, the sisters found meaning in a central tenet for many Chicago Catholics during the 1930s and 1940s.[26]

The theological concept of the Mystical Body emphasized the unity of Catholics through the Eucharist. Not a wholly new theology, it came into sharp focus in 1943 when Pope Pius XII issued an encyclical on the subject. And, in Chicago, it further motivated Catholic youth and intellectuals in the direction of social action and racial inclusiveness. Most of them were involved in Chicago Inter-Student Catholic Action (CISCA), the Summer School of Catholic Action, the Catholic Worker movement, or the Sheil School of Social Studies. During the interwar years, belief in the Mystical Body became the hallmark of their programs and inspired the extraordinary ferment in the city's Catholic circles.[27]

Activists saw themselves bound together "as living and functioning cells in . . . Christ's Mystical Body." In 1942, Auxiliary Bishop Bernard J. Sheil, a prominent spokesperson for what has been described as "the Chicago experience" of Catholic action, called Jim Crowism "the most dangerous kind of hypocrisy" and "a disgraceful anomaly" in the Mystical Body of Christ. Black poet and novelist Claude McKay explained his 1944 conversion to Catholicism in Chicago by citing "the Mystical Body of Christ, through which all of humanity may be united in brotherly love."[28]

Most sisters at Loretto Academy had participated in "the Chicago experience" of Catholic action. During summer vacations, some had attended Father Daniel Lord's Summer School of Catholic Action, but many others vividly recalled the "excitement" of weekly CISCA meetings. On Saturday mornings, hundreds of teens (male and female) gathered in downtown Chicago in the hope of "converting the world." The Lorettos also remembered the charismatic leadership of a Jesuit priest, Martin Carrabine, who directed CISCA from 1934 to 1953. He influenced thousands of young Chicagoans, "generating in them a hunger for interracial charity, just wages, adequate housing and a respect for the dignity of labor and the laborer." He worked to increase personal holiness as well as develop Catholic action—"to spread the Kingdom of Christ on earth." In 1937, Loretto Academy's seniors selected Carrabine, "CISCA's most zealous promoter," for their retreat master. As was his habit, he focused on how to act to "best help the Mystical Body."[29]

Although CISCA members had few personal friends who were black, they became "sensitized" to "the question of race" at their meetings. To "better race relations," CISCA leaders organized readings and discussions of citizenship, democracy, and tolerance that were followed by "practical thoughts on how to be a permanent force for good in the world." At a June 1938 meeting, for example, one CISCAN encouraged others to stand up to those "who object to having Negroes in their schools." And if an African American enrolled, the CISCAN advised, "shake hands with him . . . really take him in." Not all who came to CISCA meetings were white. Small groups of African Americans students from St. Elizabeth's, a coeducational black high school at Forty-first and Michigan, sometimes attended. Sister Robert Dennis, CISCA moderator there, believed that "racial contact" was crucial. This Blessed Sacrament Sister encouraged her pupils to participate and said a "splendid feeling" existed between black and white CISCANS when they did.[30]

A number of these young Catholic activists headed into convents and seminaries after graduating from high school and college. They usually joined the religious organizations they knew best—those of their teachers, parish priests, relatives, or friends. The women who entered the convent from Loretto Academy were motivated by their CISCAN experience as well as by the nuns who taught them. Many were also inspired by Mary Ward, the founder of the Loretto Sisters. She was a woman of strong conviction who went to prison rather than bow to the authority of two popes. Academy students saw her as "the modern girl's ideal" because she "dared to dissent" and valued educated women. "Always alive" among them, Ward would continue to inspire their courage.[31]

Some sisters at Loretto Academy also drew courage from events with local connections. One was the antisegregationist play *Trial by Fire*, written by Chicago Jesuit George H. Dunne, whose aunt was a Loretto nun and who had written an acclaimed *Commonweal* article, "The Sin of Segregation," in 1945. In the play, a black family is tragically burned to death as a result of a bomb that explodes in their home. Actors from the Sheil School of Social Studies performed it in Chicago in 1948. In November, Loretto Academy sponsored a command performance for students and faculty at the Eighth Street Theater on South Wabash. Mother Edwardine said it made a deep impression on her. Seven years later, she was haunted by the "death in Mississippi of that black boy from Chicago."[32]

That black boy was Emmett Till, a fourteen-year-old South Sider, who was brutally murdered on August 28, 1955. He had gone to visit relatives and was lynched for supposedly whistling at the wife of a white shop owner in Money, Mississippi. A month later, an all-white jury found the accused men innocent. Blacks especially, but also many whites, were shocked by the horrific death and courtroom verdict. When Mamie Bradley brought her son's body back to Chicago for a funeral and burial, the event received widespread coverage in the media and served as a catalyst for the nation's civil rights movement. It had immediate repercussions at Loretto Academy.[33]

The school's open-door policy came on the heels of the Till murder. Despite fears of losing financial support, lowering standards, and giving up hard-won status, the Lorettos chose to admit African Americans to their school. When others did not, Loretto Academy "welcomed black girls and continued to provide the same academic and social advantages." By the early 1960s, South Siders had tagged the academy as a "black school," a pejorative label that ultimately prevented it from attracting middle-class girls—first white, then black—and that would force it to close in 1972. As white students transferred out, according to Mother Edwardine, "even friends drifted away." It was not long before the academy "suffered the same rejection as the black girls to whom it opened its doors."[34]

For these reasons, South Side Catholic high schools such as Mercy and Mt. Carmel were reluctant to receive an influx of black students during the 1950s. As their administrators began to feel pressure from priests in nearby parishes and officials in the archdiocese, the schools gradually admitted a small number of capable African Americans. Black parents, especially Catholic ones, also grew more insistent.[35] By the 1960s, public schools—which had become almost completely segregated during the interwar period and remained so under Benjamin C. Willis, the autocratic and confrontational superintendent—were incredibly overcrowded and understaffed in black neighborhoods. At the same time, liberals and integrationists offered new arguments for the positive effects of quotas. By using them, some Catholic school administrators insisted that they could create "interracial" institutions, a goal promoted in discussions on the "tipping point."[36]

In the late 1950s, University of Chicago sociologists publicized the tipping point. It referred to a level of tolerance by whites to minorities in a neighborhood or school. According to its chief proponents, Morton Grodzins, Otis Dudley Duncan, and Beverly Duncan, whites left when the number of blacks reached a certain level that varied from neighborhood to neighborhood or school to school. Once this occurred, the change could not be reversed. Thus, to build interracial communities or institutions, the proportion of African Americans to whites had to be controlled. Only education, which worked to increase tolerance, would raise the tipping point.[37]

Community organizer Saul Alinsky testified in favor of "benign quotas" before the U.S. Commission on Civil Rights in May 1959. As a Jew, he knew all too well their insidiousness. Yet he argued that "what is an unjust instrument in one case can serve justice in another," and hence "only by using a restrictive quota can the Negro make the first break into white communities." Sister Mark Kerin, principal of Chicago's Mercy High School, which was located several miles south of Loretto Academy, presented the same arguments to Archbishop Meyer in the hope of keeping Mercy "an integrated school." Mercy subsequently adopted quotas on black admissions, as its West Chatham neighborhood changed from white to middle-class black. But quotas did not "save" Mercy High School. By 1965–66, when 45 percent of its students were African American, enrollment fell below capacity and the year's deficit was $57,000. The tipping point apparently had been passed.[38]

Loretto as a Black School

Loretto Academy was the only African American Catholic girls' high school in the archdiocese during the 1960s. In that exciting and devastating decade, things got better and also worse. The early years, however, were thrilling. Mother Irene Gavin, principal from 1961 to 1965 and native Chicagoan from an Irish Catholic family on the South Side, recalled that the sisters worried less about the future than before, despite their financial concerns. They instead threw themselves into "a new apostolic venture"—still considered "missionary work" by some—that both challenged and changed them. What they needed to know about black history and life, they learned quickly on the job and over time through study and experience. As they became more identified with their students and more involved with their neighbors, they ceased feeling rejected or isolated in their black school.

Mother Irene distinguished herself as principal during the civil-rights decade. With one foot in the past and another in the future, she built on the foundation laid during the 1950s. A 1938 honors graduate of Loretto High School and ardent CISCAN, she remained faithful to the gospels and papal encyclicals on social justice yet advocated many of the changes in religious life that Belgian Cardinal Leon Suenens proposed in *The Nun in the World* (1962). Convinced that "injustice anywhere is a threat to justice everywhere," Mother Irene was very much inspired by King's 1963 "Letter from a Birmingham Jail." During her tenure at Loretto, she became president of the Catholic High School Principals' Association, a member of the Archdiocesan School Board, and a leader in the Urban Apostolate of the Sisters.[39]

In 1961–62, Mother Irene helped execute the merger of Englewood's Loretto High School with Woodlawn's Loretto Academy. Less than three miles apart, these small institutions faced declining enrollments. Follow-

ing years of debate and off-and-on consultations with archdiocesan officials, the Lorettos announced in May 1962 that their Englewood students
(124 of them, and mostly black) would join those in Woodlawn (220 African Americans and a few Hispanics) the following September. Speaking
for the administration in Toronto, Mother Denise Adams said the merger
offered "the best solution" and promised a new reading laboratory, better
library facilities, and an honors program at Loretto Academy.[40]

Mother Irene and the faculty succeeded in keeping these promises,
but not without a struggle. Even after the merger of the Englewood and
Woodlawn schools, Loretto Academy operated on a shoestring budget,
never having more than a few thousand dollars in reserve. Earlier in
1959, when the school board discussed possible consolidation of the two
schools, their desperate straits became known. The minutes correctly
recorded that "the Sisters' situation is simple—they are broke." One
board member suggested that they plead bankruptcy, but the Lorettos
managed to avoid doing so by living on less, making only essential repairs
to their quarters on the academy's top floor, and accepting occasional aid
from the motherhouse in Toronto.[41]

The sisters also succeeded in securing funds from sources other than
tuition and Toronto. In 1963, for example, Mother Alice Whitehead, the
librarian and audiovisual director, who also taught English and journal-
ism, received a 3M Company National Award of $3,000 for her proposal
on creative use of overhead equipment. The students earned money from
their dramatic and musical productions, as well as by selling chocolate
bars. And the fundraising efforts of the parents' club sustained several
projects. According to Mother Irene, club members knew the sisters were
"not there to make money." For that, she said, parents "respected us"
and worked hard for the school. Still, in June 1963, it was "just barely
afloat."[42]

The same could be said about the neighborhoods where most Loretto
students lived. In 1950, Woodlawn boasted "over eight hundred commercial and industrial establishments" that were largely gone by the early
1960s. The widely touted affluence of the 1950s conveniently hid what
was happening in "the other America" of older inner cities.[43] Without
fully understanding what they experienced, the sisters witnessed more
than the change of Woodlawn and Englewood from white to black; they
saw the disintegration of "a black community that was vibrant." Phyllis Crockett, a Loretto student from Englewood, said that, although she
saw few whites, "we had everything we needed." By the mid-1960s,
though, she knew "things ain't what they used to be." Decent jobs for
the unskilled had disappeared; buildings were abandoned and burned;

and middle-class blacks, who took advantage of new employment and housing opportunities, followed the exodus of middle-class whites. What was left behind was a destitute and often illiterate population, the "truly disadvantaged."[44]

In 1961, the Ladies of Loretto became directly involved in neighborhood problems, following establishment of The Woodlawn Organization (TWO). This community group, organized temporarily with support from the Archdiocese of Chicago and the United Presbyterian Church, developed into a permanent institution that operates today out of the former Loretto Academy. Under Saul Alinsky's leadership, TWO directed its members to protest local merchants' unfair business practices, double shifts and overcrowding in public schools, and the University of Chicago's aggressive urban-renewal tactics. On August 26, 1961, TWO also sponsored a caravan of forty-four "awe-inspiring" school buses carrying about two thousand people—including a contingent of Loretto Sisters—to City Hall, where they renewed their voter registrations.[45]

The Lorettos had advocated racial justice for African Americans since the early 1950s, when they joined Chicago's Catholic Interracial Council and began admitting black girls without restriction to their school. Yet it was not until 1961 that they publicly demonstrated their support for civil rights. Mother Irene recalled meeting Alinsky through Monsignor John Egan, another organizing pioneer and activist, and admitted to Alinsky's lifelong influence. She said he explained that "conflict is the price of change," a premise she never forgot; he also pointed out that individuals who are different racially and religiously can be united through a common principle, once discovered and fostered. For the Lorettos, said Mother Irene, the unifying element was "belief in the dignity of the human person." This conviction, along with their students' encounters with poverty and injustice, transformed the sisters. They remained educators, to be sure, but they became activists as well.[46]

Following the 1961 voter registration drive, the sisters joined TWO. They attended annual conferences as well as regular meetings, hosting several of them at the academy, and became committed to doing more "for the general welfare." During a gathering at Rosary College, sponsored by the Archdiocesan Office of Urban Affairs, Mother Irene told attendees that involvement in neighborhood organizations was not "something over and above, [but] it is the very ingredient of being a good Christian." In January 1963, she and Mother Aileen O'Connor, superior at Loretto convent, attended the ambitious and successful National Conference on Race and Religion at the Edgewater Beach Hotel. The *Chicago Defender*, which showcased the event, carried a photograph of the two sisters and remarked on Loretto Academy's commitment to African American students on the South Side. Months later, when spring came, Mother Aileen encouraged the nuns to extend their reach—"to walk around the neighborhood" and see how they could serve those who lived there. The Second Vatican Council was well under way, and ideas about change and renewal enveloped the convent, making 1963 "a wonderful time to be alive."[47]

The sisters' walks through the neighborhood resulted in an adult-education program. After canvassing several hundred people in a ten-block area, the Lorettos learned that their black neighbors wanted, above all, decent and secure jobs. Of the 125 individuals who responded to a questionnaire, 110 asked for assistance in preparing for civil-service exams; 99 also indicated a desire for typing classes, and only eight expressed an interest in black history. In short, what Woodlawn residents felt they needed, the nuns had in abundance: the tools of literacy. During the fall of 1963, Mother Aileen and several colleagues consulted educators and literacy specialists in Chicago and observed a community-based program in Flint, Michigan. In January 1964, when the Loretto Adult Education Center opened, sixty-four students "braved a new educational adventure" one night each week for six months.[48]

Mother Peter Claver Rooney, a graduate of Loretto High School and DePaul University, directed this center for twelve years. She had become conscious of racial problems during the late 1930s, when she met several black students from St. Elizabeth's at CISCA meetings. She remembered asking her sophomore religion teacher why there were no African Americans at other Catholic high schools and was told simply that "it was a question of finances." Much later, she began to understand the full implications of that brief response. As an American history teacher at Loretto Academy in the early 1960s, she relied heavily on historian John Hope Franklin's *From Slavery to Freedom*. Because so little black history appeared in commonly used textbooks at that time, she began including it in her courses, much as she had previously incorporated material on Catholics. When assigned to direct the Loretto Adult Education Center in 1964, she knew she faced "a big challenge" but one for which she was not totally unprepared.[49]

Four years later, more than five hundred adults from Chicago's South Side and West Side neighborhoods had taken classes at the center. The faculty of one expanded to include another nun and, at various times, from twelve to twenty lay volunteers (Catholics, Protestants, and Jews) with wide-ranging specialties: reading and writing, job training, civil-service requirements, typing, community and human relations, sewing, and fund-raising. In the beginning, the center received support from the

Lorettos (mostly in-kind services) and the archdiocese. Larger donations came later from Chicago-based corporations and foundations, along with federal funds from the 1964 Manpower Development and Training Act and the 1966 Model Cities Act. Through the efforts of Alderman Leon Despres, the center secured a $30,000 grant to coordinate an educational pilot project for the Illinois Employment Security Bureau. With this backing, the center's offerings multiplied, leading Loretto Academy to keep its doors open three nights each week. The nuns also began a day program for high school dropouts, many of whom were unemployed.[50]

Prominent Chicago Catholics recognized that the Lorettos had "pushed into uncharted waters" and developed a good deal more than "a paper program." In 1965, when the entire community voted overwhelmingly to call themselves "sisters" (rather than "ladies" or "mothers"), they gave striking evidence of the change that had occurred in their view of themselves and their work. Having crossed the boundaries of race, class, and religion, they began to discard what they saw as indicators of deference and privilege. In championing the cause of civil rights, they had not only "touched reality" but embraced it. They could not afford to travel to Selma in March 1965, but they were present in spirit. By then, the Lorettos had been "directly involved with those living on the fringes of society" for more than a decade.[51]

This new sense of ministry explains why the sisters took such pride in their adult-education center. Because of its attack on local adult illiteracy, nearly two hundred Woodlawn residents, according to the *Chicago Tribune*, had completed their elementary or secondary education by 1968. A number of lives also had improved dramatically through work. A tally of thirty-six graduates "with confirmed employment" indicated that "from September 1965 to October 1968, their total income, excluding welfare payments, rose from $12,931 to $146,806." Eleven families became newly self-supporting. In an attempt to assist poor women, the center created the popular "Coretta King Program" for black mothers, many of whom were on welfare and wanted to give education another chance. But like other antipoverty initiatives of the Great Society, the center failed to survive the Nixon administration, which did away with the Office of Economic Opportunity and the Model Cities program.[52]

Throughout the 1960s, the high school continued (along with the center) and was a hub of activity. Since the sisters lived on the building's top floor, students found the academy a convenient place to spend late afternoons and Saturdays. Truancy was almost never a problem. Sister Irene Gavin remarked that "the girls were around all the time"; and Sister Mary Patrick Simpkin, who became principal in 1966, said that they responded well to Loretto hospitality and discipline. Because of her firm jaw and serious demeanor, she was called "Jimmy Cagney" behind her back. Yet, when she stood at the door each morning, many "gave her a hug and wished her a good day." She remained committed, however, to a single rule: "measure up."[53]

Much of what happened inside Loretto Academy was "as it always was," despite the change in the school's racial composition. Helen Ellis Stanton-Hawkins, who graduated in 1962, remembers the "small, nurturing, friendly environment" and the "excellent academic program." The sisters were "well-educated," "diverse in their interests and talents," and "very upbeat." According to 1968 graduate Phyllis Crockett, they encouraged hard work and "stressed discipline." Upon graduation, she felt prepared "to compete intellectually at the highest level." Sheila McDonald, who "hated" the discipline, generally "loved [her] years at Loretto." In 1971, when she served as a student representative on a minority board at Marymount College in Salina, Kansas, she wrote appreciatively to Loretto's principal and told her of a $45,000 scholarship fund for which black high school students could apply.

Although the sisters created a positive learning environment, on occasion their African American students saw "signs of racism." For instance, Crockett recalled that she and her friends did well but sometimes found their ability "questioned," almost as if the nuns "really did not expect us to meet the challenge." She also mentioned that one classmate, who was "the smartest in our school," was encouraged to apply to a few local colleges for scholarships rather than "all over the country." Others complained that one nun treated them like children. Sister Eleanor Holland, principal from 1969 until 1972, who knew this sister well, did not think her behavior was racially motivated. She told the students: "She treats me like that [too] and I'm the principal." A 1958 graduate who never felt patronized by the Lorettos recalled objecting to the role of an ignorant black maid in a school play and arguing with her history teacher over the treatment slaves received from their masters. The part of the black maid, at least, was removed.[54]

None of these graduates believed they received anything less than a first-class education. Yet during the 1967–68 school year, rumors spread that standards at Loretto Academy had deteriorated. They resulted from an agreement that Sister Mary Patrick had made with the archdiocesan superintendent of schools to add a program for slow learners—one that emphasized reading and writing skills—to their traditional college-preparatory and commercial offerings. The Lorettos knew that such a program would "endanger our reputation," but they also recognized the special needs of many of their students.[55]

Other South Side Catholic schools responded in their own ways to racial change. During the 1960s, Mercy and Mother McAuley high schools continued to admit an increasing number of better-qualified black students from middle-class homes, though newcomers from poorly funded, segregated schools in the South remained at an academic disadvantage. Then, in June 1967, the Sisters of the Blessed Sacrament closed what remained of St. Elizabeth's, the first black coed Catholic high school in the archdiocese. Five years before, it had become a girls' school when Hales Franciscan High School, which was heavily subsidized by the archdiocese, opened for African American boys on the South Side. Of the 161 black girls who remained at St. Elizabeth's in 1967, some "found it difficult to qualify scholastically" at Catholic schools and others were unable "to pay the added tuition." Without another Catholic school to accept them and without aid from the archdiocese, they would have gone to public schools that, according to a Blessed Sacrament Sister, did not have "a very good reputation." It was in this context that the Loretto Sisters inaugurated an additional program aimed at helping disadvantaged young women.[56]

With these new students, Loretto Academy's enrollment increased to 370 and the school received funding from the archdiocese. Sister Mary Patrick's workload as principal and part-time teacher expanded as she oversaw major building repairs, including the outfitting of a reading laboratory. Students claimed that she created her own "Project Renewal." She also secured federal funds from the National Youth Corps and Job Corps programs. They enabled the academy to offer after-school internships to individuals enrolled in commercial courses. Besides gaining office experience, many earned enough to pay for their tuition and books.[57]

These improvements and opportunities made up that "something extra" touted in *Chicago Tribune* headlines in August 1969. But they—along with Loretto's traditional college-preparatory program and its faculty of sixteen qualified and dedicated teachers—were not sufficient to keep Loretto from closing. Numerous individuals and families on Chicago's South Side had benefited from the sisters' efforts. Yet in the end their commitment, and the antipoverty programs of the 1960s on which so many of their initiatives depended, failed to address the heart of the matter: racial discrimination and the disappearance of blue-collar and manufacturing jobs, particularly in the steel mills.[58]

The Closing

The Sisters of Loretto were aware of the severity of the problems that confronted them. They did not fully understand, however, the devastating social and economic forces that increasingly marginalized inner-city black families and insidiously undermined their own educational efforts. Hence they responded to local needs by acting on "the possession of literacy," a traditional value they shared with African Americans. The sisters strongly believed that literacy would give their students a chance for a better future, as it had over time for legions of poor Catholic immigrants. Hardly naive, they were instead women of faith whose religious and democratic ideals moved them "from the security of 'what has always been' to the risk of the unknown."[59]

During the 1960s, the Loretto Sisters faced unimagined difficulties. The largest of these, in addition to financial distress, was the problem of image. On the one hand, they had built up their students' self-esteem by introducing African American material into the curriculum, emphasizing the Catholic Church's teachings on racial justice, and hiring black teachers. On the other hand, they had watched with dismay and sadness as middle-class black families who wanted "integrated" schools with "high" standards rejected their academy. By 1968, according to Loretto's last principal, Sister Eleanor Holland, there was "no chance of being integrated," nor was there any possibility that the nuns would walk away from those who needed them most. They had grown accustomed to doing what they believed was right, whether their school survived or not. "Survival," she said, "is not a gospel value."[60]

From their experiences in Woodlawn, the Lorettos knew that an integrated, equal-opportunity society would take time to create and also cause conflict. Nevertheless, the destruction and polarization between blacks and whites that occurred in Chicago following King's assassination in the spring of 1968 shook their deepest beliefs. Looking back, they realized that 1968 signaled the beginning of the end for Loretto Academy. They also learned that great change causes "two things [to] happen at one time": things get better, and they get worse.[61]

Loretto Academy's location in Woodlawn continued to work against its survival. Although Chicago's South Side did not experience the rioting and looting that occurred on the West Side after King was shot in Memphis on April 4, the area surrounding the school (from Stony Island Boulevard west to Cottage Grove) became an armed camp once the National Guard settled in. The principal canceled classes for several days, and the sisters, who still lived in the building, received offers of protection from the local police as well as from Woodlawn's infamous gang, the Blackstone Rangers. But no one ventured out. When it appeared safe, the students returned with tales of confusion and terror.[62]

From then on, nothing was ever quite as good as it had once seemed. The sisters began to live with caution and stress during their remaining years in Woodlawn. As neighborhood drug deals, random shootings, and convent break-ins became more prevalent, Loretto's enrollment took an expected nosedive. In early 1972, with the school again on the brink of bankruptcy, only eighteen potential freshmen applied for admission for the next fall. Thus, acting on a suggestion from the archdiocesan school board, the Lorettos decided to join forces with the Mercy Sisters and create the new Unity High School for black teenage girls on the city's South Side. The Lorettos left Woodlawn in 1972 not because their students were black, poor, or non-Catholic but because they could no longer afford to stay.[63]

The Loretto Sisters never regretted their years in Woodlawn. But since the closing, they have wondered if their academy might not still be in operation had it been a boys' school. Would the archdiocese have supported it more generously—the way it had Hales Franciscan High School during the 1960s? The sisters know that their Woodlawn location and open-door admissions policy were important factors in Loretto's demise, but they also know that these two factors do not explain entirely the academy's closing. The Sisters of Mercy, whose school was located in a middle-class neighborhood and who had used quotas in admitting African Americans, failed as well. But Mt. Carmel High School, just two blocks from Loretto Academy on Sixty-fourth and Dante streets, survived. In fact, while celebrating its 100th anniversary in 2000, it boasted that "the fires of change" during the 1960s had not turned this "all-boys Catholic high school into Dante's inferno."[64]

Despite the changed neighborhood and a rigorous entrance exam, Mt. Carmel maintained a solid enrollment. Even during the most turbulent years, it had drawn approximately eight hundred young men from the South Side. Yet, for a long time, Mt. Carmel "did not take blacks" and then "only selectively." After Alderman Despres spoke at the school in March 1967, the principal of Mt. Carmel wrote him, "Perhaps I should have warned you of the strong feelings our students have. The great majority live on the fringe of the negro-white areas. Because of parental concern and/or ignorance, they find the economic problems of integration rather distressing. All they can see is what they feel they are about to lose, and, of course, the negro [*sic*] ends up being the culprit. Actually they are not as aggrieved as they appeared."[65] Perhaps not, but as late as 1997, about 25 percent of its total student population were African American, 10 percent Hispanic, and 2 percent Asian. And, not surprisingly, "only a small number of Mt. Carmel students [came] from the surrounding Woodlawn community."[66]

What contributed significantly to Mt. Carmel's survival, along with its cautious use of quotas, was that it catered to male students. Its athletic prowess, cultivated during the twentieth century and displayed with regularity in winning football seasons, enhanced the school's reputation and contributed to its recruitment efforts. Mt. Carmel's "amazing" alumni support resulted in major plant improvements. Because of their graduates, the school could expand its campus and modernize its facilities; and, when it mattered most, Mt. Carmel could inaugurate an extensive system of buses that "went out to all the South Side parishes" where alumni lived. Loretto Academy was unable to finance such a service, and Mt. Carmel was unwilling to share space on its vehicles. As the Blackstone Rangers took more control of the area, parents sent their sons but refused to send their daughters on public transportation. Thus, Mt. Carmel remains today "an anchor in the Woodlawn community."[67]

A decade after the closing, the Lorettos made final peace with their Woodlawn past. They leased the academy in 1983 (and sold it in 1987) to TWO for its Family Life Center, which offered job training, alcohol detoxification, and day-care services to community residents. Sister Mary Madigan, regional superior of the Lorettos, stated their hope that "the lease will safeguard as far as legally possible the purpose of serving the poor and needy of the area."[68] This contract, and the one that followed in 1987, officially ended the Loretto Sisters' seventy-year attachment to its South Side high school. But their story demonstrates how considering gender, race, religion, and education—examined together in a particular locale—result in a more complicated telling of the effects of the Great Migration and the civil-rights movement on northern cities.

Histories of race relations in the North have overlooked the role of women and the place of schools. Both usually become backdrop to a story too crowded to include them. Yet these Catholic sisters and their academy made a difference on Chicago's South Side and in America's civil-rights struggle. Located in the city's epicenter of the postwar black migration, these ordinary "local people" used their school to improve the community. In the process, they lost a cherished possession but found themselves and learned what it meant to lead a life in religion. The Sisters of Loretto also confronted with mixed results—externally defeated, internally vindicated—structural changes in urban life and the intractable realities of race relations with which American society has yet to cope with full success.

Franciscan Sisters from Dubuque, Iowa, largely of German heritage, went to Corpus Christi in 1933. The convent, a former apartment at Forty-ninth and South Parkway, had a large porch where visitors, large and small, gathered. Mother Dominica (Philippine) Wieneke, principal and superior, is pictured with several schoolchildren (c. 1939). Courtesy of the Sisters of St. Francis, Dubuque.

The Franciscans valued music and offered instruction in many forms. Sister Margaret Mary (Helen) Oestreich was a music teacher her entire life. She and her student choir perform in 1942 in the loft of Corpus Christi Church. Courtesy of the Library of Congress.

In 1946, Sister Luke (Clara) Hanig's string ensemble played before the Corpus Christi student body. Courtesy of the Sisters of St. Francis, Dubuque.

Sister Norma, formerly Alma Drexler, as a high school graduate. She went to Corpus Christi in 1933 and remained until 1953, and she remembered all her students—1,739 of them—by writing their names in a small notebook. Courtesy of the Sisters of St. Francis, Dubuque.

Sister Norma is shown with two students on an outing in Jackson Park. Courtesy of the Sisters of St. Francis, Dubuque.

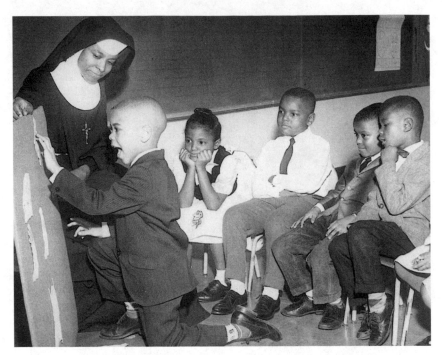

Sister Lucy Williams grew up in Corpus Christi parish. After becoming a Franciscan—the first black woman to enter the community—she returned there to teach from 1956 to 1964 (then as Sister Martin de Porres). Courtesy of the Sisters of St. Francis, Dubuque.

In 1941, five Oblate Sisters of Providence from Baltimore opened a school in Morgan Park at Holy Name of Mary parish. Before their convent was completed, they lived in a house at 112th Place and brought students into their makeshift chapel. The first five were (*from left*): Sisters Clotilde Smith; Anthony Garnier; Claude Hudlin, principal; Juliana Brent; and Providentia Pollard. Courtesy of the *Catholic New World.*

A group of energetic girls in uniform on the playground at Holy Name of Mary gathered around Sister Elise Mance during recess (c. mid-1950s). Courtesy of the Oblate Sisters of Providence, Baltimore.

Before arriving at Holy Angels on the South Side in 1946, Sister Hortensia (Louise) Stickelmaier, a School Sister of St. Francis, taught African Americans in Yazoo City, Mississippi. She was photographed with a science class in 1945. Courtesy of the School Sisters of St. Francis, Milwaukee.

Pupils at Holy Angels lined up on the playground each morning and entered school with their class and teacher (c. 1946–47). Courtesy of the School Sisters of St. Francis, Milwaukee.

Holy Angels always attracted a large number of local children. The size of Sister Laurissa Sibbel's first- and second-grade class in 1947–48 was typical. Courtesy of the School Sisters of St. Francis, Milwaukee.

Nineteen Franciscans, the teaching staff at Holy Angels in 1947–48, assembled in the convent community room for this photograph. Courtesy of the School Sisters of St. Francis, Milwaukee.

On the playground at Holy Angels, several sisters joined in the winter games of their students (c. late 1940s). Courtesy of the School Sisters of St. Francis, Milwaukee.

Loretto Academy (1906–72), located at 65th and Blackstone, belonged to the Sisters of Loretto, who are also known as IBVMs (Institute of the Blessed Virgin Mary). The academy was the first Catholic high school in the archdiocese to welcome large numbers of black students. It is now owned by The Woodlawn Organization (TWO) and provides extensive community services. Courtesy of the Sisters of Loretto.

A 1948 performance of *Trial by Fire*, in which a black family is burned to death as a result of a bomb thrown into their home, made a deep impression on sisters at Loretto Academy (several were in this audience). Actors from the Sheil School of Social Studies staged the play at the Eighth Street Theatre. Courtesy of the Archdiocese of Chicago's Joseph Cardinal Bernardin Archives and Records Center.

Mother Edwardine (Mary Gene) Partridge, principal from 1950 to 1957, opened Loretto's doors to all students, white and black. By the 1960s, the white girls had transferred to other schools, and Loretto Academy became the only black Catholic girls' high school in Chicago. Courtesy of the Sisters of Loretto.

Mother Callista (Olive) McGuire, admired by the students for her musical ability, feared the loss of Loretto Academy as the student population changed from white to black. Courtesy of the Sisters of Loretto.

Sister Irene (Mary) Gavin, principal from 1961 to 1965, relied on Loretto parents, particularly mothers, for assistance in raising funds and with other services. Courtesy of the Sisters of Loretto.

Each year, members of Loretto's junior class visited Springfield: Lincoln's boyhood home, the state capitol, and Lincoln's tomb were among the highlights. Sisters Peter Claver (Therese) Rooney and Francesca Esch led the group (c. 1963). Courtesy of the Sisters of Loretto.

Sister Sebastian (Elizabeth) Mallon of Loretto was the 1967 choice of the National Association of Biology Teachers to be "Illinois' Outstanding Biology Teacher." Here she joined her students in 1962 at the Illinois State Science Fair, where Loretto students regularly competed. Courtesy of the Sisters of Loretto.

In 1963, Sisters Irene Gavin and Alice Whitehead from Loretto Academy participated in a conference on community improvement sponsored by The Woodlawn Organization (TWO). With the sisters are several lay participants and Fathers Maurice Foley, pastor of St. Laurence (*left*), and Martin Farrell, pastor of Holy Cross (*right*). Courtesy of the *Catholic New World*.

Prior to the 1960s, Catholic sisters were often photographed at summer picnics and fun fairs—on merry-go-rounds, roller coasters, and baseball diamonds—but not marching for social justice. That changed in 1963. Courtesy of the Archdiocese of Chicago's Joseph Cardinal Bernardin Archives and Records Center.

At a race-relations workshop sponsored by Friendship House in June 1963, several School Sisters of St. Francis attended Mass. A month later, a group of them protested the discriminatory polices of the Illinois Club for Catholic Women. Courtesy of the Archdiocese of Chicago's Joseph Cardinal Bernardin Archives and Record Center.

On July 1, 1963, seven Franciscan nuns—six from Milwaukee and one from Joliet—along with Father Dan Mallette, assistant pastor of St. Agatha's, joined a demonstration in front of the Illinois Club for Catholic Women at Loyola University's Lewis Tower campus at 820 North Michigan. Courtesy of the *Catholic New World.*

Sister Angelica (Ann) Seng, a teacher at Alvernia High School, became a spokesperson for the sisters who picketed in July 1963. She is shown here with an Alvernia student four months later. Courtesy of Ann Seng.

Marillac House, on West Jackson Boulevard, was one of the nation's largest settlement houses. The Daughters of Charity, who remain active on the West Side, purchased the building (formerly St. Mary's Episcopalian Orphanage) in 1947. Courtesy of the Daughters of Charity, Evansville, Indiana.

Sister Jane Breidenbach, a nurse and former missionary to China, came to Marillac House in 1948 and remained until 1983. She assisted Puerto Rican families who lined up for free chest x-rays in August 1955. Courtesy of the Archdiocese of Chicago's Joseph Cardinal Bernardin Archives and Records Center.

In October 1964, Sister Mary William Sullivan, director of Marillac House, awarded Martin Luther King Jr. the John F. Kennedy Award of the Catholic Interracial Council of Chicago. The award honored King's courageous leadership in the cause of justice. Courtesy of the Daughters of Charity, St. Louis.

A "Neighbors at Work" cleanup parade on April 24, 1964, caught the attention of the city and its mayor. Marillac volunteers received a citation from Mayor Richard J. Daley and an invitation to visit his office, where they asked for additional local services such as more frequent garbage collection. Courtesy of the Daughters of Charity, Evansville, Indiana.

Sister Mary William (Florence) Sullivan appears here (*left*) when she graduated from Xavier High School in St. Louis in 1943, and (*below*) after she became a professional social worker, enjoying the children and babies at Marillac House in (c.) 1964. Courtesy of Sister Mary William Sullivan, DC, and the Archdiocese of Chicago's Joseph Cardinal Bernardin Archives and Records Center.

Five of the six Daughters of Charity who were arrested at State and Madison on June 12, 1965, being led to the police van. Courtesy of the Archdiocese of Chicago's Joseph Cardinal Bernardin Archives and Records Center.

The six sisters arrested in June 1965 appeared in a courtroom for sentencing in August. They were each fined $25 plus $5 costs. Unwilling to pay, they were saved from the House of Correction when two black lawyers, who had no connection with the case, paid the fines. They are (*left to right*): Sisters Jane Breidenbach, Edwardine Henjum, Pauline Cefolia, Gloria Briganti, Bridget Gemlo, and Andrea Orford. Courtesy of the Archdiocese of Chicago's Joseph Cardinal Bernardin Archives and Records Center.

Nuns from outside Chicago volunteered their services during summer months. In 1965, Sister Viatrix Mach of Rochester, Minnesota, helped coordinate the Cabrini Project. Here she talked with young people at Cabrini-Green public housing. Courtesy of the Sisters of St. Francis, Rochester, Minnesota, and Sister Mary Luke Baldwin, SSND.

7 Marching for Racial Justice in Chicago in the 1960s

Seven Franciscan nuns created a spectacle in the streets of downtown Chicago in the summer of 1963 by joining a picket line in front of the Illinois Club for Catholic Women.[1] They were protesting racial restrictions on club facilities and memberships. In novel fashion, these Catholic sisters made it clear that they would act publicly and decisively for racial justice—even against other Catholics. Their dramatic and controversial move ended an era in which American nuns remained sequestered and silent.

Two years later, another demonstration, again with sisters at the center, focused increased national attention on the city's mounting racial crisis. In June 1965, six Daughters of Charity from Marillac [Settlement] House took to the streets to protest Chicago's segregated public schools and their autocratic superintendent, Benjamin Willis. The nuns were arrested at State and Madison, held in detention at the State Street lockup, and arraigned for obstructing traffic. When the sisters were released to Sister Mary William Sullivan, director of Marillac House, she defended them. They had acted, she said, as "Christian American citizens" and "as representatives of the Church and the Daughters of Charity." In short, she believed that their public demonstration was in accord with the vision of their founder, St. Vincent de Paul, who had advised the first sisters two centuries earlier to have "no cloister but the streets of the town." Acting on old advice, these "new nuns" had entered the fray of the modern civil rights movement.[2]

The consequences of what the Franciscans and Daughters of Charity did—and why they did it—proved significant to the Catholic Church and American society. Their actions, though commonly misunderstood at the time and surprisingly overlooked since then, were motivated by a desire to do what they believed "before God had to be done." In seeking justice and dignity, they ignored parish boundaries and public sensibilities, brought knowledge and hope to their black neighbors, and forged new identities for themselves.[3]

Startling photographs and newsreel footage in 1963 marked the beginning of a general discussion on the role of nuns in the modern world.[4] Catholics and non-Catholics alike held strong opinions, most of them formed from what they had experienced in their own lives or seen in the media. Although there was little agreement among them (or among the nuns themselves), it was clear that the images of Catholic sisters marching in the streets of Chicago, or later in Selma, Alabama, bore no resemblance to people's old memories of their favorite grade-school teachers or genial photographs of nuns playing baseball.

The popular award-winning 1963 film *Lilies of the Field*, which dramatized the hardships of five German-refugee sisters in the Arizona desert, offered few useful insights. Despite exceptional performances by Sidney Poitier (as Homer Smith) and Lilia Skala (as Mother Maria), the movie—with its "happy-go-lucky Negro" and color-blind sisters—seemed almost upon release to belong to another era. By spring 1963, as a Chicago priest wrote to Cardinal Albert G. Meyer, "drastic change" had occurred "in the temper and tempo of the movement for human rights." Five years later, the place of Catholic sisters (along with that of African Americans) would never be the same. Once nuns had been "on a picket line," they could no longer be kept "behind convent walls."[5]

Convent Life

Before the 1960s, the lives of Catholic sisters bore striking resemblance to those of American soldiers. Sisters and soldiers led highly regimented and tightly ordered lives that were hierarchical at every turn. For centuries, women called to service in the Catholic Church were trained as "sisters in arms" and taught to develop traits—such as obedience, self-control, and sacrifice—that would befit them as soldiers of Christ.[6] The twin promise of a collective sense of purpose and of mutual support in challenging assignments attracted recruits to convent life, as they did secular soldiers. Rules and customs, often dating from the founding of their religious communities hundreds of years before, as well as canon law prescriptions that Vatican authorities strengthened in 1917, determined in large measure how contemporary nuns lived day to day (even hour by hour in some cases) well into the twentieth century. Despite the fact that society changed and placed new demands on them, their minutely structured lives and conspicuously clothed bodies remained largely unaltered in a Catholic Church that prided itself on its immutability. Crossing a convent threshold almost always took one back in time.

Yet wherever sisters were stationed or "missioned," they lived full and busy lives. Beginning in the 1880s, when the needs of the Catholic Church as defined by its bishops centered on classroom instruction in parish schools, most young women who entered religious congregations became teachers. As such, their "waking hours" were "crammed with communal prayers, devotional exercises, care of the convent and sacristy, a heavy teaching load, the training of children for first communion (or May procession, or confirmation), rehearsing of the choir and coaching of altar boys." Even when time allowed, women-religious—over 175,000 strong in 1963—were not permitted to leave their convents for a walk in the park or a trip to the local library. Nor could they visit the homes of their students or their own parents and siblings, attend a concert, or eat in public. They had left the world, according to one nun, "in order not to be corrupted by it."[7]

In hindsight, the time was ripe for change. The call came in *The Nun in the World*, a popular book by Cardinal Leon Joseph Suenens of Belgium. It was first published in 1962 and again in 1963, the year that Betty Friedan's *The Feminine Mystique* became an instant best-seller. Speaking about his book to an assembly of four thousand sisters in New York, Suenens said he had come not "to preach peace, but to call for a revolution, a revolution in the lives of active nuns, the nuns in the world." Catholic sisters, he insisted, "ought to be able to say, 'The world is my convent.'"[8]

What Cardinal Suenens proposed in his book received overwhelming support from nuns and others genuinely interested in their welfare. In late 1963, a prominent Catholic layman wrote that Suenens's contribution was "to have put the present situation of the nuns in historical, spiritual, and sociological context; he has been frank and has at last given official voice to the conflicts and difficulties many sisters suffered." Suenens clearly recognized that women-religious, treated as minors by convent traditions and canon law, had been unable to be fully effective as witnesses for Christ and the gospels. He encouraged them, therefore, to become "initiated into the great social problems" of the times. One nun, who taught on Chicago's South Side, recalled years later the book's impact on her and her friends. It was "read by almost every sister" and discussed endlessly. Indeed, one priest remarked to her that he guessed "every sister in Chicago puts a copy of it under her pillow every night."[9]

The excitement that resulted from reading *The Nun in the World* capped a movement for change that had been under way for nearly two decades. It began quietly in the 1940s with publication of a little noticed but landmark book called *The Education of Sisters* (1941). Sister Bertrande Meyers, its author, presented a well-argued case for the extended, integrated, and broader training of sister-teachers. A native Chicagoan and Daughter of Charity, she encouraged religious orders to insist on adequate preparation for young nuns before sending them out to teach. Twenty years before Suenens's critique, Sister Bertrande observed that sisters had for too long followed "a system of in-bred education conditioned largely by tutorial methods which seldom took them beyond their convent walls."[10]

As school enrollments climbed at the end of the 1940s, nuns became increasingly aware of "the killing schedules they undertook, and of the shoddy teaching this often made inevitable." A presentation before the National Catholic Education Association in 1949 on "The Education of Our Young Religious Teachers" dramatized the experiences of a hypothetical Sister Lucy. Its author, Sister Madeleva Wolffe, president of St. Mary's College of Notre Dame, expressed the feelings of teachers at every level. She insisted that their professional work was a "crucial component" of their religious vocation and therefore required strengthening.[11]

Attempts to remedy this situation were not supported by most local priests and bishops. They continued to request more teaching sisters for their burgeoning schools. By the early 1950s, when women-religious created the Sister Formation movement, they knew that the task of properly educating the nation's nuns would not be easy. In fact, for the first time, according to one who would become a major superior in the 1960s, many Catholic sisters became conscious of a long-standing unfairness. They saw more clearly "the injustice of an ecclesiastical system which built large parish complexes, expended huge amounts of time and money on the education of candidates for the priesthood, and begrudged sisters even the time to prepare themselves personally and professionally for their lifelong service to the church."[12]

During the 1950s and 1960s, congregations of women-religious in the United States instead came together in many joint efforts. They made immense strides in providing the nation's nuns with an integrated spiritual, academic, and professional education. The Daughters of Charity, for example, founded Marillac Sister Formation College in St. Louis in

1955 and opened it to all sisters. By 1960, the college had been expanded at a cost of $5 million; it then accommodated nearly three hundred students. Sisters from fifteen religious communities were represented on the faculty, which resulted in one of the earliest and largest experiences of intercommunity contacts among American nuns. Eighty-six Catholic women's colleges also admitted women-religious "at heavily discounted tuitions" and collectively "earmarked thirty full scholarships for them." But few sisters attended class with lay students. When they did, they were prohibited from speaking to them unnecessarily or mingling with them outside the classroom.[13]

The structures of convent life remained largely unchanged despite these educational advances. Yet as young nuns regularly asked probing questions in their classes, they also began to question traditional convent customs and practices. As a result, many who had accepted them "as almost a divine order found few humanly (or divinely) reasonable answers to justify much" of what they did. In short, the Sister Formation movement had educated a large population of seriously committed women-religious and readied them for the writings of Cardinal Suenens and the teachings of the Second Vatican Council (1962–65). Sister Elizabeth Carroll, major superior of the Sisters of Mercy in Pittsburgh, said in 1974 that Vatican II had made it possible for nuns to better understand "the system" within the Catholic Church and how it operated. It was, she observed, "an extraordinarily well-integrated and buttressed organization for the domination and controlled usefulness of women religious." Thus, the "assault on structures" and the feminist critique of patriarchy that began in the 1960s grew out of an honest desire by a large number of contemporary sisters "to serve God best" rather than serve a system that often felt oppressive.[14]

What had been learned through the Sister Formation movement and what was happening in society colored the lenses through which American nuns studied Vatican II documents. In undertaking a renewal of religious life, which had been urged in the early 1950s by Pope Pius XII and then mandated in the 1960s by Pope Paul VI's *Ecclesiae Sanctae* and *Perfectae Caritatis,* Catholic sisters took a number of issues into consideration. They sought above all to understand their vocation through the teachings of the gospels, the spirit of their orders' founders, the needs of the times, and the directions of church leaders as reflected in council documents.[15]

The Second Vatican Council affirmed the equality of women "both in domestic and in public life" and opposed all forms of racial discrimination. In a document on the "Universal Call to Holiness," the council also democratized the church by stating that all baptized Catholics were called to holiness. Thus nuns had not chosen "the better part," as they had been led to believe. Nor did their enclosed lives and private pieties assure them of salvation. Indeed, distance from the world was no longer the ideal. Like the laity (of which nuns were actually a part), sisters required a new theological orientation that emphasized society and its concerns, particularly those of the poor and alienated. For many in the church, this revolutionary view of what it meant to be contemporary Christians caused dismay and distress. What had been "a vertical religion from the worshiper up through the priest to God," noted one Chicago priest, became almost overnight "a horizontal religion, a joining together of many people."[16]

By the mid-1960s, significant changes had begun to occur in theological thinking as well as in church and convent life. The Second Vatican Council was not as revolutionary as it seemed at first glance, but it helped to alter substantially the lives of Catholic sisters. Despite the turmoil and tussles it provoked, it was "a wonderful time to be alive" for many, as a nun at Loretto Academy on Chicago's South Side observed in 1963. Pre–Vatican II convent life had not been "devoid of meaningful work, warm human relationships, or humor," according to another sister, but it had "made inroads into our sense of self."[17]

Following Vatican II, the alterations in religious habits, daily routines, and decision-making practices were accompanied by equally important changes in ministry. In Chicago, a good number of sisters had been forced by circumstances to start making such changes earlier. During the 1950s, when hundreds of thousands of black migrants from the rural South settled on the West Side, where housing was more available, the Daughters of Charity at Marillac House did not turn away from them or their children. Sister Mary William Sullivan, one of several who tried to assuage their fears and address their needs, said that she and her colleagues worked largely "in isolation, feeling and believing that no one was really interested in the Poor." By spring 1965, their attitude improved as they felt the winds of change within the church—winds so strong that "virtually no group of religious women [would be] left untouched by the [Second Vatican] Council's emphasis on ministry for justice." Yet for those who lived and worked in black neighborhoods, the council only affirmed what they had been doing for a long time.[18]

Early Signs of Change

In June 1955, Sister Mary William arrived at Marillac House, which was three miles from Chicago's Loop at 2822 West Jackson Boulevard in East Garfield Park. She was thirty years old and fresh from graduate studies in social work at Catholic University. Nine Daughters of Charity of St. Vincent de Paul were already on the job. This large Catholic settlement house had opened in 1947, with the primary objective of combating juvenile delinquency in a neighborhood that was predominantly white with strong Irish (42 percent) and Italian (22 percent) populations. The sisters had no way of knowing what the future would bring, but they had the good sense to follow their Catholic traditions and womanly instincts. They incorporated Marillac House as a social service center committed to promoting "the physical, spiritual, and educational welfare of persons of any race, creed, or color" who lived nearby.[19]

By 1955, as a result of the migration of black southerners to Chicago, East Garfield Park grew to more than seventy thousand people. Lawndale had become the new port of entry, and black settlement spread steadily into the Garfield Park and Austin communities. The Daughters of Charity watched their neighbors become mostly African Americans (48 percent), although some Irish (10 percent), Italians (11 percent), and Puerto Ricans (13.5 percent) remained. Less than ten years later, the area around Marillac House was 97 percent black. A housing shortage that began during World War II persisted into the 1950s. The massive influx of people contributed to the problem, for although Chicago may have been able to offer the migrants work, "the city was much less able to provide them with shelter." And the demolition of dwellings in the path of the new Congress (later Eisenhower) Expressway made conditions worse. Many of the residential structures that survived were dilapidated, and nearly half of them had no private baths as late as 1960.[20]

In this new ghetto, Marillac House stood out because of its size and reputation. One of the largest settlement houses in the United States, this four-story brick building (with a basement and smaller two-story additions) had become known for its warm hospitality and range of services. In the early years, local Catholics participated regularly and eagerly in core programs that were designed for all age groups from "two years to one hundred." The most popular ones, Tiny Tot Town and Kiddieville, provided day care five days a week from 7:00 A.M. to 6:00 P.M. for children from two years of age to five. There was also before- and after-school supervision for those between the ages of six and twelve. Special programs for teenagers included skating, dancing, and sports competitions (baseball, volleyball, and basketball). In a dogged attempt to live up to its slogan ("something for everyone in the family"), Marillac House provided an array of clubs and outings that attracted adults and seniors. The ten nuns who lived on the settlement's top floor and their expanding lay staff (about sixty paid workers and over a hundred volunteers by 1960) rooted their offerings "in the needs and experiences of the people themselves." As East Garfield Park shifted from white to black and from Catholic to non-Catholic, Marillac House again demonstrated its willingness to experiment.[21]

One of its most successful new ventures was Rendu House, which opened in January 1960. It was an outpost of the settlement inside the Rockwell Gardens public housing project. About a ten-minute walk from Marillac House, Rockwell consisted of eight massive high-rise buildings that provided apartments to seven thousand people. Approximately 95 percent of the residents were African American and unaccustomed to city life. Sister Mary William, who was appointed the first supervisor of Rendu House, held that position until January 1964, when she became Marillac's director.[22]

Rendu House began casually and with modest expectations. Returning from a meeting in late summer or early fall in 1959, Sister Mary William noticed through the window of a bus that several of the Rockwell high-rises were nearly completed. She and Sister Rosalie Larson, then director of Marillac House, made inquiries, fearing that their block clubs in the fifty-block area around the settlement would be adversely affected. Sister Mary William eventually met with Chicago Housing Authority officials. They encouraged the nuns to become involved at Rockwell Gardens and agreed to lease them an apartment for one dollar. To be "proximate and available," they opened an extension of Marillac House and named it "Rendu House." It honored Sister Rosalie Rendu, a nineteenth-century Daughter of Charity who labored her entire adult life in one of the most poverty-stricken districts of Paris. As a young woman, Sister Mary William had read a "very simple book" on Sister Rosalie's ministry to the poor and was inspired by it.[23]

During her years at Rendu House, Sister Mary William learned firsthand what it meant to be a "nun in the world." Through regular practice, she discovered how to reach out to individuals who were racially and culturally different and who had no previous contact with Catholic sisters. Working with a receptionist out of a small first-floor apartment (number 104 at 2517 West Adams), Sister Mary William came to know and understand African Americans in an intimate way, immediately through their day-to-day problems and over time through their dreams and disappointments. Forty years later, she remarked that Rendu House gave her "a crash course on poor black people and the conditions of their lives." And she remained grateful for it: "They taught me; they taught all of us [sisters] how to be genuinely compassionate and how to serve."[24]

Sister Mary William was born in St. Louis in 1925 and named Florence. She was the third of four children of William and Lillian O'Meara Sullivan, both Catholics. Although her parents met and married in St. Louis, where her father worked as an accountant, her mother had emigrated with a sister from County Tipperary, Ireland. Florence grew up in Our Lady of Sorrows parish in South St. Louis and went to Xavier High School, staffed by the Sisters of Charity of the Blessed Virgin Mary (BVMs). In 1941, during her sophomore year in high school, she decided to enter the convent after graduation but resolved not "to teach French and violin." Instead she hoped "to take care of orphans." Following her senior year in 1943, she joined the Daughters of Charity, where her father's two sisters were members. Headquartered in St. Louis, this community (sometimes known as "White Wings" or "White Bonnets" because of their distinctive headdress) was old, large, and had a distinguished record of "serving the sick and caring for the orphan and foundling." In 1966, when asked by a *Chicago Daily News* reporter whether her parents had supported her career choice, Sister Mary William replied that "every Irish family wants at least one religious in it. . . . they were only surprised that I, the nonconformist, was the one."[25]

The radical spirit of the times and the crying needs of the black population around Marillac House gave scope to Sister Mary William's innate nonconformity. Some who knew her well claimed that she was ahead of her time. Perhaps so. She was at least a perfect fit for them and for the leadership role she assumed. A familiar figure around Rockwell Gardens, nearly everyone recognized the tall, attractive nun, whom they often greeted as Sister Mary Williams, a common surname among African Americans. As she walked back and forth between Marillac House and Rendu House two or more times each day, she became attached to the neighborhood and its people. Before long, East Garfield Park took on new meaning and became more to her than a collection of city blocks. As a person who "loved the Lord," according to her former secretary, Maudine Wordlaw, this particular place on Chicago's West Side was a sacred community "where God, in the person of Jesus Christ, revealed himself."[26]

A year after opening Rendu House, Sister Mary William reported on what she and a few others had accomplished. There were "certain things we can 'count,'" she observed, along with all that was "immeasurable." Among the former, she and her small staff (by then a receptionist and two young assistants) had succeeded in organizing each floor of the eight high-rises into building councils that functioned like Marillac's successful block clubs. They also created a preschool cooperative for children from age two to five and an active "Play Club" at Marillac House for youngsters on a local school's afternoon shift. The staff helped volunteers from Rockwell Gardens and the surrounding area form a "Law and Order Committee," which functioned as a local "watch" group. Rendu House also sponsored a well-attended Halloween party for residents of both public and private housing.[27]

Sister Mary William had begun her assignment in Rendu House with no special directions or grandiose schemes. A professional social worker, she hoped to create an atmosphere in which she could assist those in need. When she failed in several attempts to obtain foundation funding, she was unable to put into place more elaborate programs that she had begun to dream of. She later considered this limitation a blessing. It forced her and her staff to provide what people wanted—"a direct and competent response to their problems, a means of communication, and 'love with an open hand.'" Residents came to Rendu House, according to Sister Mary William, "for just about any reason, or no reason at all." Some asked for change for a coin-operated washing machine or directions to downtown, others for advice in finding a job, and many more to introduce relatives from Alabama or Mississippi. Following a routine visit to Rendu House in June 1960, an employee of the Welfare Council of Metropolitan Chicago reported that, although Sister Mary William "looks run-ragged," all the "small questions received warm and capable consideration."[28]

By 1961, it was clear that the Daughters of Charity were serving their neighborhood's black migrants in unusual ways. The core programs continued to operate, but the sisters also began to organize local residents into a community with shared interests. "Our whole philosophy changed," said Sister Jane Breidenbach, who had been at Marillac House since 1948. "We found ourselves involved less in the prevention of juvenile delinquency and more in the development of black leadership." Much of this changed because the sisters lived in the neighborhood, where they had close daily contact with African Americans as employees, in the day-care center and block clubs, and at Rockwell Gardens. More keenly aware of how cultural and racial differences (along with poverty) handicapped these newcomers, the sisters began to think and act differently than most male leaders in the Catholic Church and officials in the city of Chicago.[29]

Saul Alinsky, a recognized community organizer, contributed to Marillac House's transformation. In 1956 he and Sister Mary William became acquainted at the National Conference of Catholic Charities in Buffalo, where he spoke about "community organization and leadership" in Chicago's Back of the Yards neighborhood. Back at home, he gave her "a great deal of encouragement" and taught her the value of organizing: that there was "power in numbers" and that "power was always taken, never given." When you meet with powerful people in the church or in government, she recalled Alinsky telling her, "You don't go in to ask, you go in to negotiate." And she agreed with him that African Americans should not have to ask for rights and privileges enjoyed by other Americans.[30]

During the same period, Sister Mary William developed a collegial relationship with Monsignor John "Jack" Egan, another well-known community organizer and social-justice activist. He headed up the archdiocese's Office of Urban Affairs. Impressed when he first heard "the nun from Marillac" at a meeting in summer 1960, he vowed to "stay close to them [Daughters of Charity] to learn more of their thinking." As he became more acquainted, Egan told other priests and nuns of their work, particularly at Rockwell Gardens.[31]

One day, Father Sebastian Lewis, a Benedictine priest at St. Joseph's parish near the Cabrini-Green housing project, "bumped into Egan, who put him in touch with Sister Mary William." After seeing her operation in Rendu House, he returned to St. Joseph's school "all excited—[you've] got to meet this nun, got to meet this nun," he told Sister Mary Benet McKinney, another Benedictine and principal of St. Joseph's. She and others eventually met Sister Mary William and her colleagues at Marillac House. In fact, during 1961, it was there and at other convents on the West Side that sisters from various religious communities gathered informally on weekends to talk about racial change and its impact on their lives and work. By the year's end, they had formed a West Side Sisters' Conference, which soon became the Urban Apostolate of the Sisters. In 1962, the year in which *The Nun in the World* first appeared and the Second Vatican Council began, Sister Mary William was released from her usual responsibilities for one day each week to become the Urban Apostolate's first coordinator.[32]

During that year, some nuns in other parts of Chicago joined the West Siders. The majority of them were teachers in black areas who were frustrated by their inability to relate to their students. Sister Mary Benet, who would become the Urban Apostolate's second coordinator and then director, remembered that "Sister Mary William would sit and talk with us about people who came up [to Chicago] from Mississippi." Because of her experiences at Rockwell Gardens, she related well to black families and warned sisters against trying "to shove white values down their [pupils'] throats." Instead, she encouraged home visits and congenial interaction—not something encouraged in most religious communities at the time. It was in homes, countered Sister Mary William, where teachers would begin to understand the daunting problems their students faced. Little by little (and usually without anyone's permission), nuns who lived in black neighborhoods began going into homes and attending meetings of local civic groups during after-school hours. "And that got us into lots of trouble," said Sister Mary Benet.[33]

For that reason, the Urban Apostolate's coordinating committee accepted Monsignor Egan's offer to work out of the archdiocese's Office of Urban Affairs, which he directed. The sisters immediately became connected to neighborhood groups throughout the city. They also received protection against complaining pastors who did not want nuns "out at these meetings" instead of training altar boys, cleaning the church sacristy, or teaching the choir. Several of them spoke directly to Egan about Sister Mary William. Her lack of deference and her "aggressiveness" caused one priest in 1963 to accuse her of being "antagonistic toward the clergy" and possibly "anti-clerical." But Sister Mary William had grown impatient and frustrated with the general reluctance of pastors to take a stand on civil rights. She also disliked their patronizing attitude and their refusal to acknowledge what she had learned about racial conditions in Chicago and what the Urban Apostolate of the Sisters was doing about them. Egan understood. In 1964, following a meeting of twenty pastors, "all from Negro parishes," he noted that the gathering was "an extraordinary and historic development, since the pastors by and large in the Negro areas have been completely quiet on the race question." Finally, the Urban Apostolate's location in the Office of Urban Affairs cleared the way for Egan to secure Cardinal Meyer's imprimatur for the fledgling organization.[34]

The cardinal's approval unleashed a flood of energy among Chicago's inner-city nuns. Following Alinsky's advice, they organized themselves into five "areas" that included all of the city's changing neighborhoods. Sisters from different religious orders cooperated across parish boundaries to address a pressing problem in their area and to become involved in community organizations already up and running. Frequent exposure to life outside convent walls often resulted in dramatic changes in individual sisters. Sister Mary Benet remembered a young Sister of the Holy Family of Nazareth who became active in the Organization of the Southwest Community. At an area meeting, Sister Mary Benet asked her how she felt about "six months of working on the street?" The sister responded enthusiastically, saying, "It has really been something! I have gone from a community [of nuns] where our motto is 'Oh, my Jesus, all for thee' to this community [of organizers] where the motto is 'We don't take no shit from no one.'" As such experiences became more common, the sisters' polite acceptance of intolerance, gradualism, outright discrimination, and sexism evaporated.[35]

Area IV of the Urban Apostolate of the Sisters functioned differently from the others. It was unique in that it was made up of only one community of women-religious, the School Sisters of St. Francis, whose motherhouse was in Milwaukee. But many of its members lived throughout Chicago, where they staffed more than thirty schools. In 1961, the entire order had begun "working in a positive and steady way to promote an awareness of racial justice."[36] A year later, in April 1962, the sisters in Chicago decided to broaden their experience by visiting homes in Cabrini-Green public housing on the near North Side. Father Damien Charbonneau, OSM, of St. Dominic's, a nearby parish without a school, had suggested the project after hearing that the nuns had participated in a series of race relations workshops at Chicago's Friendship House, a Catholic interracial institution headquartered on the South Side since 1942. On the weekends and holidays, organized teams of Franciscans made themselves available to Cabrini residents, especially the elderly and children. As their home visiting expanded during that summer, the sisters received additional instruction and training from Paul Mundy, professor of sociology at Loyola University, and Sister Mary William, who encouraged them to join the Urban Apostolate as a single area.[37]

Sister Angelica Seng, a young Franciscan who served as a project leader at Cabrini, also organized the workshops at Friendship House. She was a Chicagoan who had grown up on the North Side in St. Andrew's parish. She became a volunteer at Friendship House during the 1950s as a student at Alvernia High School. Founded by the School Sisters of St. Francis in 1924, Alvernia was located in a residential district northwest of downtown Chicago. By 1949, when Ann Seng was a freshman, the school had more than a thousand students in what it described as a "relaxed, though structured" all-girls environment. Decades later, when asked about her years at Alvernia, Seng immediately and vividly recalled her sociology teacher, Sister Rebecca Brenner. She appears to have awakened in many students their potential as women and opened their minds to the needs of the larger world. Above all, she raised their racial consciousness.[38]

Sister Rebecca taught at Alvernia for fifteen years (1937–52) and was enormously influential. Not only was she effective in the classroom, but she was a force outside it. She routinely took students off campus to

Friendship House, where they met and spent time with black people, and her pupils visited prisons where less privileged women were incarcerated. Behind the scenes in the community, Sister Rebecca prodded administrators at Alvernia and in Milwaukee to recruit black girls, Catholic or not, through tuition assistance or scholarships. Unafraid of being labeled a "'nigger lover' and radical," she openly "confess[ed] to both" in 1947. From then on, she used every opportunity to present a case for "interracial harmony." If it were to prevail, she argued, "the roots of hatred must be annihilated through sound education and the exercise of Christian justice."[39]

In 1952, after her junior year, Seng entered the School Sisters of St. Francis. By 1960, she had returned to Alvernia—then as Sister Angelica—to teach sociology. Almost immediately she began arranging for students and colleagues to participate in the interracial programs at Friendship House. Aware of the hardening racial divisions in Chicago's older neighborhoods (where the Franciscans had most of their elementary schools), Sister Angelica persuaded community leaders to cosponsor an all-day workshop on race relations at Friendship House in early 1962. Ever an "efficient organizer," Sister Angelica and Betty Plank, Friendship House's education director, assembled a mix of people and materials to instruct a new audience on how to teach children of a different racial and cultural background. More than 120 Franciscans from twenty-eight schools responded to what was a "first" for Friendship House. Other programs soon followed.[40]

In the aftermath of the historic National Conference on Religion and Race held in Chicago during January 1963, Friendship House increased its educational activities. Sister Angelica, who continued to teach at Alvernia during the week and volunteer at Cabrini-Green on the weekends, persuaded her community to send more young sisters to Friendship House. At race-relations gatherings in May and June 1963, groups of between thirty-five and forty nuns from Milwaukee were among those who heard presentations that were soon to bear unexpected results. Marillac's Sister Mary William spoke on "The Apostolate of Presence" and shared what had become part of her standard message: the importance of being "proximate and available" to poor people. Inspired by the words of Martin Luther King Jr., whose address at the Conference on Religion and Race several months earlier had received extensive local coverage, she echoed his warning. If the church were absent in a time of racial and moral crisis, it might very well become "little more than an irrelevant social club."

Dora DuPont Williams, another speaker, was more provocative. A North Shore resident from Winnetka who was unfashionably liberal, she had been among the Friendship House contingent who, in August 1962, had responded to King's call "to bear witness . . . and to stand with the people of Albany [Georgia] as they strive for freedom." After describing her experiences in Georgia, which included a night in jail, Williams asked when Catholic sisters would become visibly involved in the civil rights movement. Why was it "proper" or "appropriate," she goaded, for newspapers to carry photographs of nuns on merry-go-rounds or roller coasters at picnics and fairs but not for a cause that mattered?[41]

Before Selma

The first group of Catholic sisters to join a public demonstration in support of racial justice took place on July 1, 1963, at 820 North Michigan Avenue in downtown Chicago, the event that opens this chapter. It included seven Franciscans, of whom six were School Sisters of St. Francis and the seventh a member of the Sisters of St. Francis of Mary Immaculate in Joliet. With them was one priest, Father Daniel Mallette, associate pastor at St. Agatha's parish in Lawndale on the West Side.[42] All of the nuns had attended workshops at Friendship House, and all of the School Sisters of St. Francis had volunteered at Cabrini-Green during the previous year. They regarded their picketing against the discriminatory policies of the Illinois Club for Catholic Women in front of Lewis Towers as "an escalation of concern and commitment." Sisters Angelica Seng and Anthony Claret Sparks, who were studying sociology at Loyola that summer, attributed their final decision to take part in the student-led demonstration to Dora Williams's remarks at Friendship House and King's "Letter from a Birmingham Jail." Challenged to act on their beliefs, the Franciscans chose to join the front line rather than "stand on the sideline and merely mouth pious irrelevancies and sanctimonious trivialities." Never did they imagine that they would become the focus of local, national, and international attention.[43]

Until the nuns joined the demonstration, the marching students who organized it (members of the Student Action Committee of Greater Chicago) had been ignored. In late June, Sister Angelica first learned about the segregated policies of the Illinois Club for Catholic Women from Tom Cook, a black staff person at Friendship House. An African American student had been prohibited from using the club's swimming pool, and a qualified black woman was denied membership in the organization. The students and several of the faculty had expressed their displeasure publicly in articles and letters in the school newspaper and had staged three demonstrations, but they had drawn little publicity and no response. Cook asked Sister Angelica if she and several friends might join the demonstration. She answered with a strong "maybe" and, years later, does not recall any strategy "to get some collars [priests] and habits [nuns] involved." She wanted first to attempt to contact Julia Lewis, founder and president of the club and widow of the late Frank Lewis, a prominent Catholic philanthropist who had donated Lewis Towers to the Jesuits for their university. The women's club occupied the top several floors.[44]

Julia Lewis, a confident and proud woman, refused to back down. She viewed the club as private—and hers. Thus, its policies reflected her opinions. Despite its many good works since the 1920s, the club was, she believed, "for white Catholic women." In a June 1963 "President's Message," Lewis clearly stated what she thought about the civil rights movement and black people. "Most of the trouble in Birmingham, and elsewhere, even here, is not created by the Negroes themselves," she observed, "but by a group of so-called heroic people who want to keep the pot boiling and stir up trouble when none would exist." She reported that the Illinois Club for Catholic Women was "doing as much as possible for the needy" and would continue to do so. But, she argued, "we, too, are entitled to Civil Rights. We are taking them." Besides, Lewis reported that her "fine colored housekeeper" of some twenty years told her that black people "'don't want to mix socially with the whites. I like my own people. They know how to enjoy themselves better. . . . I loves my people.'"[45]

Sister Angelica and two other nuns tried to see Lewis on June 28, but "she was busy." The Franciscans left a note in which they expressed concern about the club's discriminatory policies and asked again if they might meet with her. The following day, Lewis called Sister Angelica. Although the conversation was polite, Lewis was unwilling to budge even when told that "some of the sisters would take a public stand . . . on Monday [July 1]." Lewis said: "Go ahead and do what you feel you have to do." Sisters Angelica and Anthony Claret, from different Franciscan communities, telephoned their respective mothers-general and explained the situation. Both were encouraged to follow through with their plan—"if it's right, go ahead," were the words of one superior. But neither they nor Julia Lewis expected what followed.[46]

Almost instantly, stories of "pickets in black" appeared locally on television and in newspapers. They were accompanied by astonishing images of Catholic sisters in full dress holding signs that read, "The Illinois Club for Catholic Women is Not Catholic," "Integration Now," and "Catholics Do Not Discriminate." The national media used similar write-ups and the same powerful pictures; in mid-July, the picketing nuns and priest found themselves in *Time* magazine. By then, Lewis had announced changes in club policies. Her son read a statement in which he complained of the sisters' action: "I don't recall a single incident other than the death of my father that hurt my mother as much as having the religious turn on her by picketing. . . . I feel they acted in extremely poor taste." Obviously angry, he questioned why nuns in "18th century garb, with 19th century rules, should suddenly vault into the 20th century."[47]

Other Catholics wondered as well. Many responses, but not all, came in the form of objections. Critics charged in phone calls and letters that the Franciscans had acted impulsively, inappropriately, and in an undignified manner. One upset "father of a nun" was especially disturbed that the sisters' protest was "so elaborately publicized in newspapers and television." Like many others, he complained to Cardinal Meyer that their picketing was "an undignified public demonstration which impairs the respect and standing of our Catholic nuns." Another critic characterized the sisters as "fools" who were "so saturated with the question of racial discrimination that they hesitated not a moment to strike out."[48]

The Franciscans also had supporters. Dora Williams, who had challenged them at Friendship House, immediately sent a bouquet of flowers. Raymond Hilliard, chairman of the National Catholic Conference on Interracial Justice, and Mathew Ahmann, its executive director, applauded their courage. They pointed out that racial injustice, not the nuns, "lacked dignity." John A. McDermott, executive director of the Catholic Interracial Council of Chicago (CIC), argued that "peaceful demonstrations against racial injustice can be an effective and proper means for Catholics to give witness to the principles of their faith." Having failed "to effect a quiet solution," the sisters chose to become public witnesses.[49]

The seven Franciscans did not act on impulse. They knew what they were about when they joined the picket line. And because they did, according to Ahmann, they gave encouragement to others and "brought the [Catholic] Church into the civil rights battle to stay." The summer of 1963 proved extraordinarily significant for that reason. More and more church leaders became committed and visible social activists. It was nearly impossible, especially after the March on Washington in August, "to stand by while their black counterparts were staging demonstrations, engaging in active civil disobedience, and increasingly becoming targets of racial violence." Sister Anthony Claret contended that women-religious also had "a part to play in the issues of the day, particularly this problem [of racial justice]." They picketed, therefore, "not because we were students at Loyola and teachers; we did this because we are religious." But they also knew that the future would not be easy. The harsh criticisms they received, remarked Sister Angelica, were "a serious indication of lack of understanding of just what is the Church." Equally indicative of the difficulties ahead was the closed swimming pool in Lewis Towers. It had been drained, "apparently to prevent any interracial swimming."[50]

Despite these denunciations and frustrations, the Franciscans' actions fit the times and the place. Not only was the Second Vatican Council well under way, but the pace of Chicago's racial-justice campaign had quickened following the success of the National Conference on Religion and Race held earlier in the year. It had been the brainchild of Ahmann and McDermott, two forceful lay Catholics who were willing to take risks and rock boats to "speed-up the process of reform in Chicago's racial patterns." Under McDermott, the Catholic Interracial Council (CIC), more than any other single entity, "provided the impetus for Catholic racial reform in the 1950s and 1960s."[51]

Its tough stance received unflagging support from Ahmann and his National Catholic Conference for Interracial Justice. On July 17, 1963, he and three of the Franciscans who had picketed met with the directors of CIC and encouraged them to approve "the use of direct action methods in the work for interracial justice and charity." Ahmann explained that although direct action was often divisive, it was necessary because "religion was in the race battle to stay" and "the CIC of Chicago was the strongest [Catholic] unit in the entire movement." The resolution passed easily, allowing McDermott—often on the front lines himself—to turn CIC into "a social action as well as an educational organization."[52]

Catholic activists understood that the recent whirlwinds of rebellion and destruction demanded a resolute response on civil rights, not gradualism or compromise. By 1964, nuns who resided in black communities spent little time in seclusion or on themselves. Although they could not alter the social and economic forces that were devastating their neighborhoods, they did not withdraw. Instead they became more active in grassroots organizing and introduced new kinds of services that addressed the everyday needs of African Americans. On the South Side, in Woodlawn, the Sisters of Loretto opened the Loretto Adult Education Center, while continuing to staff their academy for black students. Such efforts built upon those begun decades earlier when the Sisters of the Good Shepherds created a boarding school for African American girls in Hyde Park. On the North Side, at St. Joseph school, adjacent to Cabrini-Green public housing, "the old definition of teacher was greatly enlarged." Good classroom teaching remained imperative, but the Benedictines also guided parents through "the intricacies of nutrition, child psychology, and hygiene."

Finally, on the West Side, in East Garfield Park, the Daughters of Charity at Marillac House organized "Neighbors at Work." Twenty-four block clubs of more than two thousand members involved residents (about a third of whom received public aid) in programs and activities that promoted personal development and neighborhood improvement. A massive cleanup campaign and parade in April 1964 was but one example.[53]

As inner-city sisters left many of their old ways behind and increasingly crossed the boundaries of race, religion, and class, they became more connected to people living on society's fringes. As a result, Martin Luther King Jr.'s distinctly Christian message of suffering, deliverance, and justice resonated as strongly among them as among their black friends and neighbors. For it was from them that nuns found the inspiration and courage to work for racial equality. The efforts of Catholic sisters made the headlines on occasion, but, more often than not, outsiders hardly noticed. As Sister Mary William once remarked: "We deal with very poor people daily. . . . If you ever need today's food and this week's rent, just call. We're good at [providing] that." So good, in fact, she was appointed director of Marillac House in 1964. Under her energetic leadership, the Daughters of Charity at Marillac House would join the ranks of those women-religious who took a stand in Chicago in July 1963 and marched in Selma in March 1965.[54]

The Arrest

On June 12, 1965, six Daughters of Charity from Marillac House were among two hundred people arrested in the heart of Chicago's Loop during a civil-rights demonstration.[55] Once again, sisters and priests, clothed in religious garb, captured the headlines and caused the most consternation among the city's Catholics. "Fine to march in Selma, but not Chicago," Sister Mary William recalled decades later, remembering the onslaught of angry phone calls and outraged letters that Marillac House received. Only three months before, legions of priests and nuns had marched in Selma, Alabama. Father James Groppi, a Milwaukee activist, called their participation "a success," especially since it brought swift passage of a right-to-vote law. But comparing Selma to Chicago in 1965, he remarked that "it did not take one-hundredth as much courage to go to Selma as it did to get involved in an arrest situation in Chicago." In the North and in a city where there was a "law-and-order mayor," according to Groppi, "a priest [or nun] really sticks his [or her] neck on the line."[56]

The arrest of the Daughters of Charity shocked everyone. Those most surprised may have been the sisters themselves and their superior,

Sister Mary William. It was she who had informed them of the demonstration, following a telephone call earlier in the day from Father George Clements, a black priest at St. Dorothy's on the South Side. As the nuns were carted off in a police van to the State Street lockup, where they were detained and arraigned, speculation began among journalists and priests on whether or not they were the first Catholic sisters ever arrested in the United States. The desk sergeant assured reporters that "he'd never booked a nun before," and no one else had ever heard of any other such arrest. What culminated in an extraordinary event grew out of a simple decision by six women-religious to protest publicly the condition of Chicago's overcrowded, segregated public schools. Sister Mary William had given them permission to participate because they felt obliged "to represent the Poor whom they know, love, and serve" in their West Side neighborhood. She later explained to her superior in St. Louis that the sisters "stood in Witness to the Poor."[57]

One of the arrested nuns, Sister Andrea (Lucy) Orford, who was born in Chicago in 1929, believed that her commitment to racial justice began years earlier with the example of her mother, Alice Andrews Orford. Alice had grown up in a working-class family on the near West Side and belonged to Holy Family parish, where she had had the Religious of the Sacred Heart for teachers. She later married and raised four children, but she never forgot the poor. Another daughter, Sister Martin de Porres Orford, said her mother "would reach out to anyone in need," but she was devoted to a black Catholic mission, St. Joseph's, at Thirteenth and Loomis streets. In the summer, Mrs. Orford brought children from the mission into their white neighborhood for picnics. She also made regular visits to St. Joseph's with supplies of clothes and baked goods, often taking her youngest daughter, Lucy, with her. On June 13, 1965, the day after Sister Andrea's arrest, she recalled accompanying her mother to the mission and spontaneously hugging a little boy. It astonished him, and his classmates "screamed with laughter." That expression of affection, she wrote, was "perhaps the beginning of why I did what I did yesterday." She wanted to demonstrate once again that "there was no difference in me from them."[58]

Another of those arrested was Sister Jane Breidenbach, the oldest at fifty-nine and the best known. A trained nurse and an avid gardener, she had grown up on a farm near Sterling, Colorado, and spent two years working in an orphanage in China before arriving at Marillac House in 1948, a year after it opened. Before leaving in 1983, she would become a legend. When she joined the march, she was already widely respected for her care of children in the day nursery and for organizing neighborhood cleanup and voter-registration campaigns. Sister Jane joined the demonstration on June 12 because she believed there was "a need for religious [nuns and priests] to support the cause" of black children who were deprived of equal educational opportunities. In the end, she considered the entire incident, including the money paid for their release, a small price to pay "for the privilege of representing the needs of our Poor."[59]

By 1965, the Daughters of Charity at Marillac House had developed a deep sense of identification with their black neighbors. Their commitment had begun to take shape in the late 1950s when East Garfield Park changed racially. The sisters were forced to confront for the first time the indignities and desperation that resulted from the twin disadvantages of poverty and race. In 1961, they rejoiced when they heard the summons of a young Catholic president with Irish roots. Sister Mary William still remembers "standing and watching President John F. Kennedy give his inaugural address"; she said it made a profound impact on her and the other nuns. They felt energized. They wanted to serve the poor as Catholic sisters *and* as American citizens, and they felt called by the president's words to heed Isaiah's command "to 'undo the heavy burdens . . . and to let the oppressed go free.'" But it was "Preacher King" who moved the sisters more than anyone else. His message of nonviolence and his unique ability to "harness practical necessities to religious power" drew these women-religious headlong into the throes of the civil rights movement. Having previously taken up the causes of their oppressed black neighbors, the nuns quickly and ardently joined the ranks of what they saw as a religious and moral crusade that wedded Christian principles and American ideals.[60]

Determined to make Marillac House "the collective voice of the poor," Sister Mary William emphasized community organizing when she became director. The block clubs, previously established through the "Neighbors at Work" program, were the key vehicles for giving people a sense of community and of personal worth, as well as a way to address their problems. During the early months of 1964, local residents undertook a major cleanup campaign that caught Mayor Richard J. Daley's attention. Following notice that his office had awarded "Neighbors at Work" a citation for its successful efforts, Sister Mary William scheduled an appointment with the mayor and a rally at Marillac House to prepare for it. "Now we must act," she coached; "the time has come for our neighborhood to be heard." On April 2, 1964, she and five other nuns, along with forty West Siders, went to City Hall. In a closed meeting, the group told Mayor Daley that there were "no play lots, no ball fields, no playgrounds, no urban renewal program" in the fifty-block neighborhood.

Within six weeks, they said they wanted some vacant lots cleared, additional lighting installed around unoccupied buildings, and garbage collected more frequently. Daley heard them out; he refused to follow their timetable but promised action. It came slowly and incompletely.[61]

The block clubs were also an important vehicle for leadership training and political empowerment, a lesson Sister Mary William learned from Alinsky. Through the cleanup campaign, club members (more than two thousand and expanding) began to understand that "working together for a common good benefit[ed] each of them individually." From June through August 1964, they participated actively in the "Summer of Progress," the first of several intensive summer programs aimed at developing self-reliance and civic responsibility. Sister Mary William brought to East Garfield Park an army of committed volunteers not unlike the still-new Peace Corps, though on a much smaller scale. College students and local activists, including nuns and seminarians from Chicago and elsewhere, helped residents "do what they want to get done."[62]

This summer project, although structured, was democratic and diverse. It included a range of educational and tutorial services, recreational activities, neighborhood self-help initiatives, and grass-roots organizing. In between scheduled assignments, volunteers walked the streets, at the urging of Sister Mary William. She firmly believed that if residents were helped "in their homes, on their yards, or in whatever capacity the people think important, that a sympathetic and truly loving Christ would be displayed." At summer's end, nearly four thousand West Siders and volunteers had participated in a rich and satisfying experience. It proved so rewarding that plans for a 1965 "Summer of Hope" were under way before the closing sessions.[63]

Sister Mary William once described herself as a "large, loud Irish nun sitting on the corner of Jackson and California" on the city's West Side. That may have been true, but McDermott of Chicago's Catholic Interracial Council saw her differently. He described her as "a fighter for justice and a dynamic and creative woman who combines professional competence with apostolic zeal." It was probably for that reason that he invited her to serve as "Mistress of Ceremonies" at the council's annual John F. Kennedy Award Dinner in October 1964. Sister Mary William immediately accepted the invitation, without asking anyone's permission, because "it needed to be done." It needed to be done, she said, for children like nine-year-old Jimmy, who had recently told her that he was glad "he [was] a Negro" because "Martin Luther King [was] a Negro." She confessed that it was the first time in her nine years at Marillac House that she had "heard anyone say he was happy to be a Negro." She also credited King with inspiring the development of black leadership in their neighborhood.[64]

At the Kennedy Award Dinner, Sister Mary William sat next to King, who asked her about living conditions on the West Side. She told him about some of the problems in housing and in education. She was adamantly against building any more high-rise housing projects, but she was even more troubled by the segregated, underfunded, and over-crowded public schools. The Marillac House staff knew the situation well. Because of double shifts, youngsters in the area spent whole mornings or afternoons at the settlement rather than in their classrooms. By the mid-1960s, Chicago's public schools had become a major source of discontent to African Americans and civil rights activists, who organized the Coordinating Council of Community Organizers and consistently demanded the removal of the school superintendent, Benjamin Willis. In June 1965, when his appointment was renewed, citywide boycotts and protests erupted. Because the Daughters of Charity were in sympathy with the cause and always "ran with their people," it was not unusual or extraordinary that they participated in the June 12 demonstration. Sister Mary William remembered it as being "one of many" such occasions.[65]

The public unpleasantness that resulted, however, was extraordinary. On the day after the arrest, local and national media carried accounts of the march and photographs of the nuns being led into a police van. Almost immediately, hundreds of messages flooded Marillac House. A few of them offered support, but most were critical, even offensive. Maudine Wordlaw, secretary to Sister Mary William, recalled the level of anger and hate. Some said the sisters were "nigger lovers" and "traitors to the Catholic Church and America"; almost all of them repeated a single phrase: "You sisters have no right. . . ." But in a democracy, Sister Mary William insisted, "everybody's voice has to be heard—even the sisters'."[66]

In the local Catholic newspaper, letters criticized the Daughters of Charity for putting on a show and breaking the law. For example, two priests from St. Sabina's parish insisted that Willis's "neighborhood school policy" (one that kept in place a dual, segregated system) was "in the best interests of the majority of the pupils" and that "breaking the laws in our city is not justifiable." When called to appear before the provincial council of the Daughters of Charity in St. Louis, Sister Mary William and Sister Jane faced a group of their own with mixed opinions. Several, including the provincial superior, were in sympathy with the sisters' actions but disliked the publicity they received. Others considered what they had done a scandal. In Chicago, the vicar general of the archdiocese suggested that Sister Mary William be removed.[67]

In the days and weeks after the arrest, Sister Mary William said little publicly. In fact, she talked to the press only once and briefly. With bene-factors withdrawing pledges of funds and board members resigning, she was apprehensive about Marillac's summer program and her neighbors' reactions. Before long, several "elders" from the block clubs came to express their concern and appreciation. They advised Sister Mary William that the next time—never doubting that there would be another time—she consult them "before you go out and put yourselves on the line." In August, when the nuns appeared before Judge Lester Jankowski for sentencing, about forty West Siders showed up in court. One of Maril-lac's regulars brought the sisters sandwiches to show her appreciation for the many times they had "waited in clinics, welfare offices, [and] court rooms."[68]

The six Daughters of Charity were convicted of blocking traffic and fined $25 each. Sister Andrea said she and the others could not pay, because "any money that comes to us must go to help the poor." They would instead serve out the fines in the Chicago House of Correction at the usual rate of five dollars a day. That, however, proved unneces-sary. Maurice Scott Jr. and Howard D. Geter, two black attorneys not associated with Marillac House, saved the nuns from jail by paying the entire fine. Unbowed, Sister Mary William and her colleagues refused to back away from future strikes against injustice. How could they, she remarked, when "sisters have been walking in hospital and school cor-ridors for years." She did not want "all that walking to go to waste." Bound together over time in a thankless effort to awaken the American conscience, the sisters "caught courage" from one another's lives.[69]

Waste Not, Want Not

In the years between 1965 and 1968, Catholic sisters did not want for opportunities to be "proximate and available" to Chicago's black migrants. Never before or after were so many "new nuns" involved in bringing hope and knowledge to people so desperately in need; nor did these activists waste opportunities to learn from one another, including sisters who had lived among African Americans long before the 1960s. The Urban Apostolate of the Sisters provided the principal avenue of communication. Through its newsletters and regular meetings, as well as informal gatherings, members collected and shared all kinds of informa-tion and experiences. During the summer months at settlements, public housing centers, and inner-city parishes, new self-help and educational initiatives also involved nuns from outside Chicago. Nearly thirty Franciscans from Rochester, Minnesota, came to work in projects at Marillac House and Cabrini-Green; at St. Agatha's parish on the West Side, the Servants of Mary from Ladysmith, Wisconsin, taught remedial reading. Besides working to develop indigenous leadership through community organizing, Catholic sisters continued to promote literacy citywide. Summer reading programs, even in nontraditional places such as "freedom schools" and day camps, proved crucial. In 1965, when unskilled and semiskilled jobs were disappearing, 8.2 years was the average educational level of African Americans.[70]

As the civil rights campaign moved to northern cities, it became strikingly apparent that revolutionary changes in social and economic conditions were necessary if black Americans were to become equal. In Chicago, where a significant number of nuns lived in African American communities and were well aware of the teachings of the Second Vatican Council, they were no longer willing to remain on the sidelines. They committed themselves to ushering in "a new day" of racial justice, one that included the most radical goals of the civil rights movement. When King returned to Chicago in 1966 to target housing discrimination, Catholic sisters were among his strongest supporters; even after Archbishop John Cody pleaded for King to suspend demonstrations during that summer, nuns continued to participate in them. They were essential, according to Sister Angelica Schultz, a Dubuque Franciscan, "to lance the infection of racism and bring to the open the un-Christian mentality of those attending our churches and schools." In late July, during a march in Gage Park on the Southwest Side, she was knocked to the ground by a brick thrown directly at her. Yet, at the end of that violent summer, a drawing of a nun with a sign that read, "I love Rev. M. L. King" appeared in the *National Catholic Reporter* and highlighted this well-known fact.[71]

What was not widely known was that Catholic sisters learned some unanticipated lessons about freedom and equality as a consequence of their intense involvement in the civil rights movement. Not unlike female activists in the Student Nonviolent Coordinating Committee (SNCC), who began pointing out the unequal treatment of women in the movement, nuns too started drawing parallels between their position in the Catholic Church and that of blacks in American society. In 1965, at a Chicago rally in which Marillac's Sister Mary William preceded King as a speaker, she asked (and answered): "Why are Sisters like Negroes? Because they, too, are segregated, ghettoed, and because leadership is not encouraged in their ranks." It was an easy jump for many sisters to extend this analogy—"blacks and women . . . are inferior in intelligence, intuitive rather than rational, emotional, childishly irresponsible, [and] oversexed."[72]

On the fringes of church leadership, women-religious saw their experiences and talents routinely ignored or dismissed. They were treated as hired help, according to Sister Mary William, who could "build the house," then watch the pastor "put on the roof" and claim it as his. Not surprisingly, these insights and appeals for a theology of equality—generally rejected and often ridiculed—resulted in a strong feminist consciousness, particularly among nuns. It contributed over time to "the exceptionally outspoken and organized activism of feminists in the *American* Catholic Church." It would also deepen the commitment of sisters to developing democratic structures among themselves and those they served.[73]

Early in 1966, King and the Southern Christian Leadership Conference set up headquarters on the city's West Side and called for an all-out war against slums. By then, more African Americans lived in Chicago "than in the entire state of Mississippi," and more blacks "occupied the city's larger public housing projects than populated Selma, Alabama." These numbers, coupled with the power of the Daley machine in both black and white communities, presented the northern branch of the civil-rights movement with an arduous challenge. Nevertheless, "Neighbors at Work" from Marillac House immediately joined other organizations in King's Chicago campaign. Despite "long, tedious, rambling meetings" and innumerable workshops on nonviolence, Sister Mary William and her staff grew hopeful as they observed "the development of [local] people, the shedding of apathy, the rise and fall of hostility." This experience—plus the neighborhood's support of Marillac House following the nuns' arrest and a small grant of $7,000—prompted Sister Mary William to adopt what she called a strategy of "secondary leadership."[74]

What this strategy meant in real terms became clear in early spring. Sister Mary William announced that the 1966 summer program, "Leadership through Learning," would be staffed entirely by individuals "living right in the community." Marillac House employees subsequently recruited, trained, and paid local people to work as recreation directors, tutors, bus drivers, baby sitters, club coordinators, and more. No longer were outside volunteers, who were mostly white and middle-class, invited to participate. The sisters and staff, although involved in training sessions, became "secondary"; they stepped back and depended on the community's black leaders to carry the program to a successful end. The following spring, their efforts were rewarded when the Metropolitan Welfare and State Street councils chose to honor Wilmon L. Carter, president of Neighbors at Work. He received an award as Chicago's 1967 Volunteer-of-the-Year at a luncheon in the Palmer House Hotel.[75]

The good news, however, did not outweigh the bad. It was simply "a beautiful rainbow amid a storm." Tragic and destructive violence erupted in 1966, when police turned off a fire hydrant in ninety-degree heat, and again in 1968, when news of King's murder reached the West Side. Although vandalism was widespread, Marillac House, which was protected by local teenagers and adults, "suffered not even a broken window." Still, seething and disheartened, Sister Mary William was forced to admit that "little [had] changed on the West Side." Unemployment rates there and on the South Side remained higher than national rates had been during the Great Depression, and living conditions had hardly improved. One West Side teen sounded off: "We just ain't taking it no more. Sure some of us died. But are we really living?" Nothing was "more dangerous," Sister Mary William responded, "than a man who has lost his hope." In May 1968, she willingly left Marillac for a period of rest and a new assignment in Dallas. She subsequently learned that Rendu House, her creation in Rockwell Gardens, had closed.[76]

In June 1968, poet Gwendolyn Brooks commented that "the people have marched enough." In Chicago and elsewhere, an era had ended. Circles of trust had been broken, and the backlash had begun. The *Chicago Defender* reported that outbreaks of violence and calls for racial separation had sent "white folks scurrying for shelter to halt the progressive march of the civil rights movement." That may have been true of many white Americans, but it did not describe most Catholic sisters who had worked hand in hand with African Americans to secure justice and equality. Some, like the Daughters of Charity at Marillac House, had earlier recognized the need to pull back and allow black people to free themselves of dependence on whites. Not all nuns, however, accepted this idea so readily, since they continued to believe in integration rather than separation. Most were also "shocked at the anger and distrust" reflected in the separatists' new mood. Sister Anthony Claret, who had picketed in front of the Illinois Club for Catholic Women in 1963, admitted feeling rejected. Yet she "moved on," as did others, and eventually found that her feelings "led to a clearer understanding of the rejection many black people had felt."[77]

The civil rights movement, with its local variations and complexities, must rank high in the history of unintended consequences. What began as a struggle for civil rights for African Americans developed into a revolutionary and ongoing quest for equality and self-determination for all people, including Catholic sisters. They were, like many of the movement's most ardent women activists (both black and white), religiously motivated. Their faith in God and the human conscience, in fact, "made it easier for them to have faith in social change" and work to achieve it. They believed deeply that "a new world [was] coming." And through their involvement, especially through grass-roots organizing and hands-on teaching, participants gained a better appreciation for developing in others the ability to draw on their own resources and make their own decisions. One woman remarked: "The primary lesson I learned is that ordinary people can do the most extraordinary things." Such conscious-ness-raising resulted in a firm commitment to democracy and a strong aversion to hierarchy.[78]

Influenced by the rhetoric of the civil rights movement and the docu-ments of the Second Vatican Council, many Catholic sisters sought to redefine for themselves what it meant to be modern women in the Ameri-can Catholic Church. The experiences of the School Sisters of St. Francis are a case in point. In 1960 they had committed themselves to working for racial justice at Cabrini-Green, and in 1963 six of them protested the discriminatory policies of the Illinois Club for Catholic Women. By 1966, the year in which the National Organization of Women was founded, the Franciscans were already involved in a thorough examination of the rules and customs governing their lives and ministries. Above all, they sought to "remove some of the authoritarian, outmoded practices which no longer fit with modern society." In 1970, one of the largest religious communities in the United States, with over 3,500 members and some thirty schools in Chicago, adopted a new constitution that embodied "a fully representative, democratic system." It called for "deeper involve-ment in social issues, greater emphasis on democratic decision-making, and increased autonomy for individual sisters in regard to the personal use of money and time." When the document was reviewed in Rome, a Vatican representative, Cardinal Ildebrando Antoniutti, who responded by letter, accused the Franciscans of creating an "exaggerated cult of freedom . . . nullifying authority on all levels." Sister Francis Borgia Rothluebber, the superior general, who would eventually travel to Rome "to plead to live the Gospel," was not surprised or intimidated. She believed, once the members' views were polled, that "our new directions are certain to be continued." And indeed they were.[79]

During this period of reexamination and renewal, many sisters chose to leave religious life for an array of reasons too complex to discuss here. But for the women-religious who chose to stay, their lives became quite different from those depicted less than a decade earlier in *Lilies of the Field*. As "new nuns" adjusted their views of themselves and their work in the contemporary world, they identified themselves more frequently as feminists and refused to submit to patriarchal or paternalistic social structures similar to those that had resulted in white dominance over blacks. For Catholic sisters, as for other women in the movement, their commitment to civil rights heightened their awareness of injustice and launched them into new avenues of advocacy. As "faithful and fearless" women of the church, they continued, often against great odds, to support the disadvantaged and powerless in their struggle for human dignity. A thorough examination of these good-hearted efforts in cities and towns across America will eventually make possible an overall assessment of their record of achievement—something we now lack. It will also result in new "angles of vision" on the nation's struggle for social justice and produce more "untold stories of ordinary people."[80]

NOTES

Introduction

1. I am grateful to Anita Therese Hayes, BVM, archivist of the Sisters of Charity of the Blessed Virgin Mary, in Dubuque, Iowa, for sending me statistics on Holy Name convent and school.

2. In the decades after World War II, young Catholic women were attracted to religious life by the "vibrancy" of nuns. As Sister Mary Andrew Matesich, a Dominican, recently recalled, the sisters "were fun, they were educated, and they lived lives of significance." See the *New York Times*, July 26, 2004. On figures in text, see *New World* [of the Archdiocese of Chicago], January 17, 1999; the *Chicago Sun-Times*, June 20, 1999; and the *New York Times*, January 16, 2000. In 2004, only 108 nuns taught full-time in the Chicago archdiocese (*Chicago Sun-Times*, March 29, 2004). The quote appears in Margaret Mac Curtain, OP, "Tending the Wells of Memory—Sharing Sources of Hope," in *Distance Becomes Communion: A Dominican Symposium on Mission and Hope*, ed. Geraldine Smyth, OP (Dublin: Dominican Publications, 2004), 44.

3. Quotes are from Ann M. Harrington, BVM, *Creating Community: Mary Frances Clarke and Her Companions* (Dubuque, Iowa: Mt. Carmel Press, 2004), 92; and Peter Steinfels, *A People Adrift: The Crisis of the Roman Catholic Church in America* (New York: Simon & Schuster, 2003), 279.

4. Quotes are from Harrington, *Creating Community*, 116; and Sister Mary Agatha [O'Brien] to Sister Mary Elizabeth [Strange], June 28, 1851, Sisters of Mercy Archives, Province Center, Chicago.

5. Joan W. Scott, "Feminism's History," *Journal of Women's History* 16, no. 2 (2004): 10–29 (quote on p. 22). What is true of Catholic sisters is also true of other women who are members of conservative religious traditions.

6. Carol K. Coburn and Martha Smith, in the preface to their prize-winning book *Spirited Lives: How Nuns Shaped Catholic Culture and American Life, 1836–1920* (Chapel Hill: University of North Carolina Press, 1999), ix.

7. Chicago's distinctiveness also stemmed from the presence of a number of important organizations. From the 1930s into the 1960s, Chicago Catholics benefited from programs and activities sponsored by Chicago Inter-Student Catholic Action (CISCA), Friendship House, the Sheil School of Social Studies, the Catholic Worker movement, the Catholic Interracial Council of Chicago, the National Catholic Conference for Interracial Justice, and the Christian Family movement.

8. Quotes are from Leslie Woodcock Tentler, "On the Margins: The State of American Catholic History," *American Quarterly* 45 (March 1993): 108; and

Mary Jo Weaver, *New Catholic Women: A Contemporary Challenge to Traditional Religious Authority* (Bloomington: Indiana University Press, 1995), 11. For a recent example in which the efforts of Catholic sisters are overlooked, see Gail Collins, *America's Women: Four Hundred Years of Dolls, Drudges, Helpmates, and Heroines* (New York: William Morrow, 2003).

9. Ellen Skerrett, "Chicago's Irish and 'Brick and Mortar Catholicism': A Reappraisal," *U.S. Catholic Historian* 14 (Spring 1996): 53–71 (quote on p. 54).

10. Catherine McAuley is quoted in Joy Clough, RSM, "Chicago's Sisters of Mercy," *Chicago History* 32 (Summer 2003): 42.

11. Maureen Fitzgerald, "Irish-Catholic Nuns and the Development of New York City's Welfare System, 1840–1900" (Ph.D. diss., University of Wisconsin–Madison, 1992), 37. In addition to the activities of the Sisters of Mercy, see those of the Religious of the Sacred Heart and the Little Sisters of the Poor. Located in what would become known as the Hull-House neighborhood, the Religious of the Sacred Heart taught about nine hundred students annually from 1867 to 1899. In 1876, the Little Sisters of the Poor opened a home for the elderly in the Hull mansion—the building in which Jane Addams and Ellen Gates Starr would later begin their settlement. See Ellen Skerrett, "The Irish of Chicago's Hull-House Neighborhood," in *New Perspectives on the Irish Diaspora*, ed. Charles Fanning (Carbondale: Southern Illinois University Press, 2000), 189–222.

12. Karen Armstrong, *The Spiral Staircase: My Climb out of Darkness* (New York: Alfred A. Knopf, 2004), 200.

13. On creation of the parochial school system, see Mary J. Oates, *The Catholic Philanthropic Tradition in America* (Bloomington: Indiana University Press, 1995), 142–64. The last two quotes are from Kevina Keating, CCVI, and Mary Peter Traviss, OP, *Pioneer Mentoring in Teacher Preparation: From the Voices of Women Religious* (St. Cloud, Minn.: North Star Press, 2001), 35, 124.

14. Ibid., 38, 49. In the interviews done for the Keating and Traviss book, the authors noted that in only three of the sixty interviews did sisters say, "I was a good teacher." Most said "we." One remarked, for instance: "we knew we were powerful as a community. We could do things together that by ourselves there would be no way in the world we would have the opportunity to accomplish." See p. 88.

15. Ellen Skerrett, "The Catholic Dimension," in *The Irish in Chicago*, ed. Lawrence J. McCaffrey, Ellen Skerrett, Michael F. Funchion, and Charles Fanning (Urbana: University of Illinois Press, 1987), especially pp. 45–46.

16. My father, Christopher J. Hoy, was the son of Irish immigrants. He grew up in St. Columbanus parish, where he had the Adrian Dominicans for teachers. He went to Leo High School, staffed by the Christian Brothers, and entered DePaul University in 1935 on a football scholarship. As a young man, he worked as a clerk for the Pennsylvania Railroad; when he retired, he had served for nearly twenty-five years as conference manager of the American Library Association.

17. See, for example, Lynne Olson, *Freedom's Daughters: The Unsung Heroines of the Civil Rights Movement from 1830 to 1970* (New York: Scribner, 2001.)

18. Quotes are from Michael McGerr, *A Fierce Discontent: The Rise and Fall of the Progressive Movement in America, 1870–1920* (New York: Free Press, 2003), 196; Judith Ann Trolander, *Professionalism and Social Change: From the Settlement House Movement to Neighborhood Centers, 1866 to the Present* (New York: Columbia University Press, 1987), 93; and Jane Addams, "The Subjective

Necessity for Social Settlements," in *Twenty Years at Hull-House*, ed. James Hurt (Urbana: University of Illinois Press, 1990), 76.

19. See June O. Patten, "Williams, Fannie Barrier," and Koby Lee-Forman, "Woolley, Celia Anna Parker," in *Women Building Chicago, 1790–1990: A Biographical Dictionary*, ed. Rima Lunin Schultz and Adele Hast (Bloomington: Indiana University Press, 2001), 977–79 and 993–95, respectively. Williams and Woolley were active members of Jenkin Lloyd Jones's All Souls Church, a "progressive, national center that supported female ministers." See Mary Jo Deegan, ed., *The Collected Writings of Fannie Barrier Williams, 1893–1918* (DeKalb: University of Northern Illinois Press, 2002), xxxv.

20. Quotes are from Celia Parker Woolley, "The Frederick Douglass Center, Chicago," *Commons* 9 (July 1904): 328–29; Cynthia Grant Tucker, *Prophetic Sisterhood: Liberal Women Ministers of the Frontier, 1880–1930* (Bloomington: Indiana University Press, 1990), 185; and Fannie Barrier Williams, "The Frederick Douglass Center," *Southern Workman* 35 (July 1906): 334.

21. The Archdiocese of Chicago is divided into parishes demarcated by specific geographical boundaries. For a discussion of parish boundaries and how they function, see John T. McGreevy, *Parish Boundaries: The Catholic Encounter with Race in the Twentieth-Century Urban North* (Chicago: University of Chicago Press, 1996), 20–25.

22. When settlement workers adopted this practice, it was not new—rather, it was tried and true. Sisters and priests who lived in black neighborhoods heard the words of Martin Luther King Jr., for example, differently than did city and church officials who lived elsewhere. Mathew Ahmann, director of the National Catholic Conference for Interracial Justice, remarked on this difference: "The gap between chancery office understanding and vision and the vision held by the priest or sister serving the ghetto is huge." See Mathew Ahmann, "Strategies for the Future," in *The Church and the Urban Racial Crisis*, ed. Mathew Ahmann and Margaret Roach (Techny, Ill.: Divine Word Publications, 1967), 233. The first quote in the text is from an interview with Sister Mary William Sullivan, DC, on February 7, 2002, Chicago. She served as director of the Marillac House settlement on the West Side from 1964 to 1968. The remaining ones are from Jeff Kelly Lowenstein, "King's Chicago Harvest," *Chicago Tribune*, January 25, 2004; Mary Peter Traxler, SSND, "The New Nun—Ministry of Presence," *Community* 26 (February 1967): 6; and Francis Borgia Rothluebber, OSF, "Pastoral Planning: Gospel by Design," *Origins* 3 (September 13, 1973): 192.

23. M. Anthony Claret Sparks, OSF, "A Sister Survey: A Study of Attitudes, Awareness, and Involvement of Religious Women in the Race Issue," *Community* 26 (March 1967): 8–12 (quote on p. 10). For "caught courage," see Carolyn G. Heilbrun, *The Last Gift of Time: Life Beyond Sixty* (New York: Ballantine Books, 1997): 138. An example of a woman who "caught courage" is Mary Griffin, formerly Sister Mary Ignatia, BVM, who was on the faculty at Mundelein College for several decades. In her autobiography, she admitted that it was "that single outrageous act" of the seven Franciscan Sisters who picketed the Illinois Club for Catholic Women in July 1963 that changed her forever. She later marched at Selma. See Mary Griffin, *The Courage to Choose: An American Nun's Story* (Boston: Little, Brown and Company, 1975), 38–45 (quote on p. 38).

24. Dorothy Day, unlike most Catholic sisters before the 1960s, sought to effect social change. Yet, in many ways, she and the "good hearts" who are the subject

of this study had much in common. All of them lived and worked in poor neighborhoods among those they tried to serve. They also placed great value on the
works of mercy and on ordinary, daily acts of kindness; they spent more energy
and attention on doing good than on discussing it or writing about it; they believed
public service and responsibility were more important than individual freedom
and personal fulfillment. None of them was self-indulgent or undisciplined, and
all of them were deeply religious, especially conscious of God's presence in the
world. A thoughtful study of Dorothy Day in this regard is June E. O'Connor,
The Moral Vision of Dorothy Day: A Feminist Perspective (New York: Crossroad,
1991).

Chapter 1: The Journey Out

1. Sister Mary Eustace Eaton to Archbishop William J. Walsh, April 26, 1899,
Archbishop William J. Walsh Papers, Dublin Diocesan Archives, Drumcondra,
Dublin. A *sister* is a woman who has taken either temporary (occasionally a *novice*) or final vows in a religious order; a *postulant* is a woman who is living in a
convent but in an apprentice-like status; an *aspirant* is a young woman who has
only informally committed herself to entering a religious congregation at a later
time. Religious *order, community,* and *congregation* are used interchangeably.
A *sodality* was not a religious order but a kind of young people's club that combined devotional and recreational functions.

2. Mrs. William O'Brien, *Sister Mary Eustace* (Dublin: M. H. Gill and Son, 1923),
20–21. See also Sister Mary Eustace to Archbishop Walsh, March 16, 1892, Walsh
Papers. Throughout the nineteenth century, *dowry* referred to a sizable amount
of money. See note 28 in this chapter for a further explanation.

3. There are two different 1905 lists (written in Sister Mary Eustace's hand)
reporting "Statistics of the Archbishop of Dublin's Sodality." On one list, 642
are reported to have entered religious life; on the second, 778. On the first list,
371 young women are reported as entering religious life in the United States; on
the second, 411. Sister Mary Eustace to Archbishop Walsh, January 1905, Walsh
Papers. In response to a 1902 request for statistics from Archbishop Walsh, Sister
Mary Eustace responded that 603 "nuns from the Sodality are now in convents"
and that 639 "have gone out from it [the Sodality] to convents (including those
who have died or left.)" We can perhaps assume that Sister Mary Eustace was
making the same distinction in her 1905 lists. Sister Mary Eustace to Archbishop
Walsh, January 31, 1902, and December 25, 1905, Walsh Papers.

4. The Ursulines returned to Cork because promises made to them by the vicar
general of New York were not kept. See Ursuline Sisters, "Annals," 1:177, 257–
63, Ursuline Convent Archives, Blackrock, Cork; Bishop Francis Moylan (Cork)
to Bishop John Carroll (Baltimore), January - 1813, Baltimore Diocesan Archives
(original) and Ursuline Convent Archives (copy); and R. F. O'Connor, "An Interesting Centenary," *American Catholic Quarterly Review* 35 (January–October
1910): 479–80. I am grateful to Ursula Clarke, OSU, for sending me this information.

5. My long-standing curiosity about the ubiquitous Irish nun was reawakened by
a description of "major drives in Ireland to gain new members" in Hasia R. Diner,
Erin's Daughters in America: Irish Immigrant Women in the Nineteenth Century

(Baltimore, Md.: Johns Hopkins University Press, 1983), 130. However, not all Irish nuns were recruited as adults in Ireland. Many came to the United States as children and subsequently entered religious life; others joined religious communities in France or elsewhere in Europe and later found themselves assigned to missions in the United States. Still others were the daughters of Irish emigrants, who were born in the United States, attended parochial schools, and decided at some point to become nuns. Despite American birth, these too have been included among "Irish nuns." But my concern is not with these. Based on figures listed in Catholic directories, there were approximately forty thousand nuns in the United States in 1900 and about seventy-five thousand in 1915. See also Eileen Mary Brewer, *Nuns and the Education of American Catholic Women, 1860–1920* (Chicago: Loyola University Press, 1987), 15. Probably between four and seven thousand Irish women, or 10 percent of these totals, emigrated to America as nuns (professed, novices, postulants, or aspirants) from 1812 to the beginning of World War I in 1914. They are the subject of this chapter.

6. Mary J. Oates, "'The Good Sisters': The Work and Position of Catholic Churchwomen in Boston, 1870–1940," in *Catholic Boston: Studies in Religion and Community, 1870–1970*, ed. Robert E. Sullivan and James M. O'Toole (Boston: Roman Catholic Archbishop of Boston, 1985), 172–73, 184–85, and 197.

7. David Fitzpatrick, "'A Share of the Honeycomb': Education, Emigration, and Irishwomen," in *The Origins of Popular Literacy in Ireland*, ed. Mary Daly and David Dickson (Dublin: Trinity College Dublin & University College Dublin, 1990), 168. *Heroes of Their Own Lives* (New York: Penguin Books, 1989) is the title of Linda Gordon's study of family violence in Boston, 1880–1960. In it, she demonstrates how many family-violence victims took control of their lives by "attempting to replace with creativity and stubbornness what they lacked in resources" (p. 290). Like them, the Irish women in this essay who decided to journey out became "actors," responded creatively to an opportunity, and shaped their lives in a different way. See Louise A. Tilly, "Gender, Women's History, and Social History," *Social Science History* 13 (Winter 1989): 439–62 (especially 458–59).

8. Before the Catholic Emancipation Act of 1829, Catholic political participation in the United Kingdom (then including all of Ireland) was legally proscribed.

9. Susan O'Brien, "*Terra Incognita:* The Nun in Nineteenth-Century England," *Past and Present* 121 (November 1988): 118. Desmond J. Keenan observed that "the bishops, the canons, and the parish priests dominated the entire scene," with nuns and brothers playing a secondary role. Women-religious "in addition had the social disadvantage of being female." Desmond J. Keenan, *The Catholic Church in Nineteenth-Century Ireland: A Sociological Study* (Totowa, N.J.: Barnes and Noble, 1983), 148. Edmund M. Hogan found that the "low valuation" placed on nuns in nineteenth-century Ireland was a direct result of the condition of the church during penal times, when there were few priests to say Mass and administer the sacraments. "The reaction to this crisis," he stated, "seems to have taken the form of an inflated reverence for priesthood, so strong as to overshadow the other categories of church membership." Edmund M. Hogan, *The Irish Missionary Movement: A Historical Survey, 1830–1980* (Dublin: Gill and Macmillan, 1990), 51. And Caitriona Clear pointed out that nuns have been overlooked by contemporary historians, not only because of their low status in the church and their singular "invisibility," but also because they are often regarded as "half-

clergy, half women, and not enough of either to merit examination." Caitriona Clear, *Nuns in Nineteenth-Century Ireland* (Dublin: Gill and Macmillan, 1987), xvii.

10. Sister Mary Eustace used the word "scattering" to describe the departure of young women from Harold's Cross. Sister Mary Eustace to Archbishop Walsh, September 14, 1900, and August 8, 1903, Walsh Papers.

11. Quoted in Peter Guilday, *The Life and Times of John England, First Bishop of Charleston (1786–1842)*, 2 vols. (New York: America Press, 1927), I, 522.

12. Ursuline Sisters, "Annals," 2:81, 91.

13. Ibid., 90, 96–97.

14. Quoted in Guilday, *Life and Times of John England*, 1:530.

15. Gerald Shaughnessy, *Has the Immigrant Kept the Faith? A Study of Immigration and Catholic Growth in the United States, 1790–1920* (New York: Macmillan Company, 1925), 224–31.

16. Hogan, *The Irish Missionary Movement*, 14–16.

17. Sisters of Mercy, "Annals [1843]," Sisters of Mercy Archives, Carlow; and Mother Austin Carroll, *Leaves from the Annals of the Sisters of Mercy, in Four Volumes*, vol. 3, *Continuing Sketches of the Order in Newfoundland and the United States* (New York: Catholic Publication Society Company, 1889), 44–45. Paul Cullen was the most powerful and, subsequently, the most controversial prelate in nineteenth-century Ireland. For discussions of his influence and achievements, see Emmet Larkin, "The Devotional Revolution in Ireland, 1850–1875," *American Historical Review* 77 (June 1972): 625–52; and Patrick J. Corish, *The Irish Catholic Experience: A Historical Survey* (Wilmington, Del.: Michael Glazier, Inc., 1985), 192–225.

18. Mother Elizabeth Strange, "Diary written while crossing the Atlantic [incomplete manuscript]," Sisters of Mercy Archives, Pittsburgh; and Carroll, *Leaves*, 3:46–47, 56–61. For the phrase "floating convent," see Mother Austin Carroll, *Leaves from the Annals of the Sisters of Mercy, in Four Volumes*. Vol. 1: *Ireland* (New York: Catholic Publication Society Company, 1881), 160. See Chapter 2 for more on Sister Agatha O'Brien.

19. Sister Monica O'Doherty to Mother Vincent Whitty, April 22, 1846, Sisters of Mercy Archives, Baggot Street, Dublin.

20. Ibid. The quote on soap and the looking glass is taken from another letter dated only "1846."

21. Sister Mary Vincent Haire to Mother Vincent Whitty, June 24, 1846, Sisters of Mercy Archives, Baggot Street.

22. Sister M. Jerome McHale, *On the Wing: The Story of the Pittsburgh Sisters of Mercy, 1843–1968* (New York: Seabury Press, 1980), 22. In 1912, one Dominican Sister wrote to another in Dublin that she had spent "50 years under the scorching sun of N.O." Sister M. Xavier Gaynor to Mother M. Bertrand Maher, February 17, 1912, Dominican Convent Archives, Cabra, Dublin. On mosquitoes, see Suellen Hoy and Margaret Mac Curtain, eds., *From Dublin to New Orleans: The Journey of Nora and Alice* (Dublin: Attic Press, 1994), 87.

23. Unfortunately, no letters from any of these nuns have been preserved in the Kinsale and Midleton convents. The most detailed account of their experiences can be found in Carroll, *Leaves*, 3:468–77; Rev. Matthew Russell, *The Three Sisters of Lord Russell of Killowen and Their Convent Life* (New York: Longmans, Green, and Company, 1912), 26–33; and *Memoir of Rev. Mother Mary*

Teresa Comerford, Foundress of the Convents of the Presentation Order on the Pacific Coast, And the Missionary Novitiate, Kilcock, Ireland (San Francisco: P. J. Thomas, 1882), 24–32.

24. Mother Agnes O'Connor to Mother Vincent Whitty, March 24, 1848, Sisters of Mercy Archives, Baggot Street.

25. Sister M. Raphael Consedine, *Listening Journey: A Study of the Spirit and Ideals of Nano Nagle and the Presentation Sisters* (Victoria, Australia: Congregation of the Presentation Sisters, 1983), 282.

26. Archbishop Joseph Alemany to President Bartholomew Woodlock, March 20, 1857, Collection of Letters from Priests and Bishops, 1843–1877, All Hallows College Archives, Drumcondra, Dublin.

27. As Clear has shown, "entrants became progressively younger as the century wore on." For instance, in the Mercy convent in Limerick, Ireland, the average age at entry from 1851 to 1860 was 26.2, whereas it was 21.1 from 1891 to 1900. Clear, *Nuns in Nineteenth-Century Ireland,* 80–81. Because American convents were often willing to accept teenagers, entrants were certainly younger as the nineteenth century progressed. In the years between 1884 and 1919, 121 young women traveled to the United States as aspirants from St. Brigid's Missionary School in Callan, County Kilkenny. The average age of the women in this group was 19.76. "Register of Aspirants," 1884–1919, Sisters of Mercy Archives, Callan, County Kilkenny.

28. Dowries varied in size. Wealthy women occasionally brought large sums of money to the religious communities they joined. See Mary Peckham Magray, *The Transforming Power of the Nuns: Women, Religion, and Culture in Ireland, 1750–1900* (New York: Oxford University Press, 1998), 36–39. However, during the mid-nineteenth century at the Convent of Mercy on Baggot Street in Dublin, the usual amount for a professed choir nun was about £500. Mercy Sisters, "Account Book, Jan. 1849 to Dec. 1889," Sisters of Mercy Archives, Baggot Street. Later, in the 1880s and 1890s, most young women brought dowries of about £300 to the Convent of Mercy in Callan, although one sister contributed £1,500 in 1894. See Mercy Sisters, "Account Book," Sisters of Mercy Archives, Callan. On the economic and devotional structures upon which the revitalized Irish Catholic Church was built, see Emmet Larkin, "Church, State, and Nation in Modern Ireland," in *The Historical Dimension of Irish Catholicism* (Washington, D.C.: Catholic University of America Press, 1984), 100–101; and Magray, *Transforming Power of the Nuns,* 4–6.

29. Clear, *Nuns in Nineteenth-Century Ireland,* 27. See also Anne V. O'Connor, "The Revolution in Girls' Secondary Education in Ireland 1860–1910," in *Girls Don't Do Honours: Irish Women in Education in the Nineteenth and Twentieth Centuries,* ed. Mary Cullen (Dublin: Women's Education Bureau, 1987), 37; Sean Kierse, *Education in the Parish of Killaloe* (Killaloe, County Clare: Boru Books, 1987), 30, 68; and Catherine Mary Keane, "A History of the Foundation of the Presentation Convents in the Diocese of Kerry" (master's thesis, School of Education, Trinity College, 1976), 54, 107.

30. Sister Ann Curry, *Mother Teresa Comerford: Foundress of the Sisters of the Presentation, San Francisco, California* (San Francisco: Presentation Sisters, 1980), 3–4; and *Memoir of Rev. Mother Mary Teresa Comerford,* 11–17.

31. Kathleen Healy, *Frances Warde: American Founder of the Sisters of Mercy* (New York: Seabury Press, 1973), 3, 6–8, 31, 45, and 127; Carroll, *Leaves,* 1:263.

32. O'Brien, *"Terra Incognita,"* 116. See also Deirdre Mageean, "Catholic Sisterhoods and the Immigrant Church," in *Seeking Common Ground: Multidisciplinary Studies of Immigrant Women in the United States,* ed. Donna Gabaccia (Westport, Conn.: Praeger, 1992), 92–97; and Tony Fahey, "Nuns in the Catholic Church in Ireland in the Nineteenth Century," in *Girls Don't Do Honours,* 15.

33. Anthony Fahey, "Female Asceticism in the Catholic Church: A Case-Study of Nuns in Ireland in the Nineteenth Century" (Ph.D. diss., University of Illinois, 1982), 56.

34. Larkin, "The Devotional Revolution in Ireland," 626, 651.

35. Caitriona Clear, "The Limits of Female Autonomy: Nuns in Nineteenth-Century Ireland," in *Women Surviving: Studies in Irish Women's History in the 19th and 20th Centuries,* ed. Maria Luddy and Cliona Murphy (Dublin: Poolbeg, 1990), 21. Historian Seamus Enright, CSSR, who has studied the spirituality of nineteenth-century Irish nuns, believes that "eleven convents" is conservative.

36. Margaret Susan Thompson, "To Serve the People of God: Nineteenth-Century Sisters and the Creation of American Religious Life," *Working Paper* series 18, no. 2, Cushwa Center for the Study of American Catholicism, University of Notre Dame, February 26, 1987, p. 15.

37. Clear, *Nuns in Nineteenth-Century Ireland,* 91–99 (quote from the Mercy Rule is on p. 92). See also Caitriona Clear, "Walls within Walls: Nuns in Nineteenth-Century Ireland," in *Gender in Irish Society,* ed. Chris Curtin, Pauline Jackson, and Barbara O'Connor (Galway: Galway University Press, 1987), 134–51. Clear appropriately uses the term "life-maintaining" to describe the work of lay sisters.

38. Clear, "Walls within Walls," 146.

39. Mother M. Vincent Hartnett, *The Life of Rev. Mother Catherine McAuley, Foundress of the Order of Mercy* (Dublin: John F. Fowler, 1864), 94.

40. O'Brien, *"Terra Incognita,"* 139.

41. Quoted in David Fitzpatrick, "The Modernisation of the Irish Female," in *Rural Ireland 1600–1900: Modernisation and Change,* ed. Patrick O'Flanagan, Paul Ferguson, and Kevin Whelan (Cork: Cork University Press, 1987), 166. In the early 1880s, two women emigrants from Connemara sent money home so that their family could buy horses to do the work they had previously done, "namely carrying seaweed often for miles to manure the land." Rev. J. M. McCormick, Roundstone Glebe, Connemara, County Galway, to Vere Foster and quoted in a report entitled "Mr. Vere Foster's Irish Female Emigration Fund: Under the Auspices of All the Clergy of All Denominations in the West of Ireland" (Belfast, 1884), 7. I thank historian Kevin O'Neill for telling me about the Vere Foster Papers, Manuscripts Division, National Library of Ireland, Dublin.

42. Quote from Joseph Wade, Crookewood, Mullingar, County Westmeath, January 1955, no. 1408, in "Emigration to America Questionnaires," 5 [bound] vols., Folklore Archives, University College Dublin, Belfield, Dublin. See also Clear, *Nuns in Nineteenth-Century Ireland,* 22–23.

43. Two essays describing women's position in nineteenth-century Ireland are J. J. Lee, "Women and the Church since the Famine," in *Women in Irish Society: The Historical Dimension,* ed. Margaret Mac Curtain and Donnacha O'Corrain (Westport, Conn.: Greenwood Press, 1979), 37–45; and Clear, "Women in Nineteenth-Century Ireland," in *Nuns in Nineteenth-Century Ireland,* 1–35.

44. David Fitzpatrick, "Marriage in Post-Famine Ireland," in *Marriage in Ire-*

land, ed. Art Cosgrove (Dublin: College Press, 1985), 120–21; Lee, "Women and the Church since the Famine," 39; Pauline Jackson, "Marriage and Dowries in Post-Famine Ireland," *International Migration Review* 18 (Winter 1984): 1010–13.

45. Mothers generally supported daughters' decisions to leave and even encouraged them to do so. Not only was employment (largely domestic service) in America more constant for daughters, but they also sent back money at more regular intervals than sons. Daughters were also less likely to drink or gamble away their earnings. Margaret Mac Curtain, "Daughters and Emigration," lecture presented at University College Dublin, April 7, 1992. See also Helga E. Jacobson, "Doing Ethnography: Irish Community Studies and the Exclusion of Women," *Atlantis* 8 (Autumn 1982): 10; and Mary Douglas, Ballyhellion, Malin Head, January 1955, vol. 141, in "Emigration to America Questionnaires," who said: "In those days that is what the people grew up for—to go away to America and far, far more went than stayed at home." The quote in the text is from Sister Rosarii, December 17, 1991, Mercy Convent, Naas, County Kildare.

46. Janet A. Nolan, *Ourselves Alone: Women's Emigration from Ireland, 1885–1920* (Lexington: University Press of Kentucky, 1989), 43, 46, 67–68. See also C. H. Oldham, "The Incidence of Emigration on Town and Country Life in Ireland," *Journal of Statistical and Social Inquiry Society of Ireland* 67 (1913/1914): 208. The eight counties from which women emigrated in larger numbers than men between 1851 and 1913 were Louth, in Leinster; Kerry and Clare, in Munster; and all five counties of Connaught.

47. Figures are from Helen M. Sweeney, *The Golden Milestone, 1846–1896: Fifty Years of Loving Labor among the Poor and Suffering by the Sisters of Mercy of New York City* (New York: Benziger Brothers, 1896), 20.

48. The Sisters of Mercy were not enclosed (restricted to work within their convent or cloister) and thus were able to undertake a variety of good works. Sometimes referred to as "walking sisters," they were often the most popular with bishops. They had no central motherhouse. Each convent was autonomous and subject to the local bishop's authority, except in matters of internal governance. Even here, bishops tried to rule from time to time. Carroll, *Leaves*, 1:139.

49. Sister M. Francis Benson to Mother Vincent Hartnett, July 4, 1859, quoted in Mother Austin Carroll, *Leaves from the Annals of the Sisters of Mercy, in Four Volumes*. Vol. 4: *Containing Sketches of the Order in South America, Central America, and the United States* (New York: P. O'Shea, 1895), 23. The experiences of the Sisters of Mercy in Chicago were much like those in San Francisco. See Chapter 2.

50. Mother Frances Warde to President David Moriarty, July 20, 1851, Collection of Letters from Priests and Bishops, 1843–1877, All Hallows College Archives.

51. Mother Baptist's birth mother generously supported convents where her daughters lived. Thus she was able to live the last years of her life at the Convent of Mercy in Newry, County Down. Russell, *The Three Sisters of Lord Russell of Killowen*, 46–47, 82–85.

52. Warde to Moriarty, July 20, 1851, All Hallows College Archives.

53. Quoted in Sister Mary Hermenia Muldrey, *Abounding in Mercy: Mother Austin Carroll* (New Orleans, La.: Habersham, 1988): 28. I made three attempts to visit the Convent of Mercy in Cork, but I was told by the superior and the archivist of St. Maries of the Isle that they had nothing that would interest me.

54. "Death of Mrs. Warde, Superioress of the Convent of Mercy, Cork," *Cork Examiner*, December 18, 1879. The quotes are from Healy, *Frances Warde*, pp. 425 and 127, respectively.

55. Mother Josephine Hagarty, "Sisters of the Presentation of the Blessed Virgin Mary, San Francisco, California: Annals of the Congregation, 1854–1907," p. 8, Presentation Sisters Archives, San Francisco, California.

56. "Irish Missioners in California," *Kilkenny Journal*, March 2, 1867; and "Irish Nuns in California," in ibid., March 30, 1867. See also *Rev. Mother Teresa Comerford*, 37–39; and Hagerty, "Sisters of the Presentation of the Blessed Virgin Mary."

57. *Memoir of Rev. Mother Mary Teresa Comerford*, 75; and Curry, *Mother Teresa Comerford*, 20–23.

58. "Remarkable Events, 1865," in Presentation Sisters, "Annals," George's Hill Convent Archives, Dublin. See also Sister Amata Hollas and Sister Andrea Hubnik, *Extending the Incarnation: A Biographical, Historical and Pictorial Record of the Sisters of the Incarnate Word and Blessed Sacrament, Victoria, Texas* (Victoria, Texas: Kurtz Printing Company, 1989), 15–16.

59. Anna Shannon McAllister, *Flame in the Wilderness: Life and Letters of Mother Angela Gillespie, CSC, 1824–1887, American Foundress of the Sisters of the Holy Cross* (Notre Dame, Ind.: Centenary Chronicles of the Sisters of the Holy Cross, 1944), 271–80, especially 273, 278, and 280 for quotes.

60. Ibid., especially 275–76 and 280 for quotes. For the last one, see Larkin, "The Devotional Revolution in Ireland," 651. In 1865 the Holy Cross Sisters decided that no dowry would be required if candidates possessed an "aptitude and the qualities proper to Religious life." The nuns agreed, however, that if officials in Rome encouraged them to require dowries, fifty dollars would be the maximum they would request. Sister M. Campion Kuhn, "The Americanization of the Sisters of the Holy Cross," paper presented at the Conference on the History of the Congregations of Holy Cross, Wilkes-Barre, Pennsylvania, May 25–26, 1985, p. 21.

61. "Kilcock Convent School," *Kildare Observer*, December 6, 1879; "Death of Mother Mary Teresa Comerford," *Kilkenny Journal*, August 27, 1881; *Memoir of Rev. Mother Teresa Comerford*, 75; and Presentation Sisters, "Annals, 1879," Presentation Convent Archives, Kilcock, County Kildare.

62. The one lay postulant, Kate Stapleton, who was accepted without a dowry was from County Tipperary. Another candidate, Maria Tierney, who did not persevere, was awarded £170 after leaving the Kilcock novitiate. Solicitor Stephen J. Brown to Reverend Thomas Geoghegan, September 21, 1888, Presentation Convent Archives, Kilcock. See also Curry, *Mother Teresa Comerford*, 25–32.

63. Quotes are from Kevin Condon, *The Missionary College of All Hallows, 1842–1891* (Dublin: All Hallows College, 1986), 86, 244. Mother Teresa Comerford received support from All Hallows administrators and graduates. See Archbishop Joseph Alemany to President Bartholomew Woodlock, May 5, 1859; and Mother Teresa Comerford to President Thomas Bennett, June 13, 1862, All Hallows College Archives.

64. Condin, *The Missionary College of All Hallows*, 219; Presentation Sisters, "Annals," George's Hill, Dublin; and Roland Burke Savage, *A Valiant Dublin Woman: The Story of George's Hill (1766–1940)* (Dublin: M. H. Gill and Son, 1940), 248–49.

65. Healy, *Frances Warde*, 126.

66. The society (or association, as it is called in Ireland) was founded in 1822 in Lyons to support the Catholic Church's missionary activities. On Propagation of the Faith funding and All Hallows, see Hogan, *The Irish Missionary Movement*, 64–65. See also "A Second All Hallows," *Irish Catholic*, March 17, 1906; and "An Irish Apostolic School: The Mission of Ireland," *Irish Catholic and Nation*, September 7, 1895.

67. Madeleine Sophie McGrath, *These Women! Women Religious in the History of Australia: The Sisters of Mercy Parramatta 1888–1988* (Kensington, New South Wales, Australia: New South Wales University Press, 1989), 11–15. Mother Michael Maher's father, Patrick Maher from Athy, was Cardinal Paul Cullen's uncle.

68. "Our Apostolic Nuns" (on Mother Joseph Rice), *Irish Catholic*, July 12, 1913. See also McGrath, *These Women!* 14, 26. This is a good example of how women-religious made their efforts "invisible."

69. "Countries—St. Brigid's [Aspirants]," undated, Sisters of Mercy Archives, Callan. According to the individuals listed in the enrollment register, 1,958 went to the U.S. between 1884 and 1959. See "Register of Aspirants," St. Brigid's Missionary School, Callan.

70. Sister M. Joseph to Rev. Mother, October 8, 1892, Sisters of Mercy Archives, Athlone, County Westmeath. I thank Sister Sheila Lunney for sharing this letter with me. Monitressess served as "teaching assistants"; they were paid small salaries and trained to become teachers in the national school system. See Keane, "A History of the Foundation of the Presentation Convents in the Diocese of Kerry," 57–58, 137–43.

71. "Our Future Nuns" circular, September 24, 1895, Sisters of Mercy Archives, Callan. See also note 27.

72. "Book of Rules," St. Brigid's Missionary School, Callan; An Aspirant, "Apostolic School for Women," *St. Joseph's Sheaf* 2 (1898): 201–2; and "Our Future Nuns" circular, September 24, 1895.

73. Bishop Eugene O'Connell to President William Fortune, May 25, 1870, All Hallows College Archives.

74. Quoted in Jay P. Dolan, *The American Catholic Experience: A History from Colonial Times to the Present* (New York: Doubleday and Company, 1985), 272. He also noted: "The major reason why parochial schools made it at all financially was because the sisters subsidized them through their low salaries" (pp. 288–89).

75. Sister Mary Eustace Eaton, "Annals of the Sodality of the Children of Mary, 1888–94," Sisters of Charity Archives, Harold's Cross, Dublin. Sister Mary Eustace made the same complaint in a letter to Archbishop Walsh, November 20, 1902, Walsh Papers. Unfortunately, she did not identify those in Chicago requesting teaching nuns. She said that they were "earnestly begging for Postulants. The very next day, Sunday, a cable arrived from the Bishop [Patrick A. Feehan] saying that two of the nuns were going to New York *this* week and to let him know how many aspirants I could send, also name of vessel they would travel by! *Answer prepaid!* It was evidently a case of now or never!"

76. Quoted in Clear, *Nuns in Nineteenth-Century Ireland*, 142.

77. Larkin, "The Devotional Revolution in Ireland," especially pp. 644–46. See also Magray, *Transforming Power of the Nuns*, 88–99; and T. I. Mulcahy, *The*

Sodality Manual: Official Manual of the Sodality of Our Lady in Ireland (Dublin: Society of Jesus, 1934), 5–6.

78. "Annals of the Children of Mary" and "List of Sodalists' Convents, 1857–1915," Presentation Convent Archives, George's Hill. There is no record of the number of recruits who went out to Houston with Mother Gabriel Dillon. However, in 1879 the bishop of Galveston acknowledged that the Houston convent was "formed almost exclusively with dear pupils raised in your house." Bishop Claude Dubuis to Mother Bridget Carroll, August 1879, Presentation Convent Archives, George's Hill.

79. Much about Sister Mary Eustace's life prior to joining the Sisters of Charity remains unknown. See Mrs. O'Brien, *Sister Mary Eustace*, 9–23.

80. "Part I: 1860–1906," *The Sodality of Our Lady, Harold's Cross, Dublin: An Account of the Life of the Sodality, 1860–1935* (Dublin: Sisters of Charity, 1935), 2; and Mrs. O'Brien, *Sister Mary Eustace*, 22–23.

81. Sister Mary Eustace to Archbishop Walsh, September 12 and 18, 1890, Walsh Papers. There are several accounts of the strike in the *Irish Times*, September 15–18, 1890.

82. Archbishop Walsh often compared the sodality to All Hallows when he addressed its members during retreats. See, for example, "Our Nun Missionaries," *Irish Catholic and Nation*, September 12, 1896. See also Mrs. O'Brien, *Sister Mary Eustace*, 20, 28–29.

83. Sister Mary Eustace to Archbishop Walsh, October 5, 1889 and February 8, 1900, Walsh Papers.

84. "Statistics of Children of Mary," and "Register for the Children of Mary, Opened August 1860," Sisters of Charity Archives, Harold's Cross. See also "Our Missionary Nuns: Our Lady's Mount, Harold's Cross," *Irish Catholic*, August 27, 1904; and Sister Mary Eustace to Archbishop Walsh, November 20, 1899; also May 10 and August 25, 1904, Walsh Papers.

85. "Irish Lady Missionaries," *Tipperary People*, September 21, 1900; and Sister Mary Eustace to Archbishop Walsh, August 6, 1900, Walsh Papers. See also Sister Mary Helena Finck, *The Congregation of the Sisters of Charity of the Incarnate Word of San Antonio, Texas: A Brief Account of Its Origins and Its Work* (Washington, D.C.: Catholic University of America, 1925), 131, 188. I am grateful for the biographical data sent to me from the Incarnate Word Archives, San Antonio, Texas.

86. The quote appears in Susan Carol Peterson and Courtney Ann Vaughn-Roberson, *Women with Vision: The Presentation Sisters of South Dakota, 1890–1985* (Urbana: University of Illinois Press, 1988), 88. Short descriptions of Mother Joseph Butler's four visits to Kinsale in 1903, 1906, 1910, and 1913 are recorded in the convent's "Annals," Sisters of Mercy Archives, Kinsale, County Cork.

87. "Religious Vocations," *Irish Catholic*, August 20, 1898. This same ad continued to run almost every week from August 20, 1899, to February 18, 1900.

88. Sister Mary Loyola Hegarty, *Serving with Gladness: The Origins and History of the Congregation of the Sisters of Charity of the Incarnate Word, Houston, Texas* (Houston: Bruce Publishing and Sisters of Charity of the Incarnate Word, 1967), especially 279, 307, and 366; see also the chapter entitled "The End of the French Period (1877–1887)." The ads of this congregation can be found during the summer months of most years; they usually gave the name of the recruiter and

told where and how she could be contacted. The ad quoted in the text appeared in *Tipperary People*, July 15, 22, and 29, 1904.

89. "Register of Presentation Convent National School," Roll Number 6215, Parish: Castleisland, 1876–1884, Presentation Convent National School Records, Castleisland, County Kerry.

90. "Nuns as Teachers," reprinted in the *Kilkenny Journal*, October 4, 1884.

91. Rev. James Canon Waldron, Ballyhaunis, County Mayo, to Vere Foster and quoted in "Mr. Vere Foster's Irish Female Emigration Fund."

92. I am grateful to Elizabeth O'Toole, Bray, County Wicklow, for telling me about her aunt Molly Mackey and sharing her letters with me. I was made aware of this small collection by an entry in Francis X. Blouin Jr. and Robert M. Warner, eds., *Sources for the Study of Migration and Ethnicity: A Guide to Manuscripts in Finland, Ireland, Poland, The Netherlands, and the State of Michigan* (Ann Arbor, Mich.: Bentley Historical Library, 1979), 253. I also appreciate biographical data from Ann Dolores, CSJ, Sisters of St. Joseph of Carondelet Provincial House Archives, Latham, New York.

93. Molly Mackey to her parents, undated, in the possession of Elizabeth O'Toole, Bray, County Wicklow.

94. Mackey to her mother, February 12, 1900, ibid.

95. See "Postulants and Novices Who Went from Cabra to New Orleans," Dominican Convent Archives, Cabra. See also Hoy and Mac Curtain, eds., *From Dublin to New Orleans*.

96. "Mother Mary John Flanagan, O.P. (1827–1904)," *Immaculata* [Cabra] 2 (1960): 16–21.

97. Walter Nugent, *Crossings: The Great Transatlantic Migrations, 1870–1914* (Bloomington: Indiana University Press, 1992), 153.

98. "Our Missionary Nuns," *Irish Catholic*, August 22, 1903.

99. Fanny Taylor, *Irish Homes and Irish Hearts* (London: Longmans, Green, and Company, 1867), 6, 42. See also Diner, *Erin's Daughters*, 28–29.

100. Monsignor Laurence Forde (for Cardinal Paul Cullen) to Monsignor Edward McCabe, March 21, 1870, Cardinal Paul Cullen Papers, Dublin Diocesan Archives, Drumcondra, Dublin. The superior at the Presentation convent in Maynooth wanted to use money from "the school fund" to support a young woman. Monsignor Forde responded negatively and said that "his Eminence" did not think "it wise to place implicit reliance on the recommendations of nuns from the remote country parts of Ireland." In another case, Archbishop William J. Walsh agreed to allow Mary Russell, a widow who was over the age limit but had a dowry of £1,000, to enter the Holy Faith Sisters at Glasnevin in Dublin. At the same time he refused permission for the nuns to accept Elizabeth Lillis, who was seventeen years old but could not bring the required dowry. See letters between the superior general of the Holy Faith Sisters (M. Agnes Vickers) and Archbishop William J. Walsh, December 30, 1904 and January 23, 1905, Walsh Papers.

101. Mary Carbery, *The Farm by Lough Gur: The Story of Mary Fogarty* (Cork: Mercier Press, 1986 ed.), 47.

102. Mary Lavin, "The Nun's Mother," in *The Stories of Mary Lavin*, 3 vols. (London: Constable, 1987 ed.), 2:63. "Offload" is a word I heard several times as Irish nuns explained the parents' reaction to sending a daughter away. Nineteenth-century newspapers continually referred to women-religious as having chosen

"the better part." See, for example, "Religious Profession at Portlaw," *Tipperary People*, November 25, 1887.

103. I am grateful to Charline Sullivan, CSJ, for information on this recruitment trip and a photograph from the Sisters of St. Joseph Carondelet Archives, St. Louis Province.

104. "Irish Postulants for American Convents," *Cork Examiner*, March 1, 1898. According to this account, postulant groups made a practice of staying at Hennessy's because "nothing could exceed the care and attention displayed by Mr. Hennessy and his staff in providing for the comforts of the young ladies and their guardians." When I visited Cobh on February 27, 1992, Mary Broderick, who has written a history of Cobh, introduced me to Jack Hennessy, Richard's grandson, now in his eighties. He told me what he remembered about the hotel, formerly at 7 Beach Street, and gave me a postcard representation of it.

105. Ellie Hogan (on board the *Celtic*) to her parents, August 10, 1924. I thank Eileen Hogan, Bawnreigh, Gortnahoe, County Tipperary, for responding to one of my newspaper ads and sending me this letter.

106. Interview with Sister Mary Ailbe O'Kelly, by Sister Marie O'Connor, St. Anthony's Convent, Syracuse, New York, January 23, 1981. A transcript is in the Sisters of St. Joseph of Carondelet Provincial House Archives, Latham, New York.

107. A [Mercy] Novice, "American Glimpses: What Irish Missionary Nuns Are Accomplishing," *Irish Catholic*, August 1, 1908. On Irish familiarity with American cities, see Kerby A. Miller, *Emigrants and Exiles: Ireland and the Irish Exodus to North America* (New York: Oxford University Press, 1985), 425.

108. "Annals of the Sodality of the Children of Mary, 1905–1915," Sisters of Charity Archives, Harold's Cross. The annalist explained that those who returned "were according to previous arrangement sent back to Dublin at the expense of the convent wherein they failed." This practice seems to have been adopted by most religious communities in the United States.

109. Sister Mary Lawrence Franklin, "The Lay Sisters," *Archival Gleanings* [of Sisters of Mercy, Erie, Penn.] 6 (November 1991): 3.

110. Thompson, "To Serve the People of God," 14–16; and Margaret Susan Thompson, "Sisterhood and Power: Class, Culture, and Ethnicity in the American Convent," *Colby Library Quarterly* 25 (September 1989): 152–60.

111. Antonia White, *Frost in May* (London: Virago Press, 1991; reprint of 1933 ed.), 180.

112. Franklin, "The Lay Sisters," 4.

113. Sisters M. Juanito Joseph Malone and Mary A. Healey, BVM, "The Girls from Ballyferriter," *SALT* [quarterly magazine for friends of the Sisters of Charity of the Blessed Virgin Mary] 19 (Winter 1991): 8–9.

Chapter 2: *Walking Nuns*

1. For the term *walking nuns*, see M. Angela Bolster, RSM, *Catherine McAuley: Venerable for Mercy* (Dublin: Dominican Publications, 1990), 55. See also Mary Carmel Bourke, RSM, *A Woman Sings of Mercy: Reflections on the Life and Spirit of Mother Catherine McAuley, Foundress of the Sisters of Mercy* (Sydney, Australia: E. J. Dwyer, 1987), 8; and E. A. Ryan, SJ, "The Sisters of Mercy:

An Important Chapter in Church History," *Theological Studies* 18 (June 1957): 259–60.

2. This has also been true in Catholic Church history, as Mary Jo Weaver correctly observed in *New Catholic Women: A Contemporary Challenge to Traditional Religious Authority* (Bloomington: Indiana University Press, 1986). Since the 1990s, there has been some progress in all regards. For an overview, see Kathleen Sprows Cummings, "Change of Habit," in *American Catholic Studies Newsletter* [of Cushwa Center for the Study of American Catholicism, University of Notre Dame] 29 (Spring 2002): 1, 8–11.

3. The quote is from William J. Onahan, *A Little History of Old Saint Mary's Church, Chicago* (Chicago: Privately published, 1908), 24. For an example of such neglect, see Sarah Deutsch, *Women and the City: Gender, Space, and Power in Boston, 1870–1940* (New York: Oxford University Press, 2000). Deutsch looked closely at how women "actively shaped their environment, reconceiving the city to redefine their place in it" (p. 24). She creatively demonstrated how a variety of women struggled to make a place for themselves in Boston. But Catholic women, including nuns, received almost no attention. In contrast, an extraordinarily expansive and useful book on Chicago, which was published a year later, gave serious consideration to the contributions of individual women-religious. See Rima Lunin Schultz and Adele Hast, eds., *Women Building Chicago: A Biographical Dictionary, 1790–1990* (Bloomington: Indiana University Press, 2001).

4. Mother Frances Xavier Warde (1810–84) was among the first seven Sisters of Mercy to make profession of vows under the direction of Catherine McAuley, the community's founder. Mother Frances became the founding superior of the Sisters of Mercy in Carlow, from which she and six companions, including postulant Margaret O'Brien, set out for Pittsburgh in 1843. (See Chapter 1.) Three years later, Mother Frances led a founding group to Chicago. In addition to Mother Agatha (Margaret) O'Brien, the pioneers were Sisters Gertrude (Catherine) McGuire, Vincent (Mary Ann) McGirr, Josephine (Elizabeth) Corbett, and Veronica (Eva) Schmidt. Biographical data on them can be found in the Sisters of Mercy Archives, Province Center, Chicago.

5. The quote is from Mother Austin Carroll, *Leaves from the Annals of the Sisters of Mercy, in Four Volumes.* Vol. 3: *Continuing Sketches of the Order in Newfoundland and the United States* (New York: Catholic Publication Society Company, 1889), 245. On lay sisters, see Caitriona Clear, *Nuns in Nineteenth-Century Ireland* (Dublin: Gill and Macmillan, 1987), 91–99.

6. A description of the new building appeared in the 1848 *Catholic Directory*. It is quoted in Mary Eulalia Herron, RSM, *The Sisters of Mercy in the United States, 1843–1928* (New York: Macmillan Company, 1929), 56. See also Joy Clough, RSM, *First in Chicago: A History of Saint Xavier University* (Chicago: St. Xavier University, 1997), 34–36.

7. William K. Beatty, "When Cholera Scourged Chicago," *Chicago History* XL (Spring 1982): 5–8 (quote); Sister Mary Fidelis Convey, "Mother Agatha O'Brien and the Pioneers" (master's thesis, Loyola University, 1929), 126; Roland Burke Savage, *Catherine McAuley: The First Sister of Mercy* (Dublin: M. H. Gill and Son, 1950), 147–53; and Joy Clough, RSM, *In Service to Chicago: The History of Mercy Hospital* (Chicago: Mercy Hospital, 1979), 18. The final quote is from Mother Agatha O'Brien to Sister Scholastica Drum, February 7, 1851, Mercy Archives.

8. These quotes are taken from letters written by Mother Agatha O'Brien on November 12, 1850; February 7, 1851; September 4, 1851; and November 12, 1851, all in Mercy Archives.

9. On the Galena foundation, see Carroll, *Leaves*, 247. Sister Gertrude McGuire died of tuberculosis and Sister Veronica Schmidt of typhoid fever. See Clough, *In Service to Chicago*, 13. Mother Agatha O'Brien to Charles O'Brien, September 4, 1851 (quote), Mercy Archives. According to the 1860 manuscript federal census, for example, fifty-seven Mercy Sisters lived on Wabash Avenue, of whom thirty-nine were born in Ireland.

10. Quotes are from Clough, *In Service to Chicago*, 18–19. On the average number of patients, see "General Hospital of the Lake," *Western Tablet*, February 28, 1852. The total number admitted in a year (1851–52) was 220.

11. Convey, "Mother Agatha O'Brien," 203, 228. Although Convey noted that Saint Patrick's free school for girls opened in 1854, the *Western Tablet* indicated that it began in 1852 (and quite possibly in late 1851). See *Western Tablet*, February 21 and March 27, 1852. Frances Willard, the well-known temperance reformer, stated in an 1894 lecture in Cleveland that she wanted "to help make the world so homelike that women could freely go out into it everywhere." See "Frances Willard's Work," *New York Times*, November 17, 1894. The Sisters of Mercy had been doing so for decades.

12. Mother Agatha O'Brien to Sister Elizabeth Strange, June 28, 1851, Mercy Archives.

13. "Reception of Nuns," *Western Tablet*, August 21, 1852 (quote). See also John Gilmary Shea, *A History of the Catholic Church within the Limits of the United States from the First Attempted Colonization to the Present Time* (New York: John G. Shea, 1892), 617–18. On this incident, see Thomas M. Keefe, "Chicago's Flirtation with Political Nativism, 1854–1856," *Records of the American Catholic Historical Society of Philadelphia* 82 (September 1971): 149, 156 (quote).

14. Convey, "Mother Agatha O'Brien," 212–13; Clough, *First in Chicago*, 36–39; and A Sister of the [Mercy] Community, "The Sisters of Mercy: Chicago's Pioneer Nurses and Teachers," *Illinois Catholic Historical Review* 3 (April 1921): 353. For a recent, detailed description of the property disputes, see Kathleen A. Brosnan, "Public Presence, Public Silence: Nuns, Bishops, and the Gendered Space of Early Chicago," *Catholic Historical Review* 90 (July 2004): 490–92.

15. Beatty, "When Cholera Scourged Chicago," 10; Suellen Hoy, *Chasing Dirt: The American Pursuit of Cleanliness* (New York: Oxford University Press, 1995), 62; Onahan, *A Little History of Old Saint Mary's Church*, 24 (quote); and Convey, "Mother Agatha O'Brien," 338.

16. Carroll, *Leaves*, 271–72; Convey, "Mother Agatha O'Brien," 343; editorials in *Chicago Daily Tribune*, June 7 (quote) and 16, 1854, and May 1, 1855; also Beatty, "When Cholera Scourged Chicago," 10.

17. "Mother Mary Agatha (Margaret O'Brien)," *Metropolitan Catholic Almanac and Laity's Directory, for the Year of Our Lord 1855* (Baltimore: Lucas Brothers, 1856), 285.

18. See Ellen Skerrett, "Chicago's Irish and 'Brick and Mortar Catholicism': A Reappraisal," *U.S. Catholic Historian* 14 (Spring 1996): 53–71 (quote on p. 53); and Charles Shanabruch, *Chicago's Catholics: The Evolution of an American Identity* (Notre Dame, Ind.: University of Notre Dame Press, 1981), 130.

19. Quotes are from "Saint Angela's Female Academy" prospectus, 1857, and "Saint Agatha's Academy for Young Ladies" prospectus, n.d., in Mercy Archives. On the curriculum, see Eileen Mary Brewer, *Nuns and the Education of American Catholic Women, 1860–1920* (Chicago: Loyola Press, 1987), 48–51 (quote on p. 48).

20. On Mother Francis Monholland, see Isidore O'Connor, RSM, *Life of Mary Monholland: One of the Pioneer Sisters of the Order of Mercy in the West* (Chicago: J. S. Hyland and Company, 1894); and Ann Leonard, "Monholland, Mother Mary Francis de Sales (Mary Monholland)," in *Women Building Chicago*, 594–98. See also Ellen Ryan Jolly, *Nuns of the Battlefield* (Providence, R.I.: Visitor Press, 1927), 223–39. Colonel James Mulligan's wife, Marian Nugent, had been a student at St. Xavier's Academy. On Mulligan, see Lawrence J. McCaffrey, "Preserving the Union, Shaping a New Image: Chicago's Irish Catholics and the Civil War," in *At the Crossroads*, 53–62.

21. "The Sisters of Charity," *Chicago Tribune*, June 21, 1862 (quote); "Obituary—Sister Anne Regina," *Chicago Times*, March 19, 1867; and Jolly, *Nuns of the Battlefield*, 67–68, 232–36.

22. O'Connor, *Life of Mary Monholland*, 107–13; George Levy, *To Die in Chicago: Confederate Prisoners at Camp Douglas, 1862–1865* (Evanston, Ill.: Evanston Publishing, 1994), 22–23, 28, 183; and "Honor Their Dead: . . . Reminiscences of Miss Sweet," *Chicago Tribune*, May 26, 1895 (quote). For more on Ada C. Sweet, see Suellen Hoy, "Sweet, Ada Celeste," in *Women Building Chicago*, 862–64.

23. On Chicago's Mercy Sisters as "ministering angels," see "Nurses for the Western Army," *Chicago Tribune*, October 18, 1861; and on the respect earned, see David Gollaher, *Voice for the Mad: The Life of Dorothea Dix* (New York: Free Press, 1995), 414.

24. Quotes are from Protestant Female Nurse Association, "To the Ladies' Hospital Aid Societies of the Northwest," *Chicago Tribune*, May 23, 1862. On Dorothea Dix, see Gollaher, *Voice for the Mad*, 413–14.

25. Robert E. Riegel, "Mary Ashton Rice Livermore," in *Notable American Women, 1607–1950: A Biographical Dictionary*, ed. Edward T. James and others (Cambridge, Mass.: Belknap Press of Harvard University, 1971), 2:410–13; and Lana Ruegamer, "Livermore, Mary Ashton Rice," in *Women Building Chicago*, 512–14. The 1883 quotes can be found in Sister Mary Denis Maher, *To Bind Up the Wounds: Catholic Sister Nurses in the U.S. Civil War* (New York: Greenwood Press, 1989), 39.

26. Catharine Beecher, *The True Remedy for the Wrongs of Women* (Boston: Phillips, Sampson, and Company, 1851), 51. In James Hurt's introduction to a recent edition of *Twenty Years at Hull-House*, Jane Addams and Ellen Gates Starr are described as "fashionable young ladies" who moved to "a dilapidated mansion in the heart of Chicago's slums determined to be 'good neighbors.'" Jane Addams, *Twenty Years at Hull-House: With Biographical Notes* (Urbana: University of Illinois Press, 1990), ix. For a different view of the Hull-House neighborhood, see Ellen Skerrett, "The Irish of Chicago's Hull-House Neighborhood," in *New Perspectives on the Irish Diaspora*, ed. Charles Fanning (Carbondale: Southern Illinois University Press, 2000), 189–222. See also Donald L. Miller, *City of the Century: The Epic of Chicago and the Making of America* (New York: Simon

and Schuster, 1996), 417–20. In a National Public Radio interview (May 1996), Miller called Addams a "gutsy" woman for living and working among Chicago's poor. Ellen Gates Starr was the niece of Eliza Allen Starr, a prominent Catholic convert in Chicago. She had "the greatest childhood influence on Ellen" and always considered the Sisters of Mercy her "old and true friends." See Allen F. Davis, "Ellen Gates Starr," in *Notable American Women*, 3:351–53 (quote on p. 351); and Reverend James J. McGovern, *The Life and Letters of Eliza Allen Starr* (Chicago: Lakeside Press, 1905), 169 (quote).

27. Leonard I. Sweet, *The Minister's Wife: Her Role in Nineteenth-Century American Evangelicalism* (Philadelphia: Temple University Press, 1983), 88–90 (quote).

28. Ibid., 91 (quotes). On Emily Judson, see Barbara Welter, "She Hath Done What She Could: Protestant Women's Missionary Careers in Nineteenth-Century America," in *Women in American Religion*, ed. Janet Wilson James (Philadelphia: University of Pennsylvania Press, 1980), 114–15. Later in the century, Protestant single women were at times permitted to become missionaries themselves. Then their lives more closely resembled those of Catholic sisters; both groups experienced "meaning and joy," and their lives were "infused by a sense of privilege at being a special recipient of God's grace" (p. 124).

29. Florence Jean Deacon, "Handmaids or Autonomous Women: The Charitable Activities, Institution Building and Communal Relationships of Catholic Sisters in Nineteenth-Century Wisconsin" (Ph.D. diss., University of Wisconsin, Madison, 1989), 119 (quote). On the severe inadequacies of famine refugees, see Lawrence J. McCaffrey, "Forging Forward and Looking Back," in *The New York Irish*, ed. Ronald H. Bayor and Timothy J. Meagher (Baltimore: Johns Hopkins University Press, 1996), 214.

30. Marta Danylewycz, *Taking the Veil: An Alternative to Motherhood and Spinsterhood in Quebec, 1840–1920* (Toronto: McClelland and Stewart, 1987), 105–9 (quote on p. 105). See also Carol K. Coburn and Martha Smith, *Spirited Lives: How Nuns Shaped Catholic Culture and American Life, 1836–1920* (Chapel Hill: University of North Carolina Press, 1999), 68–70.

31. Danylewycz, *Taking the Veil*, 85–87 (quote on p. 85). In the baptismal registry at St. Patrick's, Sister Callista's name appears as "Mary Ellen Mangin." She was born on November 19, 1855, and baptized two days later; she died on October 9, 1883, Sisters of Mercy Register, Mercy Archives.

32. Joseph G. Mannard, "Converts in Convents: Protestant Women and the Social Appeal of Catholic Religious Life in Antebellum America," *Records* [of the American Catholic Historical Society] 104 (Winter–Spring 1993): 90; and James K. Kenneally, *The History of American Catholic Women* (New York: Crossroad, 1990), 43.

33. Convey, "Mother Agatha O'Brien," 190–91, 212–14. On the legal powers the Sisters of Mercy received from the State of Illinois through the 1847 charter and act of incorporation of St. Francis Xavier Female Academy, see Clough, *St. Xavier University*, 31–32; and also Mary Livermore, *My Story of the War: A Woman's Narrative of Her Personal Experience as Nurse in the Union Army* (Hartford, Conn.: A. D. Worthington and Company, 1887), 436. Historian Lori D. Ginzberg has noted that although middle-class Protestant women rarely discussed incorporating, their very interest in doing so (and some did) "challenges

their insistence on a protected female sphere." Lori D. Ginzberg, *Women and the Work of Benevolence: Morality, Politics, and Class in the Nineteenth-Century United States* (New Haven, Conn.: Yale University Press, 1990), 48.

34. For a fine discussion of the nineteenth-century worldview of Irish men and women, see Hasia R. Diner, *Erin's Daughters in America* (Baltimore, Md.: Johns Hopkins University Press, 1983), 139–53 (quote on p. 139). See also Mary P. Ryan, "The Public and the Private Good: Across the Great Divide in Women's History," *Journal of Women's History* 15 (Summer 2003), 22–23 (quote on p. 23).

35. Quotes are from Robert A. Orsi, "Crossing the City Line," in *Gods of the City: Religion and the American Urban Landscape*, ed. Robert A. Orsi (Bloomington: Indiana University Press, 1999), 28; and Barbra M. Wall, "Unlikely Entrepreneurs: Nuns, Nursing, and Hospital Development in the West and Midwest, 1865–1915" (Ph.D. diss., University of Notre Dame, 2000).

Chapter 3: Caring for Abandoned Women and Girls

1. "An Act to Incorporate the Sisters of the Good Shepherd, of the City of Chicago," March 7, 1867, *Laws of Illinois 1867: Private Laws*, 1:153. Other forms of disorderly conduct were vagrancy or intoxication. During the nineteenth century, the distinction between delinquent and dependent children was not always clear. Delinquents were generally considered troublemakers; dependents were not. Dependents were victims of unfortunate circumstances (usually illness or death) and could not be cared for by their parents, and thus often were abandoned.

2. U.S. Bureau of the Census, *Thirteenth Census of the United States: 1910— Population* (Washington, D.C.: Government Printing Office, 1913).

3. Gabriel O'Brien, RSM, *Reminiscences of Seventy Years, 1846–1916* (Chicago: Fred J. Ringley Company, 1916), 57; Isidore O'Connor, RSM, *Life of Mary Monholland: One of the Pioneer Sisters of the Order of Mercy in the West* (Chicago: J. S. Hyland and Company, 1894), 132; Mary Foote Coughlin, *A New Commandment: A Little Memoir of the Work Accomplished by the Good Shepherd Nuns in Chicago* (Chicago: Sisters of the Good Shepherd, 1909); Rev. James J. McGovern, *The Life and Writings of the Right Reverend John McMullen, D.D.: First Bishop of Davenport, Iowa* (Chicago: Hoffman Brothers, 1888), 128–29; and *Chicago Tribune*, July 26, 1866.

4. Ralph Gibson, *A Social History of French Catholicism, 1789–1914* (New York: Routledge, 1989), 117–20; A. M. Clarke, *Life of Reverend Mother Mary of St. Euphrasia Pelletier: First Superior General of the Congregation of Our Lady of Charity of the Good Shepherd of Angers* (London: Burns and Oates, 1895); Claude Langlois, *Le Catholicisme au Feminin: Les Congrégations Françaises à Supérieure Générale au XIXe Siècle* (Paris: Les Editions du Cerf, 1984), 544.

5. See manuscript federal censuses, 1860 and 1910. Here and elsewhere, *sister* and *nun* are used interchangeably to describe any woman-religious who took vows. *Community, congregation,* and *order* continue to be used synonymously.

6. See Jay P. Dolan, *The American Catholic Experience: A History from Colonial Times to the Present* (New York: Doubleday and Company, 1985), 143–44; Michael F. Funchion, "Irish Chicago: Church, Homeland, Politics, and Class: The Shaping of an Ethnic Group, 1870–1900," in *Ethnic Chicago*, ed. Melvin Holli

and Peter Jones (Grand Rapids, Mich.: William B. Eerdmans, 1984), 18 (quote); Charles Shanabruch, *Chicago Catholics: The Evolution of an American Identity* (Notre Dame, Ind.: University of Notre Dame Press, 1981), 237.

7. For an extensive review of historical publications on Catholic sisters since the 1970s, see Carol K. Coburn, "An Overview of the Historiography of Women Religious: A Twenty-Five-Year Retrospective," *U.S. Catholic Historian* 22 (Winter 2004): 1–26.

8. See Chapter 1 for a fuller explanation of how and why so many Irish women became sisters in America.

9. *Annals of the Monastery of Our Lady of the Good Shepherd: The First in America, Founded from the Mother House of Angers, France* (Louisville, Ky.: Bradley & Gilbert Company, 1893), 8–24; and *"He Had Compassion on Them"* (St. Louis, Mo.: Blackwell Wielandy Press, 1927), 16. Both books were most likely written by a Sister of the Good Shepherd. On Bishop Benedict Flaget, see Dolan, *American Catholic Experience*, 119.

10. *Annals of the Monastery*, 32; *"He Had Compassion on Them"* 10–13, 25–26, 49.

11. Most Irish women were chaste. Those who were not were usually "rebellious or desperate," and their "careers" generally did not last more than several years. Not only did their earning power and health deteriorate, they were "stigmatized in the broader Irish community," where Catholic teachings and family honor were shared values. See Patricia Kelleher, "Gender Shapes Ethnicity: Ireland's Gender Systems and Chicago's Irish Americans" (Ph.D. diss., University of Wisconsin, 1995), 348–49. Kelleher found that in Chicago in 1880, "native white women made up the largest contingent among the prostitutes identified in the manuscript census" and that second-generation Irish and German women were "more likely" to become prostitutes than were their first-generation counterparts. On single Irish women (mostly widows) who successfully supported themselves and their children, see also Patricia Kelleher, "Maternal Strategies: Irish Women's Headship of Families in Gilded Age Chicago," *Journal of Women's History* 13 (Summer 2001): 80–106.

12. *"He Had Compassion on Them,"* 31–47. Obituaries of Mother Mary of St. John the Baptist Jackson, *Bulletin of the Congregation of the Good Shepherd of Angers* 19 (June–August 1911): 235–44; and Sister Mary of St. Philomene Kavanaugh, [Chicago] *New World*, January 18, 1902. The Jackson family immigrated to America in 1849, and four years later Margaret, who was the fifth of ten children, entered the Good Shepherd novitiate. Her sister Jane accompanied her; another sister followed several years later. The Kavanaughs immigrated in 1834, and Mary entered the novitiate in 1840. After arriving in Chicago in 1859, she never left; she died just short of her eighty-second birthday and is buried in Calvary Cemetery in Evanston. The other two nuns in the first group were Sisters Mary of St. Augustine (Mary) Smith and Sister Mary Martha (Bridget) Shine. They also lived the remainder of their lives in Chicago. Both died in the 1880s and are buried in Calvary Cemetery.

13. Theodore J. Karamanski, *Rally 'Round the Flag: Chicago and the Civil War* (Chicago: Nelson-Hall, 1993), xi–xii, 3–4.

14. For an unusually vivid account of the poverty of Irish peasants, see Robert James Scally, *The End of Hidden Ireland: Rebellion, Famine, and Emigration* (New York: Oxford University Press, 1995). See also Patricia Kelleher, "Young

Irish Workers: Class Implications of Men's and Women's Experiences in Gilded Age Chicago," *Eire-Ireland* 36 (Spring–Summer 2001): 151–65; Michael B. Katz, *In the Shadow of the Poorhouse: A Social History of Welfare in America* (New York: Basic Books, 1986), 4–10 (quote); "Second Report from the Matron of the City Bridewell," *Chicago Tribune*, June 6, 1859 (quote); and Bessie Louise Pierce, *A History of Chicago: From Town to City, 1848–1871* (New York: Alfred A. Knopf, 1940), 380, who found that "nearly three fourths of the paupers" in the county poorhouse were both Catholic and Irish.

15. On Archbishop John Hughes's attitude, see Maureen Fitzgerald, "The Perils of 'Passion and Poverty': Women Religious and the Care of Single Women in New York City, 1845–1890," *U S. Catholic Historian* 10, nos. 1 and 2 (1989): 49–50. See also Shanabruch, *Chicago Catholics*, 14–15; James Duggan, "Pastoral Letter" (quotes), January 6, 1860, Madaj Collection, Joseph Cardinal Bernardin Archives and Records Center of the Archdiocese of Chicago; and *Chicago Tribune*, April 7, 1859.

16. Gilbert J. Garraghan, SJ, *The Catholic Church in Chicago, 1673–1871: An Historical Sketch* (Chicago: Loyola University Press, 1921), 207; *Chicago Tribune*, April 7, 1859; *Chicago Daily Journal*, June 28, 1859; and "Special Book of Annals" (unpublished, House of the Good Shepherd, Chicago).

17. On Chicago's religious landscape, see Daniel Bluestone, *Constructing Chicago* (New Haven, Conn.: Yale University Press, 1991), 65–82. I interchange "Magdalen asylum" and "House of the Good Shepherd," but most Chicagoans called this institution "Magdalen asylum" before the fire of 1871 and "House of the Good Shepherd" after it. The Protestant institution, founded in 1863 for the same purpose, was named the "Chicago Erring Woman's Refuge" and generally referred to as the "Erring Woman's Refuge." In 1906 it became the "Chicago Refuge for Girls." Mary Linehan, "Vicious Circle: Prostitution, Reform and Public Policy in Chicago, 1830–1930" (Ph.D. diss., University of Notre Dame, 1991), 60.

18. *Chicago Daily Journal*, August 15, 1859; McGovern, *Right Reverend John McMullen*, 129–30; *Chicago Tribune*, April 14, 1860; Duggan, "Pastoral Letter" (quotes).

19. "Special Book of Annals"; Dolan, *American Catholic Experience*, 201–2; Funchion, "Irish Chicago," 35–36; Timothy Walch, "Catholic Social Institutions and Urban Development: The View from Nineteenth-Century Chicago and Milwaukee," *Catholic Historical Review* 64 (January 1978): 20–22; and Mary J. Oates, "Catholic Female Academies on the Frontier," *U.S. Catholic Historian* 12 (Fall 1994): 122, 127.

20. Joseph G. Mannard, "Maternity of the Spirit: Nuns and Domesticity in Antebellum America," *U.S. Catholic Historian* 5 (Summer 1986): 308; and Linehan, "Vicious Circle," 59.

21. On non-Catholic, antebellum charitable institutions, see Kenneth Cmiel, *A Home of Another Kind: One Chicago Orphanage and the Tangle of Child Welfare* (Chicago: University of Chicago Press, 1995), 11. The subject of Cmiel's book is the Chicago Nursery and Half-Orphan Asylum, begun by middle-class Protestant women in 1859–60. In 1864, the Sisters of St. Joseph of Carondelet replaced the Sisters of Mercy who were in charge of St. Joseph Orphanage for Boys and St. Mary Orphanage for Girls. These two institutions later merged to become St. Joseph's Orphan Asylum. At the war's end, German Catholics opened Angel Guardian Orphanage and three years later brought German nuns, the Poor Handmaids of

Jesus Christ, to staff it. See Harry C. Koenig, STD, ed., *Caritas Christi Urget Nos: A History of the Offices, Agencies, and Institutions of the Archdiocese of Chicago* (2 vols., Chicago: Archdiocese of Chicago, 1981), 2:899, 901–2.

22. Karamanski, *Rally 'Round the Flag,* xii–xiii, 176, 178. See *Chicago Tribune,* July 20, 1864, for an estimate of prostitutes and January 9, 1866, for the links between prostitution and poverty.

23. *Chicago Tribune,* February 3, 1865, and July 9, 1866. See also Hasia R. Diner, *Erin's Daughters in America* (Baltimore, Md.: Johns Hopkins University Press, 1983), 136.

24. Anne M. Butler, *Daughters of Joy, Sisters of Mercy: Prostitutes in the American West, 1865–90* (Urbana: University of Illinois Press, 1985), 65–66; *Book of Customs: For the Use of the Religious of Our Lady of Charity of the Good Shepherd in Angers* (Angers: Religious of the Good Shepherd, 1899), 295–99; and Coughlin, *New Commandment,* 46. On hierarchical authority in the American Catholic Church, see John T. McGreevy, *Catholicism and American Freedom: A History* (New York: W. W. Norton, 2003), 137.

25. "Red Book of Annals" (unpublished, House of the Good Shepherd, Chicago), 3. See also "Mother Mary of St. John the Baptist Jackson," *Bulletin,* 241. Her obituary reads: "She was transferred to Philadelphia in 1864 where she devoted herself to the minor duties imposed on her . . . with the same fidelity that distinguished her when in more honorable positions." I thank Madeleine Rufiange, RGS, Religieuses Notre-Dame-de-Charité-du-Bon-Pasteur, Pierrefonds, Québec, for biographical information on Mother Mary Nativity Noreau.

26. Draft letter of William J. Onahan to Bertha M. H. Palmer, c. 1892, William J. Onahan Papers, Archives of the University of Notre Dame, Notre Dame, Indiana.

27. *Chicago Times,* September 23, 1867. For number of residents, see *Chicago Tribune,* July 9, 1866.

28. Caitriona Clear, *Nuns in Nineteenth-Century Ireland* (Dublin: Gill and Macmillen, 1987), 82–91. Clear found the percentage of lay sisters higher among the Good Shepherds in Limerick than among other orders. She stated (and I agree) that this difference in proportion related to the kind of work they did: "probably because there was more scope for maintenance work." Although I do not have exact figures for choir and lay sisters at the House of the Good Shepherd, I have "intermittent" figures. In November 1887, there were thirty-two sisters; twenty-five were choir and seven were lay. See [Chicago] *Inter-Ocean,* November 12, 1877. On Sister Martha Shine, see *Inter-Ocean,* July 7, 1880; and a letter from Charles C. Copeland printed in *New World,* October 16, 1909. It was customary for nineteenth-century sisters with European origins to beg. However, bourgeois Catholics and bishops in America did not approve, and the custom was eventually discontinued. See Mary J. Oates, *The Catholic Philanthropic Tradition in America* (Bloomington: Indiana University Press, 1995), 100, 135.

29. Photos of these men are in Coughlin, *New Commandment,* 47, 51, 55. For biographical data on Onahan, see Mary Onahan Gallery, *Life of William J. Onahan: Stories of Men Who Made Chicago* (Chicago: Loyola University Press, 1929); and M. Sevina Pahorezki, OSF, *The Social and Political Activities of William James Onahan* (Washington, D.C.: Catholic University of America, 1942). On Brenan, see *New World,* April 14, 1900, and May 7, 1904; and on Copeland, see a small obituary in *Libertyville Independent,* June 28, 1923. Catholic lay

women were discouraged from entering the public arena; at fund-raising events, they usually remained in the background. See Oates, *Catholic Philanthropic Tradition*, 19–45; and Deirdre M. Moloney, *American Catholic Lay Groups and Transatlantic Social Reform in the Progressive Era* (Chapel Hill: University of North Carolina Press, 2002), 165–70.

30. "Red Book of Annals," 5–12; Garraghan, *Catholic Church in Chicago*, 207. On Bishop Duggan, see Ellen Skerrett, "The Catholic Dimension," in *The Irish Catholic*, ed. Lawrence J. McCaffrey, Ellen Skerrett, Michael F. Funchion, and Charles Fanning (Urbana: University of Illinois Press, 1987), 29–33.

31. "Red Book of Annals," 12.

32. Onahan and O'Hara agreed to split the fines equally between the two institutions but thought it unjust because the number of women in the House of the Good Shepherd was "on an average, five or six times greater than those in . . . the Erring Woman's Refuge." Onahan, "Our Religious Orders: The Nuns of the Good Shepherd," *Western Catholic*, April 10, 1875. See too "An Act for the Benefit of the Chicago Erring Women's [*sic*] Refuge for Reform, and the House of the Good Shepherd, of Chicago," March 31, 1869, *Laws of Illinois 1869: Private Laws*, 1:254–55; *Proceedings of the Common Council of the City of Chicago for the Municipal Year 1868–69*, May 6 and May 31, 1869; and "Report of the House of the Good Shepherd of Chicago to the Honorable Legislature Assembled at Springfield" (unpublished, House of the Good Shepherd, Chicago, 1871).

33. *Fifteenth Annual Report of the Erring Woman's Refuge of Chicago, Illinois* (Chicago: C. H. Blakely, 1877), 12; *Erring Woman's Refuge [and House of the Good Shepherd] v. City of Chicago*, January 2, 1877, G. no. 23135, Circuit Court, Cook County; *Chicago Tribune*, January 3, 1877; and Linehan, "Vicious Circle," 78. The city finally paid each institution only $1,287. See *Chicago Tribune*, January 14, 1877.

34. *Chicago Times*, April 29 (quote), June 3, and July 25, 1869; and "Red Book of Annals," 50–54 (quotes), 134.

35. *Chicago Tribune*, August 9, 1869 (quote); "Report of the House of the Good Shepherd"; and "Register of the Benefactors of the Convent of the Good Shepherd of Chicago" (unpublished, House of the Good Shepherd, Chicago, 1863–1880). Charles C. Copeland distinguished himself with a $500 contribution, but others also made one or more donations: Thomas Brenan, $40; William J. Onahan, $30; W. B. Ogden, $200; Daniel O'Hara, $130; Potter Palmer, $25; and a number of women, $5. Father John Waldron, a fierce Irish nationalist from County Mayo and pastor of St. John's at Eighteenth and Clark streets, contributed $130 in this two-year period. For more information on him, see Skerrett, "Catholic Dimension," 35–37.

36. Mother Mary Nativity to Mother General in Angers, December 20, 1871, copied in "Special Book of Annals"; and "The Chicago Fire," translated from *Lettres Annuelles de la Société du Sacre Coeur*, 1869–1871, National Archives, Society of the Sacred Heart, St. Louis, Missouri. I am grateful to Elizabeth Farley, RSCJ, for this information. The loss of $118,000 is Mother Nativity's figure; $90,000 is listed in Elias Colbert and Everett Chamberlin, *Chicago and the Great Conflagration* (Cincinnati: J. S. Goodman, 1872), 293.

37. Onahan, in "Our Religious Orders," refers to insurance and compensation but gives no figures. See also "Red Book of Annals," 158–63; and "Register of the Benefactors of the Convent of the House of the Good Shepherd" for donations,

including those from the Chicago Relief and Aid Society. According to the Relief and Aid Society, the total given to the House of the Good Shepherd was $17,400 (not $27, 025). See *Thirty Fourth Annual Report of the Chicago Relief and Aid Society to the Common Council of the City of Chicago: From October 31, 1890 to October 31, 1891* (Chicago: R. R. McCabe, 1891), 12–13. Karen Sawislak did not mention the Sisters of the Good Shepherd in *Smoldering City: Chicagoans and the Great Fire, 1871–1874* (Chicago: University of Chicago Press, 1995).

38. "Red Book of Annals," 164–65; and *Inter-Ocean*, June 8, 1872. The Good Shepherds did what most Catholics did after the fire: they returned and rebuilt on the same properties. Their working-class constituencies gave them "good reason to stay," according to Daniel Bluestone. This was not true of Chicago's Protestants. See Bluestone, *Constructing Chicago*, 90.

39. "Red Book of Annals," 164; and Onahan, "Our Religious Orders." Both refer to the Good Shepherds' special devotion to St. Joseph, protector and provider. Although St. Joseph has never ranked among the more popular saints, he was not ignored in the House of the Good Shepherd. See also Bluestone, *Constructing Chicago*, 94; and *Appeal in Behalf of the House of the Good Shepherd, Otherwise Known as the Magdalen Asylum* (Chicago: Ottaway & Colbert Printers, 1878).

40. Onahan, "Our Religious Orders" (quote); Joan Gittens, *Poor Relations: The Children of the State in Illinois, 1818–1990* (Urbana: University of Illinois Press, 1994), 1 (quote); and *Inter-Ocean* and *Chicago Tribune*, August 12, 1878. Both newspapers gave the bazaar a good deal of coverage from August 12 through November 28, 1878.

41. *Inter-Ocean*, August 19 and 23, 1878. A large ad on the "Grand Bazar [sic] for the Benefit of the House of the Good Shepherd" appeared on November 5, 1878. See also *Appeal in Behalf of the House of the Good Shepherd* (quote). The bazaar made between $10,000 and $12,000; see *Chicago Tribune*, November 28, 1878, and *Inter-Ocean*, June 13, 1879, respectively.

42. On the growth of private charitable institutions, see Cmiel, *A Home of Another Kind*, 39–41. Examples of specialized Catholic institutions are St. Joseph's Home for working girls (1876), begun by the Sisters of the Holy Heart of Mary; St. Vincent Infant Asylum (1881), operated by the Daughters of Charity; and Mission of Our Lady of Mercy (1886), opened by Father Louis Campbell for homeless boys, many of whom sold newspapers. In 1906 it became Father C. J. Quille's Working Boys' Home. See Koenig, ed., *Caritas Christi Urget Nos*, 902–3; and A. T. Andreas, *History of Chicago: From the Earliest Period to the Present Time*, 3 vols. (Chicago: Alfred T. Andreas, 1886), 3:774.

43. *Chicago Tribune*, March 7, 8, 10 (quotes), and 12, 1879. Onahan, Brenan, and Copeland were among the fourteen pallbearers.

44. "Book of the Chapter" (unpublished, House of the Good Shepherd, Chicago) lists the superiors. On Mother Mary of St. Angelique Cleary, see *Bulletin of the Congregation of the Good Shepherd of Angers* 18 (October 1910): 634–39. See too U.S. Bureau of the Census, *Tenth Census of the United States: 1880—Population* (Washington, D.C.: Government Printing Office, 1883).

45. On delinquent young women, see Mrs. Joseph T. Bowen, "The Delinquent Children of Immigrant Parents," in *Proceedings of the National Conference of Charities and Correction* (Washington, D.C., 1909), 257; and Steven Schlossman and Stephanie Wallach, "The Crime of Precocious Sexuality: Female Juvenile

Delinquency in the Progressive Era," *Harvard Educational Review* 48 (February 1978): 72. On the lack of decent work for Chicago women, see *Chicago Tribune,* February 12 and April 13, 1888. Ethnicity figures are from *Tenth Census.*

46. Sister Mary of St. Marine Verger, *Practical Rules for the Use of the Religious of the Good Shepherd for the Direction of the Classes* (St. Paul, Minn.: Convent of the Good Shepherd, 1943 [orig.1897]), quotes on 69, 126–27.

47. Jay P. Dolan, *The Immigrant Church: New York's Irish and German Catholics, 1815–1865* (Baltimore, Md.: Johns Hopkins University Press, 1975), 122–23 (quote on p. 122). See also Katz, *In the Shadow of the Poorhouse,* 61–62, who described Catholic charity as "heroic" and "less judgmental, more ready to help, less quick to condemn" than Protestant efforts.

48. Martin J. Scott, SJ, *Convent Life: The Meaning of a Religious Vocation* (New York: P. J. Kenedy and Sons, 1919), 218 (quote); the remaining quotes are from Verger, *Practical Rules,* 68, 220, 222; and *Chicago Tribune,* January 7, 1898.

49. Verger, *Practical Rules,* 176–77, 182–83, 186.

50. Ibid., 188. See too Archbishop George W. Mundelein to Sister Mary of the Good Shepherd, December 11, 1917, in *Two Crowded Years: Being Selected Addresses, Pastoral, and Letters . . . of the Most Rev. George William Mundelein, D. D., as Archbishop of Chicago* (Chicago: Extension Press, 1918), 342. For a brief discussion of the "double standard" in the nineteenth century, see Estelle B. Freedman, *Their Sisters' Keepers: Women's Prison Reform in America, 1830–1930* (Ann Arbor: University of Michigan Press, 1981), 19–20.

51. Verger, *Practical Rules,* 67 and 68 (quotes). See also Maria Luddy, *Women and Philanthropy in Nineteenth-Century Ireland* (Cambridge: Cambridge University Press, 1995), 124–27; and on conflicts between immigrant daughters and parents, Mary E. Odem, *Delinquent Daughters: Protecting and Policing Adolescent and Female Sexuality in the United States, 1885–1920* (Chapel Hill: University of North Carolina Press, 1995), 157–84.

52. Linehan, *Vicious Circle,* 91. According to Linehan, "three or four brides held their weddings at the refuge each year." On the role of single women in the family, see Janet A. Nolan, *Ourselves Alone: Women's Emigration from Ireland, 1885–1920* (Lexington: University of Kentucky Press, 1989), 70–71 (quote on p. 70); Diner, *Erin's Daughters,* 136–37; and Maureen Fitzgerald, "Irish Catholic Nuns and the Development of New York City's Welfare System, 1840–1900" (Ph.D. diss., University of Wisconsin, 1992), 303–4. These sources also described the generous contributions that Irish working women gave to their parishes and local charities.

53. Jane Barnes, *Irish Industrial Schools, 1868–1908: Origins and Development* (Dublin: Irish Academic Press, 1989), 41–45, 56–57, 89; and Mary Carpenter, *Reformatory School: For the Children of the Perishing and Dangerous Classes and for Juvenile Offenders* (New York: A. M. Kelley, 1969 [orig. 1851]), 80 (quote).

54. Mother Austin Carroll, "Joanna Reddan," *Irish Monthly* 20 (May 1892): 229; Clear, *Nuns in Nineteenth-Century Ireland,* 58–59; Barnes, *Irish Industrial Schools,* 83, 88–99; and Luddy, *Women and Philanthropy,* 122.

55. Arlien Johnson, *Public Policy and Private Charities: A Study of Legislation in the United States and of Administration in Illinois* (Chicago: University of Chicago Press, 1931), 95–96; and James Brown, *The History of Public Assistance in Chicago, 1833 to 1893* (Chicago: University of Chicago Press, 1941), 165–66.

56. Johnson, *Public Policy and Private Charities*, 97 (quote). See too "Act to Aid Industrial School for Girls," *Laws of the State of Illinois: Enacted by the Thirty-First General Assembly* (Springfield, 1879), 309–13.

57. Quotes are from *Chicago Tribune*, May 8, 1879; and "Act to Aid Industrial Schools for Girls," 313. Louise deKoven Bowen is quoted in Anthony M. Platt, *The Child Savers: The Invention of Delinquency* (Chicago: University of Chicago Press, 1977), 91. In 1908 she told probation officers of the Cook County Juvenile Court to "work to save the children, to save the souls of those whom Christ said, 'Of such is the kingdom of Heaven.'" Mary E. Humphrey, ed., *Speeches, Addresses, and Letters of Louise deKoven Bowen: Reflecting Social Movements in Chicago* (Ann Arbor: University of Michigan Press, 1937), 122. See also Sharon Alter, "Bowen, Louise deKoven," in *Women Building Chicago: A Biographical Dictionary, 1790–1990*, ed. Rima Lunin Schultz and Adele Hast (Bloomington: Indiana University Press, 2001), 101–6.

58. *Ninth Biennial Report of the Board of State Commissioners of Public Charities of the State of Illinois for 1886* (Springfield, Ill.: H. W. Rokker, 1887), 52, 75, 79 (quotes); and *Chicago Tribune*, January 29 and February 15, 1887.

59. *Tenth Biennial Report of the Board of State Commissioners of Public Charities of the State of Illinois for 1888* (Springfield, Ill.: Springfield Printing Company, 1888), 82 and 132 (quotes). On the outcome, see *Chicago Tribune*, February 12, 1888.

60. Bliss is quoted in *Chicago Tribune*, September 30, 1899. For ruling, see *Cook County v. Chicago Industrial School for Girls*, 125 Ill. 540 (1888), 191, 193. An "Abstract of Record" and "Transcript" are in the Illinois State Archives, Springfield.

61. *Chicago Tribune*, October 2, 1888, and March 18 and April 1, 1891. See also Platt, *Child Savers*, 116; Johnson, *Public Policy*, 106–9; and Joseph J. Thompson, ed., "Sisters of the Good Shepherd, Chicago Industrial School for Girls," in *The Archdiocese of Chicago: Antecedents and Developments* (Des Plaines, Ill.: St. Mary's Training School Press, 1920), 754. The Chicago Industrial School obtained a contract with the county in 1891 through the efforts of General George W. Smith and Thomas Brenan. Smith had argued the Good Shepherds' case before the Illinois Supreme Court, and Brenan had been a witness. His testimony appears in the "Abstract of Record" cited above.

62. Quotes, except for the last two, are from *Twelfth Biennial Report of the Board of State Commissioners of Public Charities of the State of Illinois for 1892* (Springfield, Ill.: H. W. Rokker, 1893), 181–83; Sanford J. Fox, "Juvenile Justice Reform: An Historical Perspective," *Stanford Law Review* 22 (June 1970): 1230; and "Section 17" of Illinois Juvenile Court Law in T. D. Hurley, *Origin of the Illinois Juvenile Court Law: Juvenile Courts and What They Have Accomplished* (Chicago: Visitation and Aid Society, 1907), 132–33 (quotes). On the Illinois Technical School for Colored Girls, see Chapter 4.

63. Fox, "Juvenile Justice Reform," 1226–29; Hurley, *Illinois Juvenile Court Law*, 13–25; *First Annual Report of the Visitation and Aid Society* (Chicago: Visitation and Aid Society, 1890), 5 (quote); and T. D. Hurley, *New World*, November 26, 1898. Funding for the work of the Visitation and Aid Society came from individual contributions. The two largest and most prominent benefactors were John and Michael Cudahy, millionaire Catholic meatpackers. Interestingly, they

had one sister who entered the Sisters of the Good Shepherd in Milwaukee in 1883 and died there in 1892. Onahan, Brenan, and Copeland were active society members.

64. Hurley, *Illinois Juvenile Court Law*, 9; *New World*, December 14, 1901; Robert M. Mennel, *Thorns and Thistles: Juvenile Delinquents in the United States, 1825–1940* (Hanover, N.H.: University Press of New England, 1973), 132; *Thirty-Second Annual Report of the Board of Inspectors of the House of Correction of the City of Chicago and of the Superintendent, City Physician and House Physician for the Year 1903* (Chicago: John Worthy School Print, 1904), 8; and Johnson, *Public Policy*, 203. Each shelter received twenty-five cents a day, and later forty cents, for minor delinquents committed by the juvenile court.

65. Quotes are from Meredith Tax, *The Rising of the Women: Feminist Solidarity and Class Conflict, 1880–1917* (New York: Monthly Review Press, 1980), 87; and unidentified newspaper clipping, 1894, Thomas J. and Elizabeth Morgan Collection, Book 2 (Scrapbooks), Illinois Historical Survey, University of Illinois, Urbana.

66. Tax, *Rising of the Women*, 66–67, 69 (quotes). See also Ann D. Gordon, "Brown, Corinne Stubbs," and Ralph Scharnau, "Morgan, Elizabeth Chambers," in *Women Building Chicago*, 123–25 and 608–10, respectively.

67. Quotes are from unidentified clipping, c. August or September 1889, Morgan Collection, Book 2. See also *Chicago Tribune*, August 3, 1889. On sectarianism, see three unidentified clippings, May, June, and August 1889, Morgan Collection, Book 2.

68. The sisters' brief version of this incident can be found in Coughlin, *New Commandment*, 102. More detail is in the *Chicago Tribune*, December 17 and 18, 1890. Mother Holy Cross McCabe's statement is in unidentified clipping, January 1891, Morgan Collection, Book 2. Fannie C. Kavanaugh, a convent-educated Toronto native, insisted that the alliance was "not entering into this thing because the House of the Good Shepherd is a Catholic institution." However, Tax noted that the "final episode in the Alliance's demise seems to have been its opposition to Kate Bradley's candidacy for the board of education. . . . [because] she had been reared in a convent." Bradley was also a Canadian and educated by the Ursuline Sisters. See unidentified clipping, *Chicago Times*, 1894, Morgan Collection, Book 2; and Tax, *Rising of the Women*, 87.

69. Quotes are from *Chicago Tribune*, December 17, 1890. Judge Prendergast, a Catholic, was born in Claremorris, County Mayo, Ireland, in 1854; in 1882 he was elected Cook County Judge and retired in 1890. See "Hon. Richard Prendergast," *Bench and Bar of Chicago: Biographical Sketches* (Chicago: American Biographical Publishing Company, n.d.), 605–6; and obituary in *New World*, August 26, 1899.

70. Maureen Fitzgerald has explained the "ethos common to all nuns' charities for women." In short, Catholic sisters generally opposed background investigations. They would not "subject women to the kind of public shaming" from which they sought to protect them. As a consequence, sisters frequently made little or no effort to record family histories. Maureen Fitzgerald, "Losing Their Religion: Women, the State, and the Ascension of Secular Discourse, 1890–1930," in *Women and Twentieth-Century Protestantism*, ed. Margaret Lamberts Bendroth and Virginia Lieson Brereton (Urbana: University of Illinois Press, 2002),

296. See also Dolan, *The Immigrant Church*, 133; Diner, *Erin's Daughters*, 106–7; and Butler, *Daughters of Joy*, 152.

71. Coughlin, *New Commandment*, 102 (quote). The 1891 statistics are from Illinois Conference of Charities and Corrections, *Hand-Book of Chicago's Charities* (Chicago: Edwin M. Colvin, 1892), 80. On the property purchase, see "Loan to the House of the Good Shepherd/Resolution for Members," March 27, 1892 (unpublished, House of the Good Shepherd, Chicago); and *Inter-Ocean*, December 13, 1892.

72. *Chicago Tribune*, December 20, 1896; and *New World*, December 26, 1896. On "redemptive places," see Daphne Spain, *How Women Saved the City* (Minneapolis: University of Minnesota Press, 2001), xii. According to Spain, redemptive places "served as safe sites of support and transition." Biographies of the women in the receiving line can all be found in *Women Building Chicago.*

73. Documents at the House of the Good Shepherd do not indicate the exact number of women and girls cared for by the Sisters of the Good Shepherd during their first fifty years. They believe that they assisted more than eighteen thousand. Coughlin, *New Commandment*, 154. It appears that these nuns influenced for good the lives of thousands. Unlike settlement workers or deaconesses, Catholic sisters did not search for locales in which to focus their work; as consecrated women of the immigrant Catholic Church, their institutions were located in the densely populated urban neighborhoods where most immigrant Catholics lived. They regularly helped those who came to them. Corporal and spiritual works of mercy included feeding the hungry, sheltering the homeless, visiting the sick, instructing the ignorant, admonishing sinners, comforting the afflicted, and praying for the living and dead.

74. On the sale of property and move to new quarters, see *Chicago Record-Herald*, November 26, 1904, and January 12, 1905. On opposition to large institutions, see Gittens, *Poor Relations*, 31–32 (quote on p. 31); and *Fifteenth Biennial Report of the Board of State Commissioners of Public Charities of the State of Illinois for 1898* (Springfield, Ill.: Phillips Brothers, 1899), 66–67 (quote). Maureen Fitzgerald argued that in New York City much of the opposition came from Protestant reformers who had lost control of public welfare to Catholic sisters. See Fitzgerald, "Irish-Catholic Nuns and the Development of New York City's Welfare System," 550–52. Municipal institutions slowly changed their ways of dealing with sexually deviant women. On Cleveland, see Marion J. Morton, "Seduced and Abandoned in an American City: Cleveland and Its Fallen Women, 1869–1936," *Journal of Urban History* 11 (August 1985): 463. In Chicago, Kenneth Cmiel showed that managers of the Chicago Nursery and Half-Orphan Asylum resisted new standards of care advocated by progressive welfare reformers. Asylum managers feared they would lose control of their institution. Cmiel, *A Home of Another Kind*, 53–55, 61–63.

75. Quotes are from William T. Stead, *If Christ Came to Chicago* (Chicago: Laird and Lee, 1893), 412. In hindsight, the challenge was evident by 1894. In a long article on "Work for the Poor," the *Chicago Tribune*, September 16, 1894, lauded Hull-House and other social settlements and made no mention of the Sisters of the Good Shepherd or any other religious community of nuns. Kathryn Kish Sklar, *Florence Kelley and the Nation's Work: The Rise of Women's Political*

Culture, 1830–1900 (New Haven, Conn.: Yale University Press, 1995), 171–205, described life at Hull-House.

76. On the settlement movement and the social gospel, see Louise C. Wade, "The Social Gospel Impulse and the Chicago Settlement-House Founders," *Register* [of the Chicago Theological Seminary] 55 (April 1965): 1–12. For a recent consideration, see several essays in Wendy J. Deichman Edwards and Carolyn De Swarte Gifford, eds., *Gender and the Social Gospel* (Urbana: University of Illinois Press, 2003). See also Victoria Bissell Brown, *The Education of Jane Addams* (Philadelphia: University of Pennsylvania Press, 2003), which examines in detail how Jane Addams struggled to fashion "a democratic, pacifist philosophy that suited her temperament" (p. 10) as she moved from the religious to the secular.

77. The sisters spoke clearly about the purpose of their work: the temporal and spiritual care of "lost sheep." For examples, see Coughlin, *A New Commandment*, 13, 23, 27. Quotes from the provincial superior and Mary McDowell appear respectively in "Book of the Chapter," 45; and Wade, "The Social Gospel Impulse," 7. On Chicago women's vision for their city (livable over profitable), see Maureen Flanagan, *Seeing with Their Hearts: Chicago Women and the Vision of the Good City* (Princeton: Princeton University Press, 2002).

78. Dolan, *American Catholic Experience*, 339–40; Patricia Byrne, CSJ, "Sisters of St. Joseph: The Americanization of a French Tradition," *U.S. Catholic Historian* 5 (Summer/Fall 1986): 271; and Oates, *Catholic Philanthropic Tradition*, 125–26, 132–33. In their 1909 history, the Sisters of the Good Shepherd acknowledged those who supported them; almost all were men. A Woman's Auxiliary was not formed until 1907. See Coughlin, *New Commandment*, 125–35, 162–72. On Catholic sisters' place in the church, see Margaret Susan Thompson, "Women, Feminism, and the New Religious History: Catholic Sisters as a Case Study," in *Belief and Behavior: Essays in the New Religious History* (New Brunswick, N.J.: Rutgers University Press, 1991), 136–63.

79. No nuns (not only the Good Shepherds) were free to challenge the status quo or actively participate in public life. See Oates, *Catholic Philanthropic Tradition*, 86–87; and Carol K. Coburn and Martha Smith, *Spirited Lives: How Nuns Shaped Catholic Culture and American Life, 1836–1920* (Chapel Hill: University of North Carolina Press, 1999), 224–25. By 1900, with the expansion of parish schools, most Catholic sisters were trained for teaching and assigned to classrooms. In 1895 the United States possessed some four thousand Catholic schools, which enrolled 755,038 children (an increase of 50 percent in a decade). See McGreevy, *Catholicism and American Freedom*, 114. See also *The Social Evil in Chicago: A Study of Existing Conditions with Recommendations by the Vice Committee of Chicago* (Chicago: Gunthorp-Warren Printing, 1911); Joanne L. Goodwin, "An American Experiment in Paid Motherhood: The Implementation of Mothers' Pensions in Early Twentieth-Century Chicago," *Gender & History* 4 (Autumn 1992): 323–42; *Chicago Record-Herald*, May 12, 1911; Sophonisba P. Breckinridge, ed., *The Child in the City: A Series of Papers Presented at the Conferences Held During the Chicago Child Welfare Exhibit* (Chicago: Chicago School of Civics and Philanthropy, 1912); and Spain, *How Women Saved the City*, 20–27, 253–54. Although Spain does not include Catholic institutions among her "redemptive places," she should.

Chapter 4: The Good Shepherds and the Illinois Technical School for Colored Girls, 1911–53

1. (Chicago) *New World,* July 30, 1965. For an extended discussion of this incident and others related to it, see Chapter 7.

2. St. Clair Drake and Horace R. Cayton, *Black Metropolis: A Study of Negro Life in a Northern City* (Chicago: University of Chicago Press, 1993 [orig. 1945]), 197–98. Black South Siders did not resent the sisters' presence nor find it unusual.

3. On the Good Shepherds in Chicago before 1911, see Chapter 3. The quote is from "Application for Charter," *Annual Report of the Chicago Industrial School for Girls for Nineteen Hundred and Eight* (Chicago: Clohesey and Company, 1909), 8.

4. From 1879 to 1911, the county paid $10 per month for each girl committed by the court; in 1911 that figure was raised to $15. See Arlien Johnson, *Public Policy and Private Charities: A Study of Legislation in the United States and of Administration in Illinois* (Chicago: University of Chicago Press, 1931), 89.

5. *Twelfth Biennial Report of the Board of State Commissioners of Public Charities of the State of Illinois for 1892* (Springfield, Ill.: H. W. Rokker, 1893), 182–83; and *Twentieth Biennial Report of the Board of State Commissioners of Public Charities . . . for the Period July 1, 1906 to June 30, 1908* (Springfield, Ill.: Illinois State Journal Company, 1909), 239.

6. A Sister of the Good Shepherd, "History of the Illinois Technical School" (unpublished, House of the Good Shepherd, St. Louis). I am grateful to Sister Mary Lourdes Langenfeld for providing me with a complete copy of this manuscript. According to it, the provincial superior decided not to sell the school after "considering how our sisters had labored for it, and [what] the sacrifice of parting with it would cost the Congregation." In the early years, the Cook County Juvenile Court sent a few delinquent girls to the school, but the practice had ended by the 1920s. See also *A School-Home for Girls between the Ages of 6 and 16* (Chicago: Sisters of the Good Shepherd, 1940). A copy is in the House of the Good Shepherd, Chicago. For a history of orphanages in the United States from 1800 to the Great Depression, see Timothy A. Hacsi, *Second Home: Orphan Asylums and Poor Families in America* (Cambridge, Mass.: Harvard University Press, 1997).

7. Allan H. Spear, *Black Chicago: The Making of a Negro Ghetto, 1890–1920* (Chicago: University of Chicago Press, 1967), 21–23.

8. Quotes are from "History of the Illinois Technical School"; and James R. Grossman, *Land of Hope: Chicago, Black Southerners, and the Great Migration* (Chicago: University of Chicago Press, 1989), 171. For more on Chicago's segregated social services and the city's reformers, see Thomas Lee Philpott, *The Slum and the Ghetto: Neighborhood Deterioration and Middle-Class Reform, Chicago, 1880–1930* (New York: Oxford University Press, 1978), 293–301, 323–41.

9. Quotes are from "History of the Illinois Technical School." On the issue of race, the Sisters of the Good Shepherd were religiously motivated. They saw Christ as the Good Shepherd and believed that "'there shall be one fold and one Shepherd.' Yes, this was the message—the poor little black lambs must not be excluded, for Christ died for all." See "Chicago (Illinois Technical School for Colored Girls)," *Bulletin of the Congregation of the Good Shepherd of Angers* 21 (February 1913): 42. For a brief history of the Illinois Division of Visitation,

see Charles Virden, "Division of Visitation of Children," *Institutional Quarterly* 12/13 (1921–22): 43–49.

10. *Chicago Defender,* November 30, 1912. For Pinckney's career, see Frank T. Flynn, "Judge Merritt W. Pinckney and the Early Days of the Juvenile Court in Chicago," *Social Science Review* 28 (March 1954): 20–30; David Spinoza Tanenhaus, "Policing the Child: Juvenile Justice in Chicago, 1870–1925" (Ph.D. diss., University of Chicago, 1997). On Pinckney's "close relations with the Chicago Woman's Club, settlements, and charities," see Joanne L. Goodwin, *Gender and the Politics of Welfare Reform: Mothers' Pensions in Chicago, 1911–1929* (Chicago: University of Chicago Press, 1997), 120.

11. "History of the Illinois Technical School." Mair's letter (undated) is quoted in this manuscript. He was a broker whose office was located in downtown Chicago; he lived at 500 North State Street. In 1893, Mair had arranged for the Little Company of Mary Sisters to come to Chicago from Rome, where they had nursed his dying wife. At his death, he left $5,000 to the Good Shepherds. See *Chicago Tribune,* March 3, 1915; John W. Leonard, ed., *The Book of Chicagoans* (Chicago: A. N. Marquis and Company, 1905), 389; *New World,* October 19, 1895; and Joseph J. Thompson, ed., *The Archdiocese of Chicago: Antecedents and Development* (Des Plaines, Ill.: St. Mary's Training School Press, 1920), 756.

12. Quotes are from "History of the Illinois Technical School." Biographical sketches of Patrick J. O'Keeffe are in Charles French, ed., *Biographical History of the American Irish in Chicago* (Chicago: American Biographical Publishing Company, 1897), 298–303; and in "Family Record," biographical folders, Chicago Historical Society. O'Keeffe married Isabelle Cecilia Kelly, also a board member of the Chicago Industrial School for Girls. A former teacher and journalist, she was the first Catholic woman appointed to the Chicago Board of Education in 1898.

13. Christopher Robert Reed, *The Chicago NAACP and the Rise of Black Professional Leadership, 1910–1916* (Bloomington: Indiana University Press, 1997), 38. For Brown's assistance to Woolley, see *Chicago Defender,* March 16, 1918. Brown believed that education could lift up "a people oppressed and persecuted . . . to equality and eminence." For his impressions of Washington and the Tuskegee students, see "Remarks of E. O. B. at Memorial Meeting for Booker T. Washington [1915]," Edward Eagle Brown Family Papers, Newberry Library, Chicago. Brown was married to Helen Eagle Brown, who was active in Catholic women's organizations and a board member of the Chicago Industrial School for Girls. The Browns lived first on Burton Place near Lincoln Park, then later on North State Street. See also Walter Nugent, "A Catholic Progressive? The Case of Judge E. O. Brown," *Journal of the Gilded Age and Progressive Era* 2 (January 2003): 5–47; and Koby Lee-Forman, "Woolley, Celia Anna Parker," in *Women Building Chicago, 1790–1990,* ed. Rima Lunin Schultz and Adele Hast (Bloomington: Indiana University Press, 2001), 993–95.

14. "History of the Illinois Technical School." During that transitional period, the archbishop denied the Good Shepherds three bequests left to the "Chicago Industrial School for Girls," which he had moved to Des Plaines. Even though the nuns requested them, the archbishop "did not feel inclined to allow them to come to us."

15. Ibid.

16. Ibid.

17. *Chicago Tribune,* March 16, 1912; Richard R. Wright Jr., ed. *Centennial Encyclopaedia of the African Methodist Episcopal Church . . .* (Philadelphia: Book Concern of the A.M.E. Church, 1916), 129–30.

18. *Chicago Tribune,* March 16, 1912.

19. Quoted in "History of the Illinois Technical School."

20. Ibid. According to the Good Shepherds, their "staunchest friends" in this "hour of need" were "notably Mr. Charles Virden and Mr. Thomas O'Connor . . . who, recognizing the good work done during the 'Chicago Industrial School' career, carried us through the battle unscathed." The sisters were also grateful to two others: "The Honorable Denis E. Sullivan proved his friendship and appreciation by his valuable legal advice gratuitously given [and] Judge Merritt W. Pinckney of the Juvenile Court was another strong advocate of our cause." See "Chicago (Illinois Technical School for Colored Girls)," *Bulletin of the Congregation,* 43. Virden was Episcopalian; O'Connor and Sullivan, Catholic; and Pinckney, Unitarian.

21. Quote is from Hacsi, *Second Home,* 2. See Table 1.3 (p. 53) for number of orphanages in 1910.

22. Quotes are from Hacsi, *Second Home,* 56, 65; and Michael B. Katz, *In the Shadow of the Poorhouse: A Social History of Welfare in America* (New York: Basic Books, 1986), 61. For the importance of Catholic institutions and the contributions of nuns, see Mary J. Oates, *The Catholic Philanthropic Tradition in America* (Bloomington: Indiana University Press, 1995); Dorothy M. Brown and Elizabeth McKeown, *The Past Belongs to Us: Catholic Charities and American Welfare* (Cambridge, Mass.: Harvard University Press, 1997); and Maureen Fitzgerald, "Irish-Catholic Nuns and the Development of New York City's Welfare System, 1840–1900" (Ph.D. diss., University of Wisconsin–Madison, 1992).

23. Hacsi, *Second Home,* 122; Clare L. McCausland, *Children of Circumstance: A History of the First 125 Years (1894–1974) of Chicago Child Care Society* (Chicago: Chicago Child Care Society, 1976), 97–99; Kenneth Cmiel, *A Home of Another Kind: One Chicago Orphanage and the Tangle of Child Welfare* (Chicago: University of Chicago Press, 1995), 126–27; and *Chicago Defender,* August 16, 1913.

24. *Chicago Defender,* August 16, 1913.

25. [Chicago] *Broad Ax,* March 6, 1915. Smith died in Florida, but her body was returned and buried in Hazelwood Cemetery in Harvey. See also David C. Bartlett and Larry A. McClellan, "The Final Ministry of Amanda Berry Smith: An Orphanage in Harvey, Illinois, 1895–1918," *Illinois Heritage* 1 (Winter 1998): 20–25; Wanda A. Hendricks, *Gender, Race, and Politics in the Midwest: Black Club Women in Illinois* (Bloomington: Indiana University Press, 1998), 45–46; and Anne Meis Knupfer, *Toward a Tenderer Humanity and a Nobler Womanhood: African American Women's Clubs in Turn-of-the-Century Chicago* (New York: New York University Press, 1996), 76–81.

26. Charles Virden, "Inspection of Institutions: Amanda Smith Industrial School for Girls," in State of Illinois Board of Administration, *Sixth Annual Report; Seventh Annual Report* (Springfield, Ill.: Illinois State Journal Company, 1917), 145. See also *Broad Ax,* July 26, 1913. Earlier it was known as the "Louise Juvenile Home" and, until the post–World War I years, it was located on the periphery of a black residential area. Two Illinois statutes (1879 and 1883) allowed the state

to subsidize industrial schools, but funds were disbursed only for children committed by the court.

27. Julius Taylor, editor of the *Broad Ax*, was an enthusiastic supporter of McDonald and printed many of her annual reports. See *Broad Ax*, December 31, 1904; October 5, 1907; January 2, 1909; and January 4, 1913. See also Knupfer, *Toward a Tenderer Humanity*, 71–76; and Sandra M. Stehno, "Foster Care for Dependent Black Children in Chicago, 1899–1934" (Ph.D. diss., University of Chicago, 1985), 40–41.

28. Bartlett and McClellan, "Final Ministry of Amanda Berry Smith," 25; "Resolution [on McDonald's leave]," October 13, 1920, folder 4, box 33; and Charles Virden, "Condensed report of the Amanda Smith Industrial School for Girls," June 18, 1915 (quotes), folder 3, box 37, both in Julius Rosenwald Papers, Department of Special Collections, University of Chicago Library. For the efforts of women's clubs, see Knupfer, *Toward a Tenderer Humanity*, 80.

29. For a fuller discussion of those school closings, see Stehno, "Foster Care for Dependent Black Children," 77–93 (quote). Stehno states that Edith Abbott and Sophonisba P. Breckinridge, prominent social welfare leaders in Chicago, believed strongly that "the preferred method of care should be placing out in family homes" and that "whites should be in control" because African Americans had problems raising money. Stehno also notes that Abbott's "home-finding program appears to be a segregated one." See pages 70 and 71. For criticisms of large institutions, see Hacsi, *Second Home*, 68 (quote).

30. Charlotte Ashby Crawley, "Dependent Negro Children in Chicago in 1926" (master's thesis, University of Chicago, 1927), 90 (quotes); "Classification of Chicago Social Agencies," 1930, folder 1, box 145, Welfare Council of Metropolitan Chicago Papers, Chicago Historical Society. See also "Financial and Statistical Summaries of the Catholic Dependent Institutions of the Archdiocese of Chicago, Illinois, for the Fiscal Year Ending December 31, 1921," Madaj Collection, Joseph Cardinal Bernardin Archives and Records Center of the Archdiocese of Chicago; Valeria D. McDermott and Annie Elizabeth Trotter, *Chicago Social Service Directory*, 2nd ed. (Chicago: John C. Burmeister Printing Company, 1918), 49; and *Chicago Defender*, October 21, 1939. On Catholic sisters as an efficient and trained workforce, see Oates, *Catholic Philanthropic Tradition*, 28–29; and Hacsi, *Second Home*, 90.

31. Marie Davis, pastoral assistant at St. Ailbe's Catholic Church, Chicago, is the daughter of a woman who attended the Illinois Technical School. Davis remembers the Good Shepherd Sisters as both "nurturing" and "flexible." After her mother graduated, married, and had children, she often visited the nuns and assisted them by taking students on outings. Young Marie always joined in. She also spent nights and a few weekends in the sisters' care when her parents went away. Interview with Marie Davis, June 3, 1999, Chicago. On the "proliferation of schools, hospitals, and orphanages" that "boggles the contemporary mind," see Carol K. Coburn and Martha Smith, *Spirited Lives: How Nuns Shaped Catholic Culture and American Life, 1836–1920* (Chapel Hill: University of North Carolina Press, 1999), 2. Maureen Fitzgerald argues that in New York City, anti-Catholicism contributed to Protestant reformers' critique of institutional care. See Fitzgerald, "Irish-Catholic Nuns and the Development of New York City's Welfare System," 550–52. For the anti-Catholicism of Charles Loring Brace, the "most outspoken critic of orphan asylums," see Hacsi, *Second Home*, 159. It is

not clear how anti-Catholicism entered into the Chicago debate. For quote, see *A School-Home for Girls*.

32. Coburn and Smith, *Spirited Lives*, 75; and Hacsi, *Second Home*, 143 and 194.

33. "Documents: Additional Letters of Negro Migrants of 1916–1918," *Journal of Negro History* 4 (July 1919): 432. On the African American migration to Chicago during World War I and the importance of education, see Grossman, *Land of Hope*, 246–58.

34. Interview with Mary Louise Higgins Mims and Marguerite (Margo) Anderson Butler, Evanston, Illinois, January 12, 2001.

35. For the curriculum, see Thompson, *Archdiocese of Chicago*, 757. All boarders said grace before meals and attended Mass as well as occasional devotions. Some who were not Catholics became Catholics. There were 119 baptisms out of a total 1,179 pupils between 1911 and 1920. See also *A School-Home for Girls*.

36. I am indebted to Margo Butler for her memories of student life at the Illinois Technical School. On music, dance, cooking, and sewing, see *New World*, April 21, 1939; and on the home-based occupations of seamstresses, see Eileen Boris, "Black Women and Paid Labor in the Home: Industrial Homework in Chicago in the 1920s," in *Homework: Historical and Contemporary Perspectives on Paid Labor at Home*, ed. Eileen Boris and Cynthia R. Daniels (Urbana: University of Illinois Press, 1989), 39–46. The final quote is in Patrick H. O'Donnell [lawyer] to J. D. Watts [executive secretary of Catholic Charities in Chicago], May 28, 1925, Madaj Collection, Bernardin Archives.

37. *A School-Home for Girls*; O'Donnell to Watts, May 28, 1925 (quote); Hacsi, *Second Home*, 180–84, 196–212; and Butler interview.

38. The Good Shepherds kept their boarding school in Chicago, although progressives thought that "moving out of the city was easily one more way to cut the children off from the physical and moral dangers of Chicago." See Cmiel, *A Home of Another Kind*, 67–68. In 1913 the sisters enclosed their acreage with a higher and sturdier fence. Their friend P. J. O'Keeffe raised the funds, to which philanthropist Julius Rosenwald contributed $250 because "of the splendid work that this Institution is doing for the colored people." Julius Rosenwald to P. J. O'Keeffe, March 27, 1913, folder 10, box 13, Rosenwald Papers. On outdoor games and softball teams, see *New World*, April 21, 1939 (quote). On scouting and special occasions, see *A School-Home for Girls*; and unpublished Christmas letters of the Sisters of the Good Shepherd, 1939 and 1941, House of the Good Shepherd, Chicago. In 1943 and 1944, Catholic Girl Scouts held retreats, sponsored by the archdiocesan Council of Catholic Women, at the Illinois Technical School. They were for black troops only. In 1944, white troops met at Barat College in Lake Forest and Our Lady of Bethlehem Academy in La Grange. See "C. C. W. Plans Four Retreats For Teenagers," newspaper clipping, June 3, 1944, folder 9, box 28, Daniel M. Cantwell Papers, Chicago Historical Society. There were few, if any, racially integrated scout troops in the United States before World War II.

39. *New World*, September 24, 1915. Quotes are from an unpublished Christmas letter, 1919, from the Sisters of the Good Shepherd, copy in the House of the Good Shepherd, Chicago.

40. On the engraving, see *New World*, September 24, 1915. See also the sisters' annual Christmas letters. In 1940, for example, their Christmas letter described their students' exhibit at the American Negro Exposition and commented that

"the visitors wanted affidavits that the children of those ages [six to eight years] had produced the work displayed." They noted too: "Very satisfying progress was also made in the cooking classes." In the 1942 Christmas letter, the nuns recorded in detail the success of a former student who "is now a reporter on a colored journal." Former student Margo Butler recalled how important the Regal Theatre was to her general education. During eight years at the school, she believes, she "saw and heard nearly every black musician." Had she gone to school in Evanston (her birthplace), she would not have been so fortunate. She feels the same way about the Billiken parades, sponsored each year by the *Chicago Defender.*

41. Vincent W. Cooke to Mother Mary of the Good Shepherd Caverly, December 19, 1952, House of the Good Shepherd, Chicago. Because the archdiocese had invested "$120,625.00 for ordinary and extraordinary repairs" during the previous decades, Cooke suggested that the Good Shepherds "give this property to his Eminence." That they did, so the Catholic Church would not "suffer a severe setback" among African Americans. The sisters also appreciated Catholic Charities' annual contributions.

42. On the "Expansion of the Black Belt," see Drake and Cayton, *Black Metropolis,* 63. During 1951–52, there were fifty-eight boarders; in September 1952, only forty-three. Quotes appear in two letters from Mother Mary of St. Urban Hanly to Mother Superior General, October 16, 1952, and undated (c. spring 1953). Both can be found in the House of the Good Shepherd, Chicago.

43. The Sisters of the Good Shepherd were not the only nuns who linked their lives to African Americans in Chicago before the 1960s, as the following chapters attest. Equally important were the Sisters of the Blessed Sacrament, the Franciscan Sisters of Dubuque, the Sisters of the Holy Family of Nazareth, the Loretto Sisters (IBVM), the School Sisters of St. Francis, the Daughters of Charity, and others. Discussions with historian James O'Toole helped me understand how religious vocation and dress assisted individuals in creating intermediate or alternative identities that escaped the polarities of black or white. See James O'Toole, *Passing for White: Race, Religion, and the Healy Family* (Amherst: University of Massachusetts Press, 2002); and Elizabeth Kuhns, *The Habit: A History of the Clothing of Catholic Nuns* (New York: Doubleday, 2003). Clearly, more research needs to be done on the role of dress in the lives of Catholic sisters, since the habit continues to cause heated debate. See also Cheryl L. Reed, *Unveiled: The Hidden Lives of Nuns* (New York: Berkley Books, 2004), 53–54.

Chapter 5: Missionary Sisters in Black Belt Neighborhoods

1. Mary Peter Traxler, SSND, "The New Nun—Ministry of Presence," *Community* 26 (February 1967): 6. For more on the "ministry of presence" in Chicago, see Chapters 6 and 7.

2. The most complete history of the Sisters of the Blessed Sacrament is Patricia Lynch, SBS, *Sharing the Bread in Service: Sisters of the Blessed Sacrament, 1891–1991* (Bensalem, Pa.: Sisters of the Blessed Sacrament, 1998). On the Catholic Church and African Americans, see Cyprian Davis, OSB, *The History of Black Catholics in the United States* (New York: Crossroad, 1995).

3. On Drexel's ancestry, see Consuela Marie Duffy, SBS, *Katharine Drexel: A Biography* (Bensalem, Pa.: Mother Katharine Drexel Guild, 1987), 23; and Dolores

Letterhouse, SBS, *The Francis A. Drexel Family* (Cornwell Heights, Pa.: Sisters of the Blessed Sacrament, 1939), 9–10. There is no evidence that the Drexels were abolitionists. Probably they were not; the Protestant character of the movement would have excluded them. But Mother Katharine and her community were not without forerunners; they resembled the ordinary northern women who fought to abolish slavery and became teachers in the South after the Civil War. On anti-Catholicism in the anti-slavery movement, see John T. McGreevy, *Catholicism and American Freedom: A History* (New York: W. W. Norton, 2003), 56–60; on women abolitionists, see Julie Roy Jeffrey, *The Great Silent Army of Abolitionism: Ordinary Women in the Antislavery Movement* (Chapel Hill: University of North Carolina Press, 1998).

4. Quote is from Paulist Walter Elliott to Sister Camper, August 15, 1894, box 2, Walter Elliott Papers, Paulist Archives, Washington, D.C. On Drexel's inheritance, see Mary J. Oates, "Mother Mary Katharine Drexel," in *Women Educators in the United States, 1820–1993: A Bio-bibliographical Sourcebook*, ed. Maxine Schwartz Seller (Westport, Conn.: Greenwood Press, 1994), 207–17.

5. On Tolton's fund-raising, see [St. Paul] *Appeal*, November 9, 1889; *Chicago Evening Journal*, May 17, 1890; and *Chicago Times*, December 1, 1890. Quotes are from Augustus Tolton to Katharine Drexel, September 30, 1890, and June 5, 1891, Sisters of the Blessed Sacrament (SBS) Archives, Bensalem, Pennsylvania.

6. Lynch, *Sharing the Bread*, 160–66; and Vincent I. Murphy, "A Local Mission Field," [Chicago] *New World*, March 6, 1938 (quote).

7. On population changes, see Allan H. Spear, *Black Chicago: The Making of a Negro Ghetto, 1890–1920* (Chicago: University of Chicago Press, 1967), 16–20. Because of the increase in student enrollment, the sisters also employed two lay teachers. See "Annual Parish Reports: St. Elizabeth," 1925, Joseph Cardinal Bernardin Archives and Record Center of the Archdiocese of Chicago. In 1924, St Monica's parishioners "inherited" St. Elizabeth's, a large church-school complex at Forty-first and Wabash. Whites had moved away following the first wave of the Great Migration.

8. Quotes are from *Three Catholic Afro-American Congresses* (New York: Arno Press, 1978 [orig. 1893]), 69, 140.

9. Drexel had hoped to interest wealthy Catholics in the work of her community, but she was not successful. Threats of violence scared away the few who expressed interest. Because of the strong prejudice and hostility aimed at African Americans, she was persuaded that her new enterprise would not succeed if she attempted to attract black and white women at the same time. Equally important was the existence of two black orders, the Oblate Sisters of Providence in Baltimore and the Sisters of the Holy Family in New Orleans. Both were as much in need of recruits as Mother Katharine. She decided never to compete with them; thus she directed African American women to them and assisted them financially. And, in the Jim Crow South, where the Blessed Sacrament Sisters initially intended to concentrate their efforts, laws and customs prohibited people of different races living under the same roof. See Lynch, *Sharing the Bread*, 40; Duffy, *Katharine Drexel*, 178–79. See also the explanation of Sister Juliana Haynes, the first black president of the community, in Lou Baldwin, *A Call to Sanctity: The Formation and Life of Mother Katharine Drexel* (Philadelphia: Catholic Standard and Times, 1987), 94. On the Jim Crow South, see Howard N. Rabinowitz, *Race*

Relations in the Urban South, 1865–1890 (New York: Oxford University Press, 1978), 330–34.

10. Lynch, *Sharing the Bread*, 56–63. Biographical data on the first sisters assigned to St. Monica's exists in the SBS Archives. Five of the six were Irish or Irish American; Sister Scholastica Borger was the daughter of German-born parents. On the sisters' education, see Sisters of the Blessed Sacrament, "Annals," 15:271–73, SBS Archives; Lynch, *Sharing the Bread*, 270–71; Oates, "Mother Mary Katharine Drexel," 215; and Edward D. McDonald and Edward M. Hinton, *Drexel Institute of Technology, 1891–1941* (Philadelphia: Haddon Craftsman, 1942), 187–91. After 1911, many Blessed Sacrament Sisters took courses at Catholic University in Washington, D.C. See also Mathilde L. Coffey, "Service and Sacrifice," *Mission Fields at Home* 1 (March 1929): 99–101.

11. Responses to the questionnaires are in the files of women who joined the community in the early years (all in SBS Archives). The last quote is from *Reflections on Religious Life Found in the Writings of Mother M. Katharine Drexel, Foundress of the Sisters of the Blessed Sacrament* (Cornwell Heights, Pa.: Sisters of the Blessed Sacrament, 1983), 36.

12. Katy Kiniry to Mother Katharine Drexel, May 14 and May 27, 1891, SBS Archives. From 1899 to 1912, Sister Paul of the Cross Kiniry taught at St. Francis de Sales in Rock Castle, Virginia. She remained in Chicago until 1915, when she became the first superior of Xavier College in New Orleans; in 1921 she was transferred to St. Mark's parish in New York City, where she died on February 16, 1927.

13. On commitment to Christian education, see Duffy, *Katharine Drexel*, 334. Like other nuns, the Blessed Sacrament Sisters learned the importance of humility and detachment from worldly goods and public notice. But, because of the nature of their apostolate, they felt they had additional reasons for not drawing attention to themselves. See Carol K. Coburn and Martha Smith, *Spirited Lives: How Nuns Shaped Catholic Culture and American Life, 1836–1920* (Chapel Hill: University of North Carolina Press, 1999), 80–81; and Baldwin, *St. Katharine*, 153–54. On Abbott, see Wallace Best, "The *Chicago Defender* and the Realignment of Black Chicago," *Chicago History* 24 (Fall 1995): 4–21.

14. *Chicago Defender*, March 8 and April 5, 1913. Although the *Defender* criticized St. Monica's, the newspaper promoted pride in Chicago's new YMCA branch—built explicitly for African Americans—and praised its white benefactors. See *Chicago Defender*, June 21, 1913; and James R. Grossman, *Land of Hope: Chicago, Black Southerners, and the Great Migration* (Chicago: University of Chicago Press, 1989), 141. See too Sister Paul of the Cross Kiniry to Mother Katharine Drexel, c. spring 1913, SBS Archives.

15. On the influence of churches in black neighborhoods, see Drake and Cayton, *Black Metropolis*, 398. There is no indication that Hull-House residents (or most settlers elsewhere) wished to live and work in African American neighborhoods or publicly confront racial prejudice. See, for example, Mina Carson, *Settlement Folk: Social Thought and the American Settlement Movement, 1885–1930* (Chicago: University of Chicago Press, 1995). She states that "though several of the white founders of the NAACP had settlement connections, institutionally the settlements failed to make any significant contribution to white Americans' consciousness of racism or to furthering black people's rights and opportunities" (p.

195). On Hull-House, see Thomas A. Guglielmo, "Encountering the Color Line in the Everyday: Italians in Interwar Chicago," *Journal of American Ethnic History* 23 (Summer 2004): 52.

16. *Chicago Defender,* August 4, 1917.

17. As the previous essay indicates, the Sisters of the Good Shepherd opened the Illinois Technical School for Colored Girls on the South Side in 1911. They should not be forgotten, but they did not consider themselves missionaries. Still, they were very much a presence in Chicago's expanding Black Belt.

18. For a history of the community, including its German origins, see Sister Mary Eunice Mousel, OSF, *They Have Taken Root: The Sisters of the Third Order of St. Francis of the Holy Family* (New York: Bookman Associates, 1954). Biographical data on the nuns assigned to Corpus Christi and elsewhere exists in the Sisters of St. Francis (SSF) Archives, Dubuque, Iowa. See also A Sister of St. Francis, *Mother Mary Dominica: A Biography of Venerable Mother Mary Dominica Wieneke, Superior General* (Dubuque, Iowa: Sisters of St. Francis, 1931). Quotes are from Nicholas Christoffel, OFM, to Mother Theodore Ruppert, OSF, October 25, 1932, SSF Archives.

19. See Mousel, *They Have Taken Root,* 247, 250–51. The Dubuque Franciscans joined the Franciscan priests from St. Louis in Chowtsun in 1931, two years before opening the Chicago mission. On the overlapping of "race" and "ethnicity," see John T. McGreevy, *Parish Boundaries: The Catholic Encounter with Race in the Twentieth Century Urban North* (Chicago: University of Chicago Press, 1996), 30. See also "[Franciscan] Volunteers for Corpus Christi, Chicago," SSF Archives.

20. Quotes are from Jay P. Dolan, *The American Catholic Experience: A History from Colonial Times to the Present* (New York: Doubleday and Company, 1985), 365. See too Timothy B. Neary, "Black-Belt Catholic Space: African-American Parishes in Interwar Chicago," *U.S. Catholic Historian* 18 (Fall 2000): 76–91.

21. On the education of settlement workers, for example, see Brown, *Education of Jane Addams.* The quote is from Mary E. Best, *Seventy Septembers* (Techny, Ill.: Holy Spirit Missionary Sisters, 1988), 138.

22. On the history of Holy Family parish, see Harry C. Koenig, STD, ed., *A History of the Parishes of the Archdiocese of Chicago* (Chicago: Archdiocese of Chicago, 1980), 1:367–82; and Ellen Skerrett, "The Irish of Chicago's Hull-House Neighborhood," in *New Perspectives on the Irish Diaspora,* ed. Charles Fanning (Carbondale: Southern Illinois University Press, 2000), 189–222. See also Raymond B. Walsh, SJ, to Mother Regina Wentowska, October 4, 1932, Sisters of the Holy Family of Nazareth (SHFN) Archives, Des Plaines, Illinois. Arnold J. Garvy, SJ, had been on the faculty at St. Louis University and St. Ignatius College (now Loyola University Chicago) before agreeing to take on St. Joseph's Mission at age sixty-five. He remained there until 1942 and cultivated an interest in black literature and history. He also kept a diary that is now in the Midwest Jesuit Archives, St. Louis, Missouri. On the Sisters of the Holy Family, he wrote on June 11, 1938: "for the princely sum of $35.00 per month for 10 months annually . . . they have carried on and transformed the moral and civic condition of the neighborhood. (Hull House cannot boast the same; and the city of Chicago owes these Sisters and the school an unpaid, unrequited, unrecognized debt.) No longer are police cars seen two and three times a day cruising about the area. . . . There is not more crime than on the Gold Coast."

23. M. DeChantal, CSFN, *Out of Nazareth: A Centenary of the Sisters of the Holy Family of Nazareth in the Service of the Church* (New York: Exposition Press, 1974), 190–97; and Koenig, *History of the Parishes*, 1:378–82. Quotes are from the Provincial Council "Minutes," November 23, 1932, SHFN Archives.

24. See Kathryn Kish Sklar, "Hull House in the 1890s: A Community of Women Reformers," *Signs* 10 (Summer 1985): 663. According to Sklar, the Hull-House women were motivated by politics, not religion: "In, but not of, the Social Gospel movement, the women at Hull House were a political boat on a religious stream." For a more recent look at women in the Social Gospel movement, see Wendy J. Deichmann Edwards and Carolyn De Swarte Gifford, eds., *Gender and the Social Gospel* (Urbana: University of Illinois Press, 2003). Jane Addams was not interested in the work of missionaries, which attracted a number of college-educated Protestant women of her time. And, when Addams spoke to Chicagoans of her plans to open a settlement, she "made no appeals to Christian duty, extolled none of the virtues of self-sacrifice. . . . She focused instead on the need among individual women of her class and education to find useful outlets for their energies and their intellectual training." Brown, *Education of Jane Addams*, 213. Finally, see Elisabeth Lasch-Quinn, *Black Neighbors: Race and the Limits of Reform in the American Settlement House Movement, 1890–1945* (Chapel Hill: University of North Carolina Press, 1993), 47–74, who shows that settlements, particularly in the South, that were religious were more successful in reaching out to and helping black families.

25. Preceding chapters in this book offer explanations and examples of this phenomenon.

26. On the missionary vocation as special, even heroic, see Angelyn Dries, OSF, *The Missionary Movement in American Catholic History* (Maryknoll, N.Y.: Orbis Books, 1998), 254–56. On lack of status for Catholic missionary-sisters, foreign or domestic, compared to priests, see Dana L. Robert, *American Women in Mission: A Social History of Their Thought and Practice* (Macon, Ga.: Mercer University Press, 1997). Despite nuns' important work among women and children, it was always "considered auxiliary to the primary missionary task of church planting, the prerogative of the male hierarchy and men's missionary orders" (p. 322). The quote in the text is from questionnaires of applicants to the Sisters of the Blessed Sacrament; copies in SBS Archives.

27. In a short autobiographical sketch written in the early 1940s, Sister Brendan (Augusta) O'Brien recalled the reaction of her aunt when she heard of her niece's plans to enter the Sisters of the Blessed Sacrament. Mother Katharine recruited her in Ireland; she taught in Chicago from 1922 to 1925. The second quote is from Dorothy C. Lichty to Mother Katharine Drexel, July 13, 1915, SBS Archives. She entered in August 1915 (became Sister Dorothea) and also taught in Chicago from 1922 to 1925. Interview with Sister Norma (Alma) Drexler, October 20, 1997, Dubuque, Iowa. She taught at Corpus Christi from 1933 to 1953. In a small notebook, she kept the names of her pupils (nearly two thousand) during those twenty years. Copy of notebook is in SSF Archives.

28. Quotes are from Drake and Cayton, *Black Metropolis*, 413–15; and Michael W. Homel, *Down from Equality: Black Chicagoans and the Public Schools, 1920–41* (Urbana: University of Illinois Press, 1984), 108–9. The Blessed Sacrament Sisters believed the "aim of education" was to help students "to lead a life of usefulness" and "to discharge [one's] duties as a good citizen on earth in prepara-

tion [for] heavenly citizenship." Dolores Letterhouse, SBS, "Why Negro Educa-tion," *Mission Fields at Home* 3 (December 1930): 39. See also Joseph J. McCar-thy, "History of Black Education in Chicago, 1871–1971" (Ph.D. diss., Loyola University, 1973), 100–101. He contends that the sisters taught children—not black children—how to learn and that the nuns' attitudes were the decisive fac-tor. They "empathized with their pupils, families, and community," and their approach was one of "consistency."

29. P. J. Wendl, SVD, "The Negro Missions of the Society of the Divine Word," *Missionary* 29 (October 1916): 568–72; Harold M. Kingsley, "The Negro Goes to Church," *Opportunity* 7 (March 1929): 91; and Joseph Eckert, SVD, "Mission Work among the Negroes of Chicago, *Our Missions* 8 (August 1925): 150–54. Quotes are from Rosemary L. Bray, *Unafraid of the Dark: A Memoir* (New York: Random House, 1998), 26, 31.

30. Quotes are from Joseph F. Eckert to Katharine Drexel, June 20, 1920, August 1920, April 8, 1930, and May 24, 1934, SBS Archives; and interview with Sister Janvier Williams, December 17, 2001, Oak Lawn, Illinois. The Blessed Sacrament Sisters did not believe that sister-teachers were superior to lay teachers. Early on, they recognized the value of black lay teachers in their schools and welcomed them. Although the hierarchy tended to see lay faculty "an expedient," these nuns saw them as "a desirable commodity." See McCarthy, "History of Black Education," 102–3. From its beginning, Xavier University in New Orleans, which was founded by Katharine Drexel, trained large numbers of African Americans to teach in rural Catholic schools in the South.

31. On the practice of home visiting, see "Annals," St. Monica's, Chicago, 1912–1922, SBS Archives; and Dorothy Ann Blatnica, VSC, *"At the Altar of Their God": African American Catholics in Cleveland, 1922–1961* (New York: Garland Publishing, 1995), 63, 108–10. See also Lynch, *Sharing the Bread,* 161–62. I have not found mention in any public documents of visits to Provident Hospital, but I have located numerous references in material kept by the sisters. For example, a note of June 1914 thanked the nuns for their "interest towards Mr. Walter Hall during his long siege of illness" at Provident. Mr. and Mrs. J. H. DeBruhl to Sister Mary Emmanuel [Mohan] and Sisters, June 19, 1914, SBS Archives. Interviews with Gwen Smith and Warner Saunders, August 1 and August 24, 2001, respec-tively, Chicago.

32. *Chicago Defender,* October 11, 1941; William B. Faherty and Madeline Oli-ver, "Sister Claude, O. S. P. (Barbara Hudlin)," in *The Religious Roots of Black Catholics of St. Louis* (St Louis: St. Stanislaus Historic Museum, 1977), 70–76; and Josephine Lockhart, "The Hudlin Family," *Proud* 7 (Fall 1976): 28–32. Besides Sister Claude Hudlin, there were Sisters Juliana Brent, Anthony Garnier, Providen-tia Pollard, and Clotilde Smith. See also Clarence J. Howard, SVD, "The Colored Sisters Come to Town," *St. Augustine's Messenger* 20 (July 1941): 2–5 (quote); and *Chicago Tribune,* July 27, 2002.

33. For a history of the Oblates and a perceptive analysis of race and religion in antebellum America, see Diane Batts Morrow, *Persons of Color and Religious at the Same Time: The Oblate Sisters of Providence, 1828–1860* (Chapel Hill: University of North Carolina Press, 2002). On the Sisters of the Holy Family, see Virginia Meacham Gould and Charles E. Nolan, eds., *No Cross, No Crown [an account by Sister Bernard Deggs]: Black Nuns in Nineteenth-Century New Orleans* (Bloomington: Indiana University Press, 2001); and Tracy Fessenden,

"The Sisters of the Holy Family and the Veil of Race," *Religion and American Culture* 10 (Summer 2000): 187–224. Quotes are from an interview with Lucy Williams, OSF, June 7, 2000, Merrillville, Indiana.

34. Edward Marciniak, "Catholic-Negro Relations . . . in Chicago," *Opportunity* 25 (Summer 1947): 140–41; and Timothy B. Neary, "Crossing Parochial Boundaries: Interracialism in Chicago's Catholic Youth Organization, 1930–1954," *American Catholic Studies* 114 (Fall 2003): 23–37. Also influential were George H. Dunne, SJ, "The Sin of Segregation," *Commonweal*, September 21, 1945, pp. 542–45; and Sister Mary Ellen O'Hanlon, OP, *Racial Myths* (River Forest, Ill.: Rosary College, 1946). The latter is a small booklet familiar to Friendship House regulars in the 1940s and 1950s. See too Rima Lunin Schultz and Benvenuta Bras, OP, "O'Hanlon, Sister Mary Ellen," in *Women Building Chicago*, 643–46.

35. Quotes are from Father Patrick Curran, "Missionary Apostolate among the non-Catholic Negroes in Chicago," *Christ to the World* 5 (Summer 1960): 297; and Cardinal Samuel A. Stritch to Mother Corona Wirfs, OSF, May 30 and June 6, 1946, School Sisters of St. Francis (SSSF) Archives, Milwaukee.

36. Koenig, *History of the Parishes*, 1:357; "Annual Parish Reports: Holy Angels," 1945–1946, Bernardin Archives; and Dorothy Austin, "Nun Puts New Ideas to Work in Old South," *Milwaukee Sentinel*, June 29, 1977. Sister Hortensia was born in 1892 in Peoria, Illinois, to German American parents. She first taught African Americans in 1940 in Yazoo, Mississippi, and she returned there after two decades in Chicago. In 1957 the city's Catholic Interracial Council honored her with its Thomas J. Crowe Award for "convincing her mother general and the order to encourage and accept vocations from Negro girls and her devotion and efforts in interracial work." Quote is from *CIC News Letter*, 4 (June–July 1957), copy in Catholic Interracial Council Papers, box 17, Chicago Historical Society. See also Roi Ottley, "Interracial Council Honors Nun Instructor," *Chicago Sunday Tribune*, June 2, 1957.

37. Koenig, *History of the Parishes*, 1:357; Curran, "Missionary Apostolate," 299–300; and Claire Sobczyk, OSF, "A Survey of Catholic Education for the Negro of Five Parishes in Chicago" (master's thesis, DePaul University, 1954), 17–21. For Eckert's influence on Richards and Father Martin Farrell, see Steven M. Avella, *This Confident Church: Catholic Leadership and Life in Chicago, 1940–1965* (Notre Dame, Ind.: University of Notre Dame Press, 1992), 283–88.

38. Sobczyk, "Survey of Catholic Education," 22–27; McCarthy, "History of Black Catholic Education," 100–102, 123; and interview with Holy Angels' principal, Helen Strueder, OSF, November 3, 2002, Chicago, Illinois.

39. Curran, "Missionary Apostolate," 299–300; *Chicago Defender* (on South Side problems), October 7, 1939; Nicholas Lemann, *The Promised Land: The Great Black Migration and How It Changed America* (New York: Vintage Books, 1992), 17–18, 70; and Mary Robert Dennis, SBS, "St. Elizabeth's Parish and the Negro" (master's thesis, Loyola University, 1940), 27.

40. Sister Hortensia Stickelmaier to Mother Corona Wirfs, August 22 and 27, 1955; and "Supervisor's Report" of Holy Angels School, March 24–25, 1955, both in SSSF Archives. See also *New World*, August 16, 1963. Many sisters at Holy Angels took courses and earned college degrees from DePaul University. The Franciscans were not alone in offering literacy courses to adults in the 1960s. At Loretto Academy in nearby Woodlawn, for example, the Loretto Sisters opened an adult-education center at about the same time. See Chapter 6.

41. Henry Lewis Gates Jr., *New York Times,* October 31, 1999. On the Daughters of Charity's 1965 arrest, see *National Catholic Reporter,* June 23, 1965, along with Chapter 7.

42. Quotes are from *Chicago Catholic,* June 1, 1979; George Clements to Judy Giesen, December 1, 1990, SSF Archives; and *Newsweek,* January 27, 1969. See also David Sutor, "We're Doing It by Ourselves," *U.S. Catholic* 37 (November 1972): 28; and McGreevy, *Parish Boundaries,* 225–26.

43. Strueder interview; Sutor, "We're Doing It by Ourselves," 28–31; and Sister Mary Gemma Schlegel, OSF, *Catholic Herald* [letter to editor], November 3, 1973.

44. Quotes are from *Chicago Sun-Times,* May 30, 1993; and Strueder interview. Father Smith was born in Baltimore in 1931 and ordained there in 1962 for the Diocese of Alexandria, Louisiana. He attended Loyola College of Baltimore and Boston College; he then earned a master's degree in administration and English from the University of Scranton.

45. Quotes are from *Wall Street Journal,* October 22, 1976; and Strueder interview.

46. "Holy Angels School: The Largest Black Catholic School [rules and regulations]," 1974–75, copy in SSSF Archives; and Strueder interview. See also William Tate, "I'm Going Home: A Journey to Holy Angels," in *Growing Up African American in Catholic Schools,* ed. Jacqueline Jordan Irvine and Michele Foster (New York: Teachers College Press, 1996), 145–47.

47. Mother Katharine Drexel to Father Arnold Janssen, December 12, 1905, Archives of the Society of the Divine Word (SVD), Chicago Province, Techny, Illinois. See also Ernest Brandewie, *In the Light of the World: Divine Word Missionaries of North America* (Maryknoll, N.Y.: Orbis Books, 2000), 185–92. Drexel's contributions to SVD schools in the South were significant. Another missionary, Father John Peil, said that "Mother Drexel had a better opinion concerning blacks than any one in the country" (p. 185).

Chapter 6: No Color Line at Loretto Academy

1. Quotes are from John Higham, ed., *Civil Rights and Social Wrongs: Black-White Relations Since World War II* (University Park: Pennsylvania State University Press, 1997): 9; and Ralph McGill, in *National Catholic Reporter,* March 24, 1965. See also photos in *New York Times* and *Washington Post,* March 11, 1965.

2. Martin Luther King Jr., in *Chicago Defender* [weekly ed.], July 31–August 6, 1965. See also James F. Findlay Jr., *Church People in the Struggle: The National Council of Churches and the Black Freedom Movement, 1950–1970* (New York: Oxford University Press, 1993); Gerald Gamm, *Urban Exodus: Why the Jews Left Boston and the Catholics Stayed* (Cambridge, Mass.: Harvard University Press, 1999); John T. McGreevy, *Parish Boundaries: The Catholic Encounter with Race in the Twentieth-Century Urban North* (Chicago: University of Chicago Press, 1996); and Charles Marsh, *God's Long Summer: Stories of Faith and Civil Rights* (Princeton, N.J.: Princeton University Press, 1997.)

3. Quote is from Maureen A. Flanagan, "Women in the City, Women of the City: Where Do Women Fit in Urban History?" *Journal of Urban History* 23 (March

1997): 252. The church hierarchy also regarded nuns as "other." This had both a positive and negative effect: they could develop their institutions as they wished, but then the hierarchy often had no real stake in supporting them. On women and the city, see important recent publications: Maureen A. Flanagan, *Seeing with Their Hearts: Chicago Women and the Vision of the Good City, 1871–1933* (Princeton, N.J.: Princeton University Press, 2002); Rima Lunin Schultz and Adele Hast, eds., *Women Building Chicago: 1790–1990: A Biographical Dictionary* (Bloomington: Indiana University Press, 2001); and Daphne Spain, *How Women Saved the City* (Minneapolis: University of Minnesota Press, 2001).

4. Thomas J. Sugrue, *The Origins of the Urban Crisis: Race and Inequality in Postwar Detroit* (Princeton, N.J.: Princeton University Press, 1996), 250–51.

5. John Dittmer, *Local People: The Struggle for Civil Rights in Mississippi* (Urbana: University of Illinois Press, 1994).

6. Quote is from Ernest Tucker, "School's Color Changing but Not Teaching," *Chicago's American*, August 7, 1960.

7. Catholic high schools in Chicago generally have relied on their own resources to survive, whereas elementary schools are usually subsidized by parishes. Such was the case for the high schools featured in this chapter. See James W. Sanders, *The Education of the Urban Minority: Catholics in Chicago, 1833–1965* (New York: Oxford University Press, 1977), 198.

8. Quote is from Margarita O'Connor, IBVM, *That Incomparable Woman* (Montreal: Palm Publishers, 1962), 56. The Institute of the Blessed Virgin Mary did not receive papal approval until 1703; in 1877, Pius IX recognized Mary Ward as founder. For more on her struggles, see Mary Peckham Magray, *The Transforming Power of the Nuns: Women, Religion, and Cultural Change, 1750–1900* (New York: Oxford University Press, 1998), 8; and Antonia Fraser, *The Weaker Vessel* (New York: Vintage Books, 1994), 123–28.

9. Loretto Academy remained a foundation of the Toronto motherhouse. Hence, if the sisters were divided over an issue or believed they needed an authoritative decision, they could call on the superior general in Toronto. See *Lorettan* (Chicago: n. p., 1955), 7, for number of students in 1906; and Therese Rooney, IBVM, *Women for All Time and Places* (Wheaton, Ill.: Institute of the Blessed Virgin Mary, 1998), 80.

10. *Loretto Convent of the Immaculate Conception, 65th and Washington Ave., Chicago, Illinois* (Chicago: n. p., 1908–9), 3. Copy in the Archives of the Sisters of Loretto, Wheaton, Illinois. Washington Avenue later became Blackstone.

11. *New World*, June 26, 1925; and *Official Catholic Directory* (New York: P. J. Kenedy and Sons, 1946), 67. See also Mother Eudoxia Fromm to Msgr. M. J. Fitzsimmons, January 28, 1916, Joseph Cardinal Bernardin Archives and Records Center of the Archdiocese of Chicago. Chicago's Cardinal Samuel Stritch, whose tenure stretched from 1939 to 1958, "made it quite clear" that Loretto Academy would receive no financial support from the archdiocese. See Rooney, *Women for All Time and Places*, 191.

12. "Records of the Corporation of the Ladies of Loretto from 1904–1950s," copy in Archives North America: IBVM, Toronto, Ontario; and Chicago Plan Commission and Woodlawn Planning Committee, *A Program for Community Conservation in Chicago and an Example* (Chicago: Chicago Plan Commission, 1946), 33, 56. Issues of the yearbook, *Lorettan*, and school newspaper, *Loretto*

Spire, highlight the students' interests and abilities. Copies of both publications are in Loretto Archives. Music was particularly important. Besides a special choral group, the "Loraleers," there were also glee clubs, a band, piano recitals, and an annual Christmas and spring concert. CISCA was a citywide Catholic action group for high school and college students.

13. Charles E. Silberman, *Crisis in Black and White* (New York: Random House, 1964), 319–20; *Chicago Commerce,* June 5, 1920; *Chicago Defender* [weekly ed.], December 29, 1962–January 4, 1963; and Nicholas Lemann, *The Promised Land: The Great Black Migration and How It Changed America* (New York: Random House, 1991), 6 (quote).

14. Interview with Colette Srill, IBVM, October 4, 1996, Wheaton, Ill.; Silberman, *Crisis in Black and White,* 319; and Lemann, *Promised Land,* 5–6, 70. See also Winston Moore, Charles P. Livermore, and George F. Galland Jr., "Woodlawn: The Zone of Destruction," *Public Interest* 20 (Winter 1973): 44–45; and Perry R. Duis and Glen E. Holt, "Checking in at the Fair: The Hotel Boom of the 1893 Columbian Exposition Left a Legacy to be Learned From," *Chicago* (July 1982): 84–86.

15. Roi Ottley, "Why Negroes Flock to the North," *Chicago Tribune,* April 29, 1956.

16. Quoted in Steven M. Avella, *This Confident Church: Catholic Leadership and Life in Chicago, 1940–1965* (Notre Dame, Ind.: University of Notre Dame Press, 1992), 307.

17. "Annals of Loretto Academy—Woodlawn: September 1945–1965," Loretto Archives. The unnamed annalist recorded exactly the mother general's letter and commented: "October 30 [1955]. A short serious meeting of the high school staff was called at 6:30 P.M. Mother General's final decision had come and was read to us by Mother Superior. Pardon! I have decided to quote this gem verbatim."

18. Srill interview, October 4, 1996. See also [Mother Edwardine Partridge], "Loretto Academy New Courses, Clings to Old Ideals," *New World,* August 21, 1953. Mother Edwardine later became Sister Mary Gene; she died on August 27, 2001.

19. Quotes, except for the last, are from *New World,* August 21, 1953. The final one is from Margaret Ordway, IBVM, in a conversation with author at Loretto Abbey in Toronto on February 5, 1997.

20. Interviews in Chicago, March 31 and April 2, 1997, respectively, with two former Loretto students. Callista [Nancy] Robinson, OSF, one of the academy's first black graduates (1958), became a Franciscan and later principal of Harambee Community School in Milwaukee; and Eleanor Holland, IBVM, a 1953 graduate, became a Loretto and returned to the academy as principal in the late 1960s. Both women said Mother Edwardine "took her job very seriously," was "a very strong person," and could be "intimidating" despite her small size. Holland, who was director of continuing education at the Catholic Theological Union in Chicago at the time of the interview, died on January 29, 2000, at the age of sixty-four.

21. Interviews with Mary Gene Partridge, IBVM, June 3 and October 4, 1996, Wheaton, Ill.; her responses to written questions, September 2, 1996; and "IBVM Biographical Dictionary," Loretto Archives. The final quote is from an October 31, 1996 letter to author from Reverend Anthony J. Vader, pastor of Holy Name of Mary parish in Morgan Park. See too his "Racial Segregation within Catho-

lic Institutions in Chicago: A Study in Behavior and Attitudes" (master's thesis, University of Chicago, 1962).

22. Mother Callista McGuire to "My dear Mother General [Victorine O'Meara]," c. winter 1955, Loretto Archives. Although Mother Callista was the convent superior, she did not have authority over Mother Edwardine in her role as school principal. Yet, because they lived together and did not hold the same opinion on a critical issue, tension resulted in the convent and school. Mother Callista (1889–1984) was born in Joliet, Illinois, and attended St. Mary's Academy (a Loretto school). She was admired for her musical ability. Her "Loraleers" and other choral groups won numerous music awards. Her obituary and autobiographical data are in Loretto Archives.

23. Quotes are from the letter of Mother Callista to "My dear Mother General."

24. "Sister Mary Constance MacMahon, 1894–1990," a biographical sketch in Archives North America: IBVM. On the August 1955 visit to Chicago, see "Annals of Loretto Academy," Loretto Archives.

25. Quotes are from notes on an undated telephone conversation between Mother Victorine O'Meara and Cardinal James McGuigan; Mother Victorine's typed notes of her meeting with Cardinal Samuel Stritch; and Cardinal McGuigan to Mother Victorine, January 21, 1955. All are in Archives North America: IBVM. Mother Victorine was especially concerned that a black student body (the majority of whom were not Catholic) would not provide many vocations to the religious life. Stritch told her he "was planning to build some new high schools" and promised to remember the Lorettos. There is no indication that he invited the Lorettos to staff any new high school during the 1950s. See also Benjamin C. Willis [of Chicago's public schools] to Monsignor William E. McManus [of Chicago's Catholic schools], May 6, 1966, Bernardin Archives; and George V. Fornero, "The Expansion and Decline of Enrollment and Facilities of Secondary Schools in the Archdiocese of Chicago, 1955–1980: A Historical Study" (Ph.D. diss., Loyola University Chicago, 1990), 278.

26. "Annals of Loretto Academy," Loretto Archives. During the discussion following Mother Constance's presentation, a sister asked what to do "if a negro girl should ask to enter" the community. Mother Constance replied that "there could be no other answer than 'yes' in light of the Mystical Body. But she did add that the girl should be told plainly what to expect." See "Loretto Woodlawn Visitation—1957," Archives North America: IBVM. Mother Constance's response suggested that although the Lorettos would admit African Americans, it would not be easy for them because of cultural differences as well as racism shown by some in the community and many more outside it. Since the 1960s, several black women have joined the Lorettos, but only one has remained. Few American sisterhoods, other than declaredly black ones, accepted African Americans before the civil-rights movement.

27. Philip Gleason, *Contending with Modernity: Catholic Higher Education in the Twentieth Century* (New York: Oxford University Press, 1995), 157–58; and "The Catholic Worker Program: The Mystical Body," *Chicago Catholic Worker,* July 1938. Many Catholic Workers first belonged to CISCA, as noted by Mel Piehl, *Breaking Bread: The Catholic Worker and the Origin of Catholic Radicalism in America* (Philadelphia: Temple University Press, 1982), 154. See too a "CISCA,

1941–42" syllabus on the Mystical Body in a small collection of CISCA material, Loyola University Chicago (LUC) Archives. The Sheil School stood as "a beacon of hope to every Catholic who takes seriously the teachings of the great social encyclicals." George H. Dunne, SJ, to Father Daniel Cantwell, July 16, 1946, box 1, folder 6, Daniel M. Cantwell Papers, Chicago Historical Society.

28. M. Cecilia [Himebaugh], OSB, "CISCA in Retrospect," May 6, 1965, LUC Archives; Andrew M. Greeley, "The Chicago Experience," in *The Catholic Experience: An Interpretation of the History of American Catholicism* (New York: Doubleday, 1967), 247–56; and "Bishop Sheil's Speech, *Chicago Defender,* September 1942, box 28, folder 6, copy in Cantwell Papers (quotes). Ellen Tarry, a black Catholic and a founder of Chicago's Friendship House (a Catholic organization begun in New York in the 1930s to promote interracial justice), recalled that the *Chicago Defender* "had a record for attacking Catholic ventures on the South Side." In the early 1940s, she and others "held a conference with the publisher" and changed his mind; they explained Sheil's efforts on behalf of racial justice. Ellen Tarry, *The Third Door: The Autobiography of an American Negro Woman* (New York: Guild Press, 1966), 235. On Claude McKay, a friend of Tarry and Sheil, see David Goldweber, "Home at Last: The Pilgrimage of Claude McKay," *Commonweal,* September 10, 1999, p. 12 (quote).

29. Interviews with several Loretto Sisters: Irene Gavin, Anastasia O'Connor, Mary Gene Partridge, Therese Rooney, and Alice Whitehead, October 3 and 4 and November 13, 1996, in Wheaton, Illinois. Sister Irene Gavin's commitment to CISCA remained so strong that she continued to attend meetings as an adult with her Loretto students. Her mother telephoned the convent one Saturday morning while she was at a CISCA meeting with students; later her mother said, "Don't tell me you're still going to those!" See also M. Cecilia Himebaugh, OSB, "School for Revolution in Chicago," *Orate Fratres,* copy in LUC; and *New World,* October 22, 1937 (quote). On Carrabine, see "Father Carrabine," *Jubilee* 12 (May 1964): 24; "Day of Recollection," *Loretto Spire,* June 4, 1937; and Mary Innocenta Montay, CSSF, *The History of Catholic Secondary Education in the Archdiocese of Chicago* (Washington, D.C.: Catholic University of America Press, 1953), 335–37.

30. Rooney interview, October 3, 1966. See a typed manuscript, "History of CISCA, 1924–1944"; and a pamphlet entitled "Crusaders in Student Catholic Action," both in LUC Archives. See also *New World,* June 3, 1938 (quote); and Mary Robert Dennis, SBS, "St. Elizabeth's Parish and the Negro," (master's thesis, Loyola University Chicago, 1940), 39–40 (quote).

31. Magray, *Transforming Power of the Nuns,* 8; and "Modern Girl Chooses Ideal," *Loretto Spire,* January 1940. The quote is from Holland interview, April 2, 1997.

32. Mary Gene Partridge, IBVM, to author, September 2, 1996; and interviews, October 4, 1996, and January 30, 1998. See too George H. Dunne, *King's Pawn: The Memoirs of George H. Dunne, SJ* (Chicago: Loyola University Press, 1990), 133–36, 177–78; George H. Dunne, "The Sin of Segregation," *Commonweal,* September 21, 1945, pp. 542–45; and *New World,* October 15, 1948. Dunne's aunt was Mother Mary Aquinas [Rose] Dunne.

33. Besides the Chicago daily newspapers, see Stephen Whitfield, *A Death in the Delta: The Story of Emmett Till* (New York: Free Press, 1988).

34. Partridge to author, September 2, 1996; also remarks of Sister Mary Gene Partridge, IBVM Conference, 1991, Wheaton, Illinois (copy in author's possession); and Holland interview, April 2, 1997.

35. William Osborne, *The Segregated Covenant: Race Relations and American Catholics* (New York: Herder & Herder, 1967), 212. In January 1955, for example, two priests from Holy Cross parish on the South Side complained to Sister Mary of the Angels Simon (SMAS), principal at Mercy High School, and to Monsignor George J. Casey at the Chancery Office that students from their parish were not admitted to Mercy. Rev. Leo T. Mahan to Sister Mary of the Angels, January 18 and 21, 1955; Rev. Robert Doyle to SMAS, January 26, 1955; and Casey to SMAS, February 4, 1955, all in Sisters of Mercy Archives, Chicago. Sister Mary of the Angels responded that the girls "did not register in time" and were "placed on a waiting list"; she also stated that "last year we registered seven colored girls who are here now and are accepted just like any other students." See Sister Mary of the Angels to Casey, February 8, 1955, Mercy Archives. There were other complaints as well, but by 1959, seventy-nine high schools offered a common admission exam. Some still refused to cooperate. Although schools could admit or reject students, the superintendent's office investigated complaints. See Sanders, *Education of an Urban Minority*, 199.

36. John L. Rury, "Race, Space, and the Politics of Chicago's Public Schools: Benjamin Willis and the Tragedy of Urban Education," *History of Education Quarterly* 39 (Summer 1999): 117–42. See too Alan B. Anderson and George W. Pickering, *Confronting the Color Line: The Broken Promises of the Civil Rights Movement in Chicago* (Athens: University of Georgia Press, 1986), 85–102; and James R. Ralph Jr., *Northern Protest: Martin Luther King, Jr., Chicago, and the Civil Rights Movement* (Cambridge, Mass.: Harvard University Press, 1993), 19–22.

37. Morton Grodzins, "Metropolitan Segregation," *Scientific American* 197 (October 1957): 33–41; and Grodzins, "Segregation in the North," *Progressive* 23 (January 1959): 66–70. See also a pamphlet that circulated among professionals interested in race: Morton Grodzins, *The Metropolitan Area and the Race Problem* (Pittsburgh: University of Pittsburgh Press, 1958); and Otis Dudley Duncan and Beverly Duncan, *The Negro Population of Chicago: A Study in Residential Succession* (Chicago: University of Chicago Press, 1957).

38. *Chicago Tribune*, May 6, 1959; Sanford D. Horwitt, *Let Them Call Me Rebel: Saul Alinsky—His Life and Legacy* (New York: Alfred A. Knopf, 1989), 313; Saul Alinsky, "The Urban Immigrant," in *Roman Catholicism and the American Way of Life*, ed. Thomas T. McAvoy, CSC (Notre Dame, Ind.: University of Notre Dame Press, 1960), 151; Sister Mark Kerin to Archbishop Albert G. Meyer, October 25, 1959, Mercy Archives; and Fornero, "Expansion and Decline," 413–18. See too Arnold R. Hirsch, *Making the Second Ghetto: Race and Housing in Chicago, 1940–1960* (New York: Cambridge University Press, 1983), 209–10.

39. Interview with Gavin, November 3, 1996. The biographical data is from "IBVM Biographical Dictionary," Loretto Archives. Born on December 11, 1919, she was baptized Mary Agnes at Our Lady of the Angels Church. Her father, Joseph Gavin, was born in County Mayo, Ireland, and became a Chicago policeman; her mother, Susan Costello Gavin, was born to Irish parents in Yorkshire, England. Trained in science, mathematics, and history, Mother Irene received a bachelor's

degree from St. Xavier University and a master's from DePaul University. The quote on injustice is from Martin Luther King Jr., "Letter from a Birmingham Jail," in *I Have a Dream: Writings and Speeches that Changed the World*, ed. James Melvin Washington (San Francisco: Harper Collins, 1986), 85. The Urban Apostolate of the Sisters began in 1961 and by 1965 grew to six hundred nuns. Its purpose was to help sisters become better prepared for teaching in the inner city. See Chapter 7.

40. "Press Release," May 16, 1962, in Loretto High School [Englewood] Closing Files; and Archdiocese of Chicago School Board, "Minutes of Meeting," December 12, 1961; January 5 and 26, 1962, Archdiocese of Chicago School Board Papers, all in Bernardin Archives. See too Mother Constance MacMahon to "My dear Mother Superior and Members of the Community," May 13, 1962, Archives North America: IBVM; and *New World*, May 25, 1962.

41. Archdiocese of Chicago School Board, "Minutes," June 10, 1959, Bernardin Archives (quote). Loretto Academy was $8,000 in debt in early 1961. It was quickly "made up from a legacy received," according to a notation on "Loretto Academy, Parents Meeting," May 4, 1961, Archives North America: IBVM. The nuns would have had more money after the merger had they been immediately successful in selling the Englewood building. In 1966, the Chicago Board of Education finally bought it and adjoining properties for a total of $297,500. See Catholic Schools Superintendent Monsignor William E. McManus to Cardinal John P. Cody, January 14, 1966; Chicago Public Schools Superintendent Benjamin C. Willis to McManus, May 6, 1956, Loretto High School [Englewood] Closing Files, Bernardin Archives; and Fornero, "Expansion and Decline," 275–78.

42. Most students paid full tuition, $125 a year; some paid a reduced fee of $100; and a few worked for tuition. As in 1969, the Toronto motherhouse usually contributed $500 a month. A 1964–65 financial statement recorded that the "Chocolate Bar Drive" yielded $4,000 and the parents' club donated $3,000. But the money was only a part; mothers and a few fathers, according to Mother Irene Gavin, gave many hours of service. The students' Christmas and spring concerts also brought in a several hundred dollars each. Notice of the 3M award, financial statements, and tuition records are in Archives North America: IBVM. Very helpful were the Gavin interview, November 13, 1966, and those with O'Connor and Whitehead, October 3, 1966. "Just barely afloat" is from Mother Irene to McManus, June 3, 1963, Loretto High School [Englewood] Closing Files, Bernardin Archives. During her years as principal, Mother Irene took advantage of her position on the archdiocesan school board to secure some funding for "the only black Catholic girls' high school in the whole diocese." She believes today, as she did then, that Loretto Academy deserved financial support from the archdiocese, which was assisting other religious communities in building big new high schools in the suburbs.

43. William Julius Wilson, *When Work Disappears: The World of the New Urban Poor* (New York: Alfred A. Knopf, 1997), 5 (quote); Michael Harrington, *The Other America: Poverty in the United States* (New York: Macmillan, 1962); and Sugrue, *Origins of the Urban Crisis*.

44. Phyllis Crockett, a former Loretto student, recorded her views in a documentary, "Growing up Segregated and Successful on the South Side," which she produced for National Public Radio's "Chicago Matters Series," 1983. Also Wil-

liam Julius Wilson, *The Truly Disadvantaged: The Inner City, the Underclass, and Public Policy* (Chicago: University of Chicago Press, 1987), 20–92; and Mary Pattillo-McCoy, *Black Picket Fences: Privilege and Peril among the Black Middle Class* (Chicago: University of Chicago Press, 1999), 22–24.

45. On TWO, see Horwitt, *Let Them Call Me Rebel*, 365–89. The bus caravan was inspired by a large turnout of Woodlawn residents to welcome several "Freedom Riders" at a meeting in the gym of St. Cyril's parish in June 1961. Many of the Lorettos were in the audience and learned to sing "We Shall Overcome." Rooney, *Women for All Time and Places*, 196; and Horwitt, *Let Them Call Me Rebel*, 400. On the voter registration drive, see *Chicago Defender* [weekly ed.], July 23–28, 1961; *Chicago Daily News*, August 23, 1961; *Chicago's American*, August 27, 1961; and a report, "TWO Drive—August 26, 1961," by Kenneth Gillis to Alderman Leon Despres, Leon Despres Papers, Chicago Historical Society.

46. This change would prompt the sisters to reexamine their role as women-religious and their place in the Catholic Church. Interview with Gavin, November 13, 1996. On the Lorettos' CIC membership, see Catholic Interracial Council of Chicago to Ladies of Loretto, February 14, 1963, Loretto Archives. On John Egan, see Margery Frisbie, *An Alley in Chicago: The Ministry of a City Priest* (New York: Sheed and Ward, 1991).

47. *New World*, May 10, 1963, and *January* 10, 1964. See too *Chicago Defender* [weekly eds.], January 14–19 and January 20–25, 1963. The last quote is from "Annals of Loretto Academy," Loretto Archives.

48. Therese Rooney, IBVM, "I Know a Man . . . and a Woman," in *New Work of New Nuns*, ed. Peter Traxler, SSND (St. Louis: B. Herder Book, 1968), 133–35; and quote in Therese Rooney, IBVM, "The Undereducated Adult," *NCEA Bulletin* (May 1968): 27. A copy is in Loretto Archives.

49. Rooney interview, October 3, 1996. In 1964 she had a bachelor's degree in education and a master's degree in history from DePaul University.

50. Rooney, "I Know a Man," 135–37; "Loretto Adult Education Center: 1973" and "Loretto Adult Education Center Overview, 1979," copies in Loretto Archives; and *Chicago Tribune*, August 9, 1964. A list of the first faculty members appears in Rooney, *Women for All Time and Places*. The Lorettos contributed in a variety of ways: subsidies from their motherhouse, donations from other convents, and volunteered services from individual sisters. The Archdiocese of Chicago gave direct financial contributions (on an irregular basis), no-interest loans, and a salary for a lay teacher to replace Mother Peter Claver at Loretto Academy. On at least one occasion, Cardinal Cody sent a personal donation of $6,000. See Cody to Sister Therese Rooney, January 13, 1972, Loretto Archives. The center's board gave money and/or services. See also Angelica Seng, OSF, "The Sister in the New City," in *The Changing Sister*, ed. Charles Borromeo Muckenhirn, CSC (Notre Dame, Ind.: University of Notre Dame Press, 1965), 242–43.

51. The first quotes are from Ed Marciniak and Monsignor John Egan. They appear in "Leap for Literacy: The Lives of Hundreds of Illiterate Adults Have Been Changed through Sister Mary Peter Claver's Pioneering Program," *Extension*, August 1965, copy in Urban Apostolate of the Sisters Papers, University of Notre Dame Archives. The remaining quotes are from an untitled and undated presentation by Mary Gene Partridge, IBVM, on the community's "mission statement" (in author's possession).

52. *Chicago Tribune*, December 19, 1968. Chicago's Kennedy-King College eventually took over the Loretto Adult Education Center.

53. Interviews with Mary Simpkin (formerly Sister Mary Patrick) and Gavin, October 3 and November 13, 1996. As principal, Sister Patrick had bachelor's and master's degrees in history from St. Xavier University and Loyola University Chicago. She also had participated in summer programs at Furman University (Asian studies) and the University of Michigan (economics). After leaving Loretto Academy, she taught for seventeen years in the public school system of Carol Stream, Illinois. She earned more and therefore could contribute more to the community in support of its elderly sisters. Although the students called her "Miss Simpkin," they and their parents knew she was a Catholic sister.

54. The first quote is from Tucker, "School's Color Changing, but Not Teaching." The others are from responses of Loretto graduates to author's questionnaire, March 1997. See also Sheila McDonald to Sister Eleanor Holland, October 5, 1971, Loretto Archives. Interviews with Robinson, OSF, and Holland, IBVM, March 31 and April 2, 1997, were helpful.

55. Robinson interview, March 31, 1997. See also Sister Therese Rooney to Mother Bernadette Culnan, July 10, 1968; and Sister Mary Patrick Simpkin to McManus, March 16, 1966. The quote is from an undated letter (c. 1967) that Sister Mary Patrick sent to administrators of Catholic elementary schools on Chicago's South Side. She explained Loretto's special program for low-ability students but made it clear that it was "operating in addition to the regular academic program." All documents are in Loretto Archives.

56. Fornero, "Expansion and Decline," 204–16 (on Hales Franciscan) and 353–58 (on St. Elizabeth). The quotations (on page 354) are from Mother M. David Young, SBS, to Cody, January 31, 1966.

57. The enrollment figure is from Sister Mary Gene Partridge (who returned to Loretto Academy as principal for a year) to McManus, July 7, 1968. On Sister Mary Patrick's contributions, see "The Principal Who Woke Up a School," *1967 Lorettan* (yearbook), 3; and "Correspondence Concerning the Career Bound Program," 1966–67. All are in Loretto Archives. Interview with Simpkin, October 3, 1996. The amount from the archdiocese in these years (1965–69) appears to be about $50,000. It came in the form of direct subsidies for building renovations and new equipment as well as in support of teacher salaries and student tuitions (especially for those who transferred from St. Elizabeth's in 1967).

58. *Chicago Tribune*, August 31, 1969. No sister teaching at Loretto Academy during the 1960s was without a college degree, and most of them had master's degrees and more. On the impact of job losses on Chicago's black neighborhoods and the failure of the 1960s' antipoverty programs, see Wilson, *When Work Disappears*, 30–32; and Sugrue, *Origins of the Urban Crisis*, 264.

59. Quotes are from Henry Louis Gates Jr., *New York Times*, October 31, 1999; and from Sister Mary Gene Partridge's remarks, IBVM Conference, 1991.

60. The 1969 yearbook, for example, demonstrates efforts made to incorporate black history and culture into the students' lives. There are commentaries and photos of Martin Luther King Jr., W. E. B. Du Bois, Jesse Jackson, and the Black Goddess who symbolized the students' "hopes of becoming great women." See "A Reflection of Black Pride," *1969 Lorettan*, Loretto Archives. Also the interview with Holland, April 2, 1997. Sister Eleanor Holland graduated from Loretto

Academy in 1953; she had Sisters Mary Gene Partridge and Irene Gavin for teachers. Both influenced her. In addition to a bachelor's degree in mathematics from St. Procopius College, Holland earned master's degrees in religious studies and business from Mundelein and Notre Dame, respectively.

61. On the nature of change, see observation in Henry Glassie, *Passing Time in Ballymenone* (Bloomington: Indiana University Press, 1982), 424.

62. Interview with Simpkin, October 3, 1996, who was principal in April 1968. On several occasions, Jeff Fort, leader of the Blackstone Rangers, assured her that Loretto Academy and the sisters' car were "off limits" to his gang. She was afraid of him only once—when he first contacted her. Although Fort and his gang members were responsible for "horrible things," she said that "there was a lot of good in that man." On gang problems on the South Side, see Robert A. Levin, "Gang-Busting in Chicago," *New Republic*, June 1, 1968. On the effect of King's death on the South Side, see Louis Rosen, *The South Side: The Racial Transformation of an American Neighborhood* (Chicago: Ivan R. Dee, 1998), 95–128.

63. For a contemporary account of Woodlawn's deterioration, see *Chicago Daily News*, July 6, 1971. As for living with stress, Sister Mary Simpkin remarked that most of it came from "identification with the students." Many had "horrendous problems" that had to be dealt with every day; she used to pray, however, that "she would not get used to it." Interviews with Simpkin and Gavin, October 3 and November 13, 1996. When Loretto closed in 1972, there were 250 students enrolled. See *Official Catholic Directory* (New York: P. J. Kenedy, 1972), 176; and Fornero, "Expansion and Decline," 413. In late 1970, the Lorettos feared they might not be able to meet the January 1971 payroll and asked for assistance from the archdiocese, which rescued them. See Father Robert Clark, Superintendent of Schools, to Cardinal Cody, December 17, 1970, Loretto Academy Closing Files, Bernardin Archives. Clark stated on the sisters' behalf: "There is no way I can praise the Sisters highly enough. They have made enormous sacrifices in order to offer an educational program to very poor children. They work at outside jobs during the summer and contribute their earnings to the operation of the school."

64. Interview with Simpkin, October 3, 1996. The quote is from Michael D. Wamble, "Mt. Carmel: A Century of Stability and Growth," *Catholic New World*, December 5, 1999.

65. Quotes are from interviews with O'Connor and Rooney, October 3, 1996; and Reverend Vernon Malley to Leon Despres, March 10, 1967, Despres Papers.

66. *Chicago Sun-Times*, January 22, 1997. Despite several attempts to obtain information from Mt. Carmel, I was not successful. Hence I have used what is available in public sources or archival collections.

67. Interview with O'Connor, October 3, 1996, and Kate Moriarty, RSM, March 5, 1997, Chicago. Quotations are from Wamble, "Mt. Carmel"; and Don Hayner, "Mt. Carmel Makes the Man," *Chicago Sun-Times*, September 30, 1984. In addition, this paragraph summarizes numerous conversations about school integration and viability with Sisters of Loretto and Mercy.

68. Mary Madigan, IBVM, to Mattie Butler, February 24, 1983; and press release from The Woodlawn Organization, "Woodlawn Organization Acquires Property for Family Life," September 17, 1987, Loretto Archives.

Chapter 7: Marching for Racial Justice in Chicago in the 1960s

1. The Illinois Club for Catholic Women, located in Lewis Towers (also the downtown campus of Loyola University Chicago), was across from the Water Tower at Michigan and Chicago avenues.

2. Quotes are from Mary William Sullivan, DC, "Statement of Sister Mary William Sullivan, Sister Servant of Marillac House, Chicago, Regarding the Demonstrations of June 12, 1965," Marillac House Papers, box 2, folder June 1965, Chicago Historical Society (CHS); and St. Vincent de Paul, in Leon Joseph Cardinal Suenens, *The Nun in the World: Religious and the Apostolate* (Westminster, Md.: Newman Press, 1963, rev. ed.), 40.

3. Despite their history of involvement in the lives of black Americans, no Catholic sisters are included in Lynne Olson, *Freedom's Daughters: The Unsung Heroines of the Civil Rights Movement from 1830 to 1970* (New York: Scribner, 2001). The quote is from Rev. John Hazard, Sermon at Holy Name Cathedral, June 20, 1965, copy in Marillac Provincialate Archives, St. Louis, Missouri.

4. See, for example, the photograph that accompanied "The Force of Conscience," *Time,* July 12, 1963.

5. For reviews of "Lilies of the Field," see *Saturday Review,* September 7, 1963; *Commonweal,* October 11, 1963; and *America,* October 12, 1963 (quote on p. 440). Additional quotes are in Msgr. Daniel M. Cantwell to Albert Cardinal Meyer, May 29, 1963, Cardinal Albert G. Meyer Papers, Chancery Correspondence, Joseph Cardinal Bernardin Archives and Records Center of the Archdiocese of Chicago; and Edward Wakin and Rev. Joseph F. Scheuer, "The American Nun: Poor, Chaste, and Restive," *Harper's,* August 1965, p. 40.

6. Jo Ann Kay McNamara, *Sisters in Arms: Catholic Nuns through Two Millennia* (Cambridge, Mass.: Harvard University Press, 1996), ix.

7. Quotes are in Garry Wills, *Bare Ruined Choirs: Doubt, Prophecy, and Radical Religion* (New York: Doubleday and Company, 1972), 26; and "Restive Nuns," *Time,* January 13, 1967, p. 66.

8. Quotes are in Arthur McCormack, MHM, "A New Era for the Nun in the World," *Catholic World* 199 (July 1964): 145; and Suenens, *The Nun in the World,* 95.

9. Quotes are from Michael Novak, "Nuns in the World," *Commonweal,* November 29, 1963, p. 275; Suenens, *Nun in the World,* 149; and author's interview with Irene Gavin, IBVM, Wheaton, Illinois, November 13, 1996. The priest referred to is Rev. John "Jack" Egan.

10. The quote is in Bertrande Meyers, DC, *The Education of Sisters: A Plan for Integrating the Religious, Social, Cultural and Professional Training of Sisters* (New York: Sheed and Ward, 1941), xxix. See also an excellent discussion of teacher training in Patricia Byrne and Debra Campbell, *Transforming Parish Ministry: The Changing Roles of Catholic Clergy, Laity, and Women Religious* (New York: Crossroad, 1989), 118–23, 134–53. See too Martin Duggan, "Teachers' Teacher," *Today* 17 (March 1962): 3–5; Mary I. Schneider, OSF, "American Sisters and the Roots of Change: The 1950s," *U.S. Catholic Historian* 7 (Winter 1988): 57–58. There is evidence as well that change began earlier than the 1940s and 1950s. See Joseph P. Chinnici, OSM, "Religious Life in the Twentieth Century: Interpreting the Languages," *U.S. Catholic Historian* 22 (Winter 2004): 27–47.

11. Quotes are from Elizabeth Carroll, "Reaping the Fruits of Redemption," in Ann Patrick Ware, ed., *Midwives of the Future: American Sisters Tell Their Story* (Kansas City, Kans.: Leaven Press, 1985), 58; and Gail Porter Mandell, *Madeleva: A Biography* (Albany: State University of New York Press, 1997), 189.

12. See Schneider, "American Sisters and the Roots of Change," 62; Carroll, "Reaping the Fruits," 58 (quote); and Colette Dowling, "The Nuns' Story," *New York Times Magazine*, November 28, 1976, p. 91. Elizabeth Carroll, who was major superior of the Sisters of Mercy of Pittsburgh from 1964 to 1974, believed that "the beginning of the maturing process of American sisters came with the unbelievable reluctance of bishops and priests to support this request" for teacher preparation.

13. Bertrande Meyers, DC, *Sisters for the 21st Century* (New York: Sheed and Ward, 1965), 119; Ritamary Bradley, CHM, "Marillac—A Sister Formation College," *Sister Formation Bulletin* 6 (Spring 1960): 169–70; and Mary J. Oates, "Sisterhoods and Catholic Higher Education, 1890–1960," in Tracy Schier and Cynthia Russett, eds., *Catholic Women's Colleges in America* (Baltimore, Md.: Johns Hopkins University Press, 2002), 184 (quote). "Marillac" refers to St. Louise de Marillac (1591–1660), who, together with St. Vincent de Paul (1581–1660), founded the Daughters of Charity in France. In addition to colleges, Sister Formation Summer Institutes also brought together nuns from different communities. And by 1956 the *Sister Formation Bulletin*, which covered new ideas related to education, was available in nearly 100 percent of American convents. On the significance of the Sister Formation movement, see Lora Ann Quinonez, CDP, and Mary Daniel Turner, SNDdeN, *The Transformation of American Catholic Sisters* (Philadelphia: Temple University Press, 1992), 6–11.

14. Quotes are in Carroll, "Reaping the Fruits," 58–59; and Dowling, "The Nuns' Story," 93. In college courses, young sisters were exposed to "new developments in theology, bible study, psychology, and so on." These exposures, not surprisingly, sharpened their analysis of the world around them. See Mary Luke Tobin, SL, "Doors to the World," in Ware, ed., *Midwives of the Future*, 183–84 (quote); and Francis Borgia Rothluebber, OSF, "The Call to Share Life," *Origins* 4 (November 21, 1974): 346.

15. Carroll, "Reaping the Fruits," 61.

16. The quote is in Pope John XXIII, "Pacem in Terris: Peace on Earth (April 11, 1963)," in Joseph Gremillion, ed., *The Gospel of Peace and Justice: Catholic Social Teaching since Pope John* (Maryknoll, N.Y.: Orbis Books, 1976), 209–10. See also Patricia Wittberg, SC, *The Rise and Decline of Catholic Religious Orders: A Social Movement Perspective* (Albany: State University of New York Press, 1994), 213–14; John T. McGreevy, *Parish Boundaries: The Catholic Encounter with Race in the Twentieth-Century Urban North* (Chicago: University of Chicago Press, 1996), 152, 218; William Osborne, "The Church and the Negro: A Crisis in Leadership," *Cross Currents* 19 (Spring 1965): 137; and Ridgely Hunt, "Chicago's Catholics in the Winds of Change," *Chicago Tribune Magazine*, November 15, 1964, p. 27. The quote is from Father William Graney, assistant editor of the *New World*, the newspaper of the Chicago archdiocese.

17. Quotes are from an unidentified sister, "Annals of Loretto Academy," 1963; and Kaye Ashe, OP, "Looking Back, Looking Ahead," in Ware, ed., *Midwives of the Future*, 220.

18. Mary William Sullivan, DC, to Clarence B. Cash, March 2, 1965, Marillac House Papers, box 2, folder January–March 1965, CHS. The sisters who staffed Loretto Academy on the South Side shared this experience. See Chapter 6. The last quote is from Margaret Mary Reher, "Sister Mary Luke Tobin (1908–): Architect of Renewal," *American Catholic Studies* 115 (Spring 2004): 89.

19. "History of Marillac House" (typescript), Daughters of Charity Archives, Mater Dei Provincialate, Evansville, Indiana; and "Articles of Incorporation," November 25, 1946, Marillac House Papers, box 1, folder Board Minutes 1946–53, CHS. Before its purchase by the Daughters of Charity, Marillac House had been St. Mary's Episcopalian Orphanage.

20. See an important discussion of "the dynamics of neighborhood change" in Arnold R. Hirsch, *Making the Second Ghetto: Race and Housing in Chicago, 1940–1960* (New York: Cambridge University Press, 1983), 1–39 (quote is on p. 17). In Chicago, between 1950 and 1960, the African American population grew by 65 percent, from 492,265 to 812,637. See also "History of Marillac House" (typescript); Chicago Fact Book Consortium, ed., *Local Community Fact Book: Chicago Metropolitan Area, 1990* (Chicago: University of Illinois at Chicago, 1995), 100; Winifred Kilday, DC, "A Sociological Study of the Reciprocal Relations between the Clientele and the Program of Services of Marillac House, Chicago, 1947–1961" (master's thesis, Loyola University Chicago, 1962), 32; and Amanda Irene Seligman, "Block by Block: Racing Decay on Chicago's West Side, 1948–1968" (Ph.D. diss., Northwestern University, 1999).

21. "History of Marillac House" (typescript); and Kilday, "A Sociological Study," 13, 17, 20–26 (quotes). See also a booklet, *How Can You Change a Community: Marillac's Answer* (Chicago: Marillac House, 1959), copy in Welfare Council of Metropolitan Chicago Records, box 370, folder Marillac House, Chicago Historical Society (CHS). Marillac's "answer" was found in block clubs, offensives against blight and vice, racial and cultural integration, organized civic efforts, wholesome recreation, and education to prevent prejudice.

22. On Rockwell Gardens, see Devereux Bowly Jr., *The Poorhouse: Subsidized Housing in Chicago, 1895–1976* (Carbondale: Southern Illinois University Press, 1978), 119–21.

23. Mary William Sullivan, DC, "My First Day in Heaven," *Daughter of Charity*, 1 (Fall 1962): 36–40; Kilday, "A Sociological Study," 82–84; and author's interview with Mary William Sullivan, DC, February 7, 2002, Chicago. On Sister Rosalie Rendu, see Rev. Daniel T. McColgan, *A Century of Charity: The First One Hundred Years of the Society of St. Vincent de Paul in the United States*, 2 vols. (Milwaukee, Wisc.: Bruce Publishing, 1951), 1:39. The book that Sister Mary William read as a young woman, written by an unidentified Daughter of Charity, is *White Wings and Barricades: A Story of a Great Adventure* (New York: Benziger Brothers, 1939). I am grateful to Ellen Skerrett for a copy of this book.

24. Kilday, "A Sociological Study," 82–84; "Marillac House Newsletter," September 24, 1960, pp. 1–2, Marillac House Papers, box 2, folder 1959–63, CHS, and Sullivan interview, February 7, 2002.

25. Ibid. The quotes are from *Sacred Heart Review* 2 (October 12, 1889): 1; and Jean O'Connor, "A Sister to the Poor," *Chicago Daily News*, July 13, 1966.

26. Sheila Blondell, "West-Side Sister," *Today* (May 1964): 3. Also important were the author's interviews with Rev. Daniel Mallette, July 18, 2001; Mary Benet

McKinney, OSB, April 2, 2002, both in Chicago; and Rev. Maudine Wordlaw, July 27, 2002, on the telephone. In an unpublished manuscript that Father Mallette wrote during the 1960s, he described Sister Mary William as an "ingenious woman" who was widely known in the neighborhood as Sister Mary Williams or Sister Williams. The manuscript is in the Daniel Mallette Papers, box 2, folder 5, Chicago Historical Society. Wordlaw, who became secretary to Sister Mary William in 1964, was most impressed by her faith in God and dedication to Marillac House and its neighbors.

27. Mary William Sullivan, DC, "Rendu House Extension, Annual Report—1960," Welfare Council Records, box 370, folder Marillac House, CHS. I thank Amanda I. Seligman for making me aware of this collection.

28. Blondell, "West-Side Sister," 4; and Sullivan, "Rendu House Extension, Annual Report." The last quote is from William Friedlander, "Weekly Log: Marillac House—6-28-60," Welfare Council Records, box 370, folder Marillac House, CHS.

29. Sister Jane Breidenbach is quoted in "Marillac House Opens Doors to 400 in Day Care Center," *Chicago Tribune*, September 14, 1969. Sister Jane was well known in East Garfield Park for her years of service and her willingness to speak for the neighborhood. In May 1960, before the Chicago Park District commissioners, she spoke *against* the use of Garfield Park for an extension of the University of Illinois. See "Elect Gately to Head Park Board Again," *Chicago Tribune*, May 11, 1960. The Cook County Department of Public Aid and the Rendu House staff developed "cases" for people in desperate need who were not eligible for public assistance. From these cases, the sisters learned the meaning of poverty, which kept them from "enshrining" or "ennobling" it. See Kilday, "A Sociological Study," 88; and Blondell, "West-Side Sister," 5.

30. Sullivan interview, February 7, 2002. At the Buffalo meeting of Catholic Charities, October 26–30, 1956, there was an "integration of personnel from faiths and disciplines outside of our own [Catholic] group." Msgr. Raymond Gallagher, "The 1956 Conference," *Catholic Charities Review* XL (November 1956): 7. This conference is important as an example of ecumenism before the Second Vatican Council.

31. Quotes are from Rev. John J. Egan, no specific date, "Daily Reports: July–December 1960," John J. Egan Papers, box 66, University of Notre Dame Archives (UNDA).

32. Quotes are from McKinney interview, April 2, 2002. Father Sebastian Lewis, OSB, served as assistant pastor from 1959 to 1969; he then became pastor. See also Angelica Seng, OSF, "The Sister in the New City," in M. Charles Borromeo Muckenhirn, CSC, ed., *The Changing Sister* (Notre Dame: Fides, 1965), 233; and "The Urban Apostolate of the Sisters," *Encounter*, June 1964, pp. 1–2, copy in Egan Papers, box 18, UNDA.

33. McKinney interview, April 2, 2002. See also Mary Benet McKinney, OSB, "Catholic Schools," *Chicago Sunday Tribune Magazine*, copy in Friendship House Papers, box 37, folder Undated 1965, Chicago Historical Society (CHS).

34. McKinney interview, April 2, 2002. See also the quotes from Egan, December 27–28, 1963, and January 21, 1964, in "Daily Reports: December 1963–January 1964," Egan Papers, box 66, UNDA.

35. Mary Williams Sullivan, DC, "The Urban Apostolate," October 19, 1963,

Egan Papers, box 18, UNDA; McKinney interview, April 2, 2002; and Margery Frisbie, *An Alley in Chicago: The Ministry of a City Priest* (New York: Sheed and Ward, 1991, 136–37 (quote).

36. The School Sisters of St. Francis originated in Baden, Germany. They came to the United States in 1874 and established their first school in the Chicago archdiocese in 1880. See Francis Borgia Rothluebber, OSF, *He Sent Two: The Story of the Beginning of the School Sisters of St. Francis* (Milwaukee, Wisc.: Bruce Publishing, 1965). The quote is from Mary Ann Erdtmann, "School Sisters of St. Francis Take Seriously Request for Serious Involvement in World," *Catholic Herald Citizen*, July 20, 1963. Although the School Sisters of St. Francis had been teaching at Holy Angels on the South Side since the 1940s (see Chapter 5), only a small number of the community had regular and direct involvement in the lives of black children and their families.

37. Angelica Seng, OSF, "Summary of Cabrini Mission Work, June 1963," Egan Papers, box 17, USDA; Erdtmann, "School Sisters of St. Francis"; and McKinney interview, April 2, 2002.

38. Author's telephone interview with Ann Seng, July 3, 2001. The quote is from "Alvernia High School, Chicago," in Msgr. Harry C. Koenig, ed., *Caritas Christi Urget Nos: A History of the Offices, Agencies, and Institutions of the Archdiocese of Chicago*, 2 vols. (Chicago: Archdiocese of Chicago, 1981), 1:416–18.

39. Seng interview, July 3, 2001. See also Terry J. Michelsen, "Brenner, Sister M. Rebecca," in Rima Lunin Schultz and Adele Hast, eds., *Women Building Chicago, 1790–1990: A Bibliographical Dictionary* (Bloomington: Indiana University Press, 2001), 116–18; and Sister M. Rebecca [Brenner] to Mother Corona [Wirfs], Feast of St. Praxedas, 1947, Archives of the School Sisters of St. Francis, Milwaukee, Wisconsin.

40. Seng interview, July 30, 2001. See also Betty Plank to Sister Angelica [Seng], February 2, 1962, and Betty Plank to Mother M. Clemens [Rudolph], February 28, 1962, Friendship House Papers, box 30, folder February 1962, CHS; "Catholic Unit to Stage Race Relations Workshop," *Chicago Defender* [weekly ed.], March 17–23, 1962; and "120 Nuns Take Part in Workshop," newspaper clipping, April 11, 1962, copy in Friendship House Papers, box 30, folder April 1–20, 1962, CHS.

41. "Race Relations Workshop, Childerly Farm, May 11 and 12, 1963," Friendship House Papers, box 34, folder May 1963, CHS; "Franciscans Praying during Retreat [June 8 and 9]," *New World*, June 14, 1963; and author's interviews with Seng, July 3, 2001, and Mary Sparks (formerly Sister Anthony Claret), June 26, 2001, Chicago. See also quotes from Martin Luther King Jr. in Michael B. Friedland, *Lift Up Your Voice Like a Trumpet: White Clergy and the Civil Rights and Antiwar Movements, 1954–1973* (Chapel Hill: University of North Carolina Press, 1998), 73; and Dora Williams, "My Freedom Busride to Jail in Georgia," *Catholic Layman* (April 1963): 3. I am grateful to Eve Williams Noonan for sending me a copy of her mother's article.

42. The six School Sisters of St. Francis were Sisters Cecilia Marie Day, M. Austin Doherty, Marita Joseph Kanaly, Andriana Miller, Angelica Seng, and M. Edgar Woefel. The seventh from Joliet was Sister M. Anthony Claret Sparks.

43. Seng, "Sister in the New City," 241; and Sparks and Seng interviews, June 26 and July 3, 2001, respectively. The quotes are from the author's second telephone interview with Ann Seng, June 18, 2002; and Martin Luther King Jr. "Let-

ter from a Birmingham Jail," in James Melvin Washington, ed., *I Have a Dream: Writings and Speeches that Changed the World* (San Francisco: Harper Collins, 1986), 96.

44. Angelica Seng, OSF, and Anthony Claret Sparks, OSF, "The Nun's [sic] Story: Why We Picketed," *Community* 23 (September 1963): 5; and Seng interview, July 3, 2001 (quote).

45. The first quote is from Tom Cook, "Report to Staff," July 25, 1963, copy in Friendship House Papers, box 34, folder July 14–31, 1963, CHS; the remaining quotes are from Mrs. Frank J. Lewis, "President's Message," copy in Friendship House Papers, box 34, folder June 1963, CHS.

46. Seng and Sparks, "The Nun's Story," 5–6.

47. "Pickets in Black," *Chicago Daily News*, July 2, 1963; "Nuns Picket at Loyola in Racial Protest," *Chicago Sun-Times*, July 12, 1963 (front-page photo of nuns holding signs); "The Force of Conscience," *Time*, July 12, 1963. The photograph in *Time*, for example, appeared "in every newspaper" in Brazil. See John Pimenta to Msgr. Daniel M. Cantwell, July 13, 1963, Catholic Interracial Council Papers, box 61, folder July 12–18, 1963, CHS; and attached to this letter is a copy of Rio de Janeiro's *Correio da Manha* (with photo). The quotes are from "Mrs. F. J. Lewis Acts in Loyola Picketing," *Chicago Tribune*, July 10, 1963; and "Open Membership at Picketed Club," *Chicago Daily News*, July 9, 1963.

48. Seng and Sparks interviews, July 3 and June 26, 2001, respectively. The quotes are from Edgar R. Bourke to Cardinal Albert G. Meyer, July 3, 1961, copy in Catholic Interracial Council Papers, box 61, folder July 1–12, 1963, CHS; and Helen C. Baker (to editor), "Nuns Picketing Called Unwise Action," *New World*, July 19, 1963.

49. Quotes are from Austin C. Wehrwein, "2 Catholic Leaders Back Clergy on Plans to Join Rights March," *New York Times*, July 11, 1963; and John A. McDermott (to editor), "CIC Replies to Criticism of Nun Pickets," *New World*, July 26, 1963.

50. "Not Words But Acts," *Commonweal*, 78 (July 26, 1963): 444. The first quotes are from Mathew Ahmann to CIC Board of Directors, July 17, 1963, Catholic Interracial Council Papers, box 61, folder July 12–18, 1963, CHS; and Robert Wuthnow, *The Restructuring of American Religion: Society and Faith since World War II* (Princeton, N.J.: Princeton University Press, 1988), 145–46. See also Seng and Sparks, "The Nun's Story," 6–7; "Minutes" of CIC Board Meeting, "Agenda Topic, No. 3: Report on Illinois Club for Catholic Women," September 17, 1963 (quote), Catholic Interracial Council Papers, box 1A (black notebook), CHS; and "Catholic Club Pool Still 'Off Limits,'" *Chicago American*, October 11, 1963. In November 1963, the Chicago Commission on Human Relations honored the Franciscans with an award. They declined to accept it, however. The superior of the School Sisters of St. Francis said that it would bring "another deluge of letters criticizing the nuns' activities." Msgr. Robert J. Hagerty, a vice chancellor of the archdiocese, counseled them "to turn down the citation." In his opinion, it was "a question of propriety, procedure, and etiquette as it applies to religious women." See Dave Meade, "7 Nun Pickets Decline Award Here," *Chicago Daily News*, November 20, 1963.

51. On the 1963 National Conference on Religion and Race, see Steven M. Avella, *This Confident Church: Catholic Leadership and Life in Chicago, 1940–*

1965 (Notre Dame, Ind.: University of Notre Dame Press, 1962), 312–15; and McGreevy, *Parish Boundaries,* 147–48. On Mathew Ahmann, John A. McDermott, and the Catholic Interracial Council of Chicago, see David W. Southern, "But Think of the Kids: Catholic Interracialists and the Great American Taboo of Race Mixing," *U.S. Catholic Historian* 16 (Summer 1998): 90; and John A. McDermott, quoted in a "Chicago Conference on Religion and Race News Release," June 28, 1963, copy in Catholic Interracial Council Papers, box 61, folder June 27–30, 1963, CHS.

52. The quotes are from "Minutes" of CIC Board of Directors, July 17, 1963, Catholic Interracial Council Papers, box 61, folder July 12–18, 1963; and John A. McDermott to Arthur Wright, June 17, 1964, ibid., Box 86, Folder Correspondence, CHS. McDermott did not like it that Wright, head of the New York Council, had described the Chicago Council as an educational organization. McDermott said, "We believe that the time for an education-only approach in race relations is long past."

53. Whitney M. Young Jr., "To Be Equal: What Negroes Want," *Chicago Defender* [weekly ed.], October 24–30, 1964. Young said that "after the confrontation of 1963—when Negroes bared their grievances in the March on Washington and in the streets of Birmingham—they now appeal for decision." Chicago's Catholic activists knew this. On the efforts of the Sisters of the Good Shepherd and Loretto Sisters, see previous chapters and Fay Robertson, "Neighbors at Work," January 17, 1964, Marillac House Papers, box 2, folder January-May 1964, CHS. The quotes on St. Joseph school are from McKinney interview, April 2, 2002; and McKinney, "Catholic Schools."

54. The quote is from Mary William Sullivan, DC, to Raymond C. Hilliard, Director, Cook County Department of Public Aid, February 6, 1964, Marillac House Papers, box 2, Folder January-May, 1964. See too Mary William Sullivan, DC, to T. R. Leach, December 6, 1967, ibid., box 5, folder November–December 1967, CHS.

55. The six Daughters of Charity who were arrested were Sisters Gloria Briganti, Jane Breidenbach, Pauline Cefolia, Bridget Gemlo, Edwardine Henjum, and Andrea Orford.

56. Quotes are from Sullivan interview, February 7, 2002; and Father James Groppi (to editor), *National Catholic Reporter,* August 18, 1965. On Richard J. Daley and his reputation, see Roger Biles, *Richard J. Daley: Politics, Race, and the Governing of Chicago* (DeKalb: Northern Illinois University Press, 1995). Among the first sisters to arrive in Selma in March 1965 were several from Chicago. Sister Mary Benet McKinney represented Chicago's Urban Apostolate of the Sisters and flew to Alabama at the request of Msgr. Jack Egan. She said her work in Chicago had prepared her: "With my interest in and concern for the Negro community strengthened by eight years in an inner city Chicago parish and my deep commitment to the Urban Apostolate of the Sisters it was a short stop to Selma!" And she was not afraid once she arrived; she had gone "to bear witness by living—by being present." Both quotes are from Mary Benet McKinney, OSB, "Brotherhood Came Alive in Selma Recalls Nun Who 'Bore Witness,'" *New World,* March 19, 1965.

57. Quotes are from Bruce Cook, "Nuns Arrest in Chicago Brings Soul-Searching in Civil Rights Ranks," *National Catholic Reporter,* August 23, 1965; "State-

ment of Sister Mary William Sullivan, Sister Servant of Marillac House, Chicago, Regarding the Demonstration of June 12, 1965," June 13, 1965; and Mary William Sullivan, DC, to "My Most Honored Mother [Superior]," June 14, 1965, both in Marillac House Papers, box 2, folder June 1965, CHS. In fact, these six were not the first nuns arrested. In 1916, Sister Mary Thomasine Hehir, a Sister of St. Joseph, was arrested in St. Augustine, Florida, for refusing to comply with a 1913 statute that prohibited white instructors from teaching in black schools. See Jane Quinn, *The Story of a Nun: Jeanie Gordon Brown* (St. Augustine, Fla.: Villa Flora Press, 1978), 205–10. I am grateful to historian Margaret Susan Thompson for telling me of this incident.

58. "Personal Statement of Sister Andrea Orford Regarding Demonstration of June 12, 1965," June 13, 1965, Marillac House Papers, box 2, folder June 1965, CHS; and author's telephone interview with Sister Martin de Porres Orford, CSA, April 15, 2001. There are numerous references to Alice Andrews Orford's kindnesses in Jesuit Arnold J. Garvy's unpublished "Diary of Work of St. Joseph's [Mission]." A copy is in the Midwest Jesuit Archives in St. Louis, Missouri. See Chapter 5 for more information on this mission and the Sisters of the Holy Family of Nazareth who staffed the school.

59. On Sister Jane Breidenbach, see "Lives of the Deceased Sisters" (typescript), 109–23, copy in Daughters of Charity Archives, Mater Dei Provincialate, Evansville, Indiana; and "Personal Statement of Sister Jane Breidenbach Regarding the Demonstration of June 12, 1965," Marillac House Papers, box 2, folder June 1965, CHS.

60. Another sister arrested in 1965 said she had participated in the demonstration as a Christian, American, and Daughter of Charity because it was her "moral obligation to represent the Poor." See "Personal Statement of Sister Gloria Briganti Regarding Civil Rights Demonstration, June 12, 1965," Marillac House Papers, box 2, folder June 1965, CHS. Sister Mary William also remembers studying John F. Kennedy's Inaugural Address. Shortly after she was appointed director of Marillac House, she received a copy of the address from Lenor K. Sullivan, congresswoman from Missouri's Third District, at the request of Sister Mary William's father. The congresswoman stated that it was her understanding that the address "will be helpful to you in your work." Lenor K. Sullivan to Sister Mary William, January 24, 1964, Marillac House Papers, box 2, folder January–May 1964, CHS. Quotes are from Sullivan interview, February 7, 2002; John F. Kennedy's Inaugural Address, January 20, 1961; and Richard Lischer, *The Preacher King: Martin Luther King, Jr. and the Word That Moved America* (New York: Oxford University Press, 1995), 3. Lischer shows how under King's leadership the civil rights movement became a powerful religious drama—one that would have been difficult for Catholic sisters living in black neighborhoods to resist.

61. Through her friendship with Saul Alinsky, Sister Mary William learned to value community organizing. See P. David Finks, *The Radical Vision of Saul Alinsky* (New York: Paulist Press, 1984), 13–18; Arthur Southwood, "Marillac House—A New Outlook for Its Changing Neighborhood," *New World*, July 1, 1964; and "Cited by Daley, Nun Returns with a Plea," *Chicago Sun-Times*, April 3, 1964. See also Mary William Sullivan, DC, "Invitation to March 31 Rally," March 25, 1964; and Mary William Sullivan, DC, to Mayor Richard J. Daley, March 31, 1964, both in Marillac House Papers, box 2, folder January–May 1964.

62. Southwood, "Marillac House." The quotes are from "Summary: 'Summer of Progress'—June 21 to August 21, 1964," Marillac House Papers, box 2, folder June–September 1964, CHS.

63. Ibid. For quote, see Mary William Sullivan, DC, to Leo Josephus, FSC, May 5, 1964, Marillac House Papers, box 2, folder January–May 1964, CHS.

64. Sullivan interview, February 7, 2002. For quotes, see Mary William Sullivan, DC, to Clarence B. Cash, March 2, 1965, Marillac House Papers, box 2, folder January–March 1965, CHS; John A. McDermott, "Nun Will Be Master [*sic*] of Ceremonies at CIC Dinner for Dr. Martin Luther King, Jr.," CIC Press Release, October 1, 1965, Catholic Interracial Council Papers, box 86, folder 64 Benefit, CHS; and "Why Nun Will Preside: Bare Role of Boy, 9, in Dr. King Banquet," *Chicago Sun-Times*, October 24, 1964.

65. Sullivan interview, February 7, 2002. Lillian Calhoun, "Willis Wins, 7–4," *Chicago Defender* [weekly ed.], May 29–June 4, 1965; Biles, *Richard J. Daley*, 109–18; and Jim Carl, "Harold Washington and Chicago's Schools Between Civil Rights and the Decline of the New Deal Consensus, 1955–1987," *History of Education Quarterly* 41 (Fall 2001): 318–19. On Willis, see also John L. Rury, "Race, Space, and the Politics of Chicago's Public Schools: Benjamin Willis and the Tragedy of Urban Education," *History of Education Quarterly* 39 (Summer 1999): 117–42.

66. Sullivan and Wordlaw interviews, February 7 and July 27, 2002, respectively. See also Friendship House Staff to Sister Mary William Sullivan, June 21, 1965, Friendship House Papers, box 37, folder April–June 1965, CHS.

67. Sullivan interview, February 7, 2002. See also "Marillac's Nuns Hurt by Marches," *New World*, July 30, 1965; and "More Pros, Cons on Demonstrations," *New World*, June 25, 1965. The two priests quoted here are James J. Duffy and Thomas C. White, both of St. Sabina's.

68. Mary William Sullivan, DC, to Sister Sylvia Brown, DC, June 29, 1965, Marillac House Papers, box 2, folder June 1965, CHS. On the resignations, Sister Mary William wrote to her friend that "as a result [of the sisters' arrest] the majority of the Men's Board and a portion of the Women's Board have resigned. You will not be surprised that the resignees were from the deadwood category." Quotes in the text are from Mary William Sullivan, DC, to author, January 15, 2001; and "Marillac's Nuns Hurt by Marches."

69. See *New World*, August 13, 1965; and Carolyn G. Heilbrun, *The Last Gift of Time: Life Beyond Sixty* (New York: Ballantine Books, 1997), 38. Heilbrun observed that women "catch courage from the women whose lives and writings they read."

70. Ed Marciniak, "The Nun in the City," *New City* 4 (May 15, 1965): 2–4; Richard M. Menges, "Urban Apostolate Nuns . . . They're Where the Action Is," *New World*, September 16, 1966. On the Rochester Franciscans, see Bruce Cook, "Project Cabrini," *Extension* 60 (March 1996): 9–13. On the Servants of Mary, see Rev. Daniel J. Mallette to Mary Patricia McLaughlin, OSM, May 6, 1964; and Mary Jane [Margaret] Valois, OSM, to Mallette, May 7, 1965, both in Mallette Papers, box 4, folder 2, CHS. On education of blacks, see Bayard Ruskin, "From Protest to Politics: The Future of the Civil Rights Movement," *Commentary* 39 (February 1965): 26.

71. On the civil rights movement in Chicago, including the Gage Park incident, see especially James R. Ralph Jr., *Northern Protest: Martin Luther King, Jr.,*

Chicago, and the Civil Rights Movement (Cambridge, Mass.: Harvard University Press, 1993); Alan B. Anderson and George W. Pickering, *Confronting the Color Line: The Broken Promise of the Civil Rights Movement in Chicago* (Athens: University of Georgia Press, 1986); and Biles, *Richard J. Daley*. See also Arthur Southwood, "Nun Injured in Violence: Shocked, But Not Bitter," *New World*, August 5, 1966; and "Negro No Stowaway Says Sister Angelica," *Chronicle of Mt. St. Francis* 7 (Summer 1966): 2 (quote); and *National Catholic Reporter*, September 28, 1966 (cartoon drawing).

72. Quotes are from James H. Bowman, "Martin Luther King in Chicago," *Ave Maria* 102 (September 25, 1965): 9; and Albertus Magnus McGrath, OP, "Women as the 'Niggers' of the Church," in *What a Modern Catholic Believes about Women* (Chicago: Thomas More Association, 1972), 99.

73. Quotes are from Sullivan interview, February 7, 2002; and Mary Fainsod Katzenstein, *Faithful and Fearless: Moving Feminist Protest Inside the Church and Military* (Princeton, N.J.: Princeton University Press, 1998), 134. On SNCC, see Mary King, *Freedom Song: A Personal Story of the 1960s Civil Rights Movement* (New York: William Morrow, 1987), 443–74. Cheryl L. Reed has recently shown "how much the feminist movement inside the Church mirrors the larger secular feminist movement." See the chapter on Chicago's Margaret Traxler, SSND, in Cheryl L. Reed, *Unveiled: The Hidden Lives of Nuns* (New York: Berkley Books, 2004), 74–103.

74. On King's 1966 campaign in Chicago, see Biles, *Richard J. Daley*, 119–38 (quotes on p. 119). See also Mary Clinch, "Dr. King's SCLC Comes to Chicago," *Community* 25 (July–August 1966): 6–8; an announcement entitled "What Do You Think of the Slum? Come Speak Your Mind to Dr. Martin Luther King," January 26, 1966, Marillac House Papers, box 3, folder January–February 1966; and Neighbors at Work, "Staff Meeting Minutes," January 31 and March 28, 1966, Marillac House Papers, box 3 folders January–February and March–April 1966, respectively, CHS. The end quotes are from Sister Mary William Sullivan, DC, to Rev. Edward M. Egan, March 4, 1966, Marillac House Papers, box 3, folder March–April 1996, CHS.

75. "Leadership through Learning Proposal," March 14, 1966. The stipend was "$1.25 per hour including pay for training time." By May, Sister Mary William reported that "many of the 75 jobs [were] filled." See Sister Mary William Sullivan to PFC Robert Mason, May 17, 1966. Both in Marillac House Papers, box 3, folders March–April 1966, and folder May–June 1966, respectively, CHS. On Wilmon L. Carter, see "Highest Service Accolade: Westsider Named Top '67 Volunteer," *Chicago Defender* [weekly ed.], April 8–14, 1967.

76. The first quotes are from Mary William Sullivan, DC, to Edwin C. Berry [Urban League], July 19, 1966 and to Jack Mabley [*Chicago American*], August 30, 1966, Marillac House Papers, box 4, folder July–August 1966, CHS. On West Side riots of 1966 and 1968, see Biles, *Richard J. Daley*, 125–27 and 144–47. See also John Linstead, "Living Conditions Blamed in Rioting," *Chicago Daily News*, June 25, 1968. The last quotes are from "Marillac Head Leaves for New Post," *New World*, May 10, 1968; and "What Is Blacks' Mood Here?" *Chicago Daily News*, August 26, 1968.

77. Quotes are from Joseph Haas, "A New More Militant Gwendolyn Brooks Says: 'It Is a Black Revolution,'" *Chicago Daily News*, June 8, 1968; "White Backlash," *Chicago Defender* [weekly ed.], October 15–21, 1966; and author's telephone

interview with Mary Sparks (formerly Sister Anthony Claret), July 10, 2002. On black power and Chicago Catholics, see McGreevy, *Parish Boundaries*, 225–34.

78. Quotes are from Charles Payne, "Men Led, but Women Organized: Movement Participation of Women in the Mississippi Delta," in Vicki L. Crawford, Jacqueline Anne Rouse, and Barbara Woods, eds., *Women in the Civil Rights Movement: Trailblazers and Torchbearers, 1941–1965* (Bloomington: Indiana University Press, 1993), 6; Berenice Johnson Reagon (words and music), "There's a New World Coming," on "Give Your Hands to Struggle" (Washington, D.C.: Smithsonian Folkway Recordings, 1997); and Dottie Miller Zellner, quoted in Debra L. Schultz, *Jewish Women in the Civil Rights Movement* (New York: New York University Press, 2001), 17. Schultz's study demonstrates that the motivation of Jewish women was different from that of most Protestant and Catholic women. Thus Zellner observed that it was her "first exposure to Black culture, and certainly my first exposure to ministers and religious people (p. 6)." Most Jewish women had to learn to adjust to a movement in which faith played such a prominent role. See also King, *Freedom Song*, 273–74; and Mary Berchmans Shea, OSU, "Protest Movements and Convent Life," in M. Charles Borremeo Muckenhirn, CSC, ed., *The New Nuns* (New York: New American Library, 1967), 59–65.

79. Quotes are from "Nuns Polled on Vatican Rebuke," *Chicago Sun-Times*, September 16, 1970; "Maverick Sisters of St. Francis," *Chicago Daily News*, November 17, 1970; and Francis Borgia Rothluebber, SSF, to Msgr. John J. Egan, c. March 1971, Egan Papers, box 73, UNDA. Although many Catholic sisters trace their commitment to democracy and feminism to the civil rights movement, others point to liberation theology. See Karen M. Kennelly, CSJ, "Foreign Missions and the Renewal Movement," *Review for Religious* 49 (May–June 1990): 445–63; Christine Vladimiroff, OSB, "God and Rice Bowls in a New Age," in Mary Hembrow Snyder, ed., *Spiritual Questions for the Twenty-First Century: Essays in Honor of Joan D. Chittister* (Maryknoll, N.Y.: Orbis Books, 2001), 57–61. On women-religious today, see Carole Garibaldi Rogers, *Poverty, Chastity, and Change: Lives of Contemporary American Nuns* (New York: Twayne Publishers, 1996); and Reed, *Unveiled*.

80. On nuns who left religious life, see Wittberg, *The Rise and Decline of Catholic Religious Orders*, especially Part Four on "The Present Collapse"; and Helen Rose Fuchs Ebaugh, *Women in the Vanishing Cloister: Organizational Decline in Catholic Religious Orders in the United States* (New Brunswick, N.J.: Rutgers University Press, 1993). On the transformation of religious life, see Quinonez and Turner, *Transformation of American Catholic Sisters*; Katzenstein, *Faithful and Fearless*; and Lucy Kaylin, *For the Love of God: The Faith and Future of the American Nun* (New York: William Morrow, 2000). The quote is from Kevin Boyle, "The Times They Aren't A-Changing," *Reviews in American History* 29 (June 2001): 308.

INDEX

abandoned women. *See* homeless
women
Abbott, Edith, and institutional care
of children, 187n29
Abbott, Robert S.: politics of, 90; and
St. Monica School, 90–91
abolition, and Drexel family, 190n3
abolitionists, as school teachers in
the South, 190n3
academies, of Mercy Sisters: and curriculum, 41; and Protestant pupils,
38–39
Adams, Mother Denise: and Loretto
Academy, 115; on Loretto Sisters as
teachers, 105
Addams, Jane: and African Americans, 7–8; and Child Welfare Conference, 70; and democracy and
pacifism, 183n76; descriptions of,
171n26, 172n26; and Good Shepherd Sisters, 68; and Hull-House, 3,
40, 47; and Hull mansion, 156n11;
and life in community, 43; and
social progress, 69; work of, and
William T. Stead, 69; and work of
missionaries, 193n24
admission policy, and Loretto Academy, 105–9, 113, 122, 198n17
adult education, and Sisters of
Loretto, 117–18
advertisements, and recruitment of
Irish nuns, 29
Africa: as foreign mission, 33; Irish
nuns in, 7, 25
African American Catholic congresses, and education, 89
African Americans: and Jane Addams,
7–8; and Blessed Sacrament Sisters,

7, 87–91, 93, 95–97; and Catholic
education, 89–91, 95–102; as Catholic sisters, 199n26; and change
in educational opportunities, 84;
in civil rights movement, 140; as
converts in Chicago parishes, 92;
and Katharine Drexel, 87–91, 102;
and House of the Good Shepherd,
58; and Illinois Technical School
for Colored Girls, 71–85; and John
T. Jenifer, 76–77; and *Lilies of the
Field*, 126; at Loretto Academy, in
Woodlawn, 103–24; as members
of CISCA, 111–12; as migrants to
Chicago, 3, 8, 72–75, 82, 88, 98, 104,
107; as Oblate Sisters of Providence,
97; and School Sisters of St. Francis,
98–102; and Sisters of St. Francis
(Dubuque), 91–93; and Sisters of the
Holy Family, 93–94; on West Side,
130, 131–32, 134, 135–36, 150
African Methodist Episcopal Church:
and John T. Jenifer, 76–77; and
Elizabeth McDonald, 79–80; and
Amanda Berry Smith, 79
Ahmann, Mathew: on attitude of
nuns in inner city, 157n22; and
civil rights movement, 142; on
picketing nuns, 141
Aid to Mothers Law, and Judge Mer-
ritt Pinckney 74
Alabama, and residents at Rockwell
Gardens, 134
Albany (Georgia), and Chicago's
Friendship House, 138–39
Alemany, Archbishop Joseph (San
Francisco): and emigrant nuns, 15–
16; missionary work of, 24

Garfield Park: and black migrants,
131; and University of Illinois,
209n29
Garnier, Sister Anthony, at Holy
Name of Mary, 194n32
Garvy, Rev. Arnold J.: family and
Hull-House, 192n22; on Sisters of
the Holy, and St. Joseph Mission
School, 93–94
Gates, Henry Louis, on education, 100
Gavin, Mother Irene: biographical
information on, 201–2n39; and
CISCA, 200n29; at Loretto Acad-
emy, 114–17, 118–19, 202n42
Gemlo, Sister Bridget, and civil rights
demonstration, 212n55
gender, and closing of Loretto Acad-
emy, 122–23
Geoghehan, Rev. Thomas, 23–24
German Americans, as Sisters of St.
Francis, 91
Geter, Howard D., and Daughters of
Charity, 148
Gillespie, Mother Angela, and recruit-
ment of Irish nuns, 22–23
Ginzberg, Lori D., on Protestant
women reformers, 172–73n33
Girl Scouts, at Illinois Technical
School, 83; and segregation, 188n38
"good hearts," Catholic sisters as, 2,
153, 157–58n24
Gordon, Linda, on women as "heroes
of their own lives," 159n7
Great Depression, 93, 151
Great Famine (Ireland), and emigra-
tion, 11, 12, 19, 20, 37, 44, 50
Great Migration, to Chicago, 72, 105,
123. *See also* African Americans
Great Northwestern Sanitary Fair, 42
Greenmount Spinning Company
(Dublin), 28
Griffin, Sister Mary Ignatia, and civil
rights, 157n23
Grodzins, Morton, and "tipping
point," 113
Groppi, Rev. James (Milwaukee), on
civil rights movement in Selma and
Chicago, 143

habits, religious. *See* clothing
Hacsi, Timothy A., on orphanages as
"second homes," 78
Hagerty, Monsignor Robert J., on
picketing nuns, 211n50
Haines, Mayor John C. (Chicago), and
Magdalen asylum, 51
Hales Franciscan High School, 120,
122
Hall, Walter, and Sisters of the
Blessed Sacrament, 194n31
Halligan, Rev. Thomas, and Good
Shepherd Sisters, 56
Hand, Rev. John, and All Hallows
College, 24
Harvey, Illinois, and Amanda Smith
Orphan Home, 79
Hast, Adele, and place of nuns in
American history, 169n3
Heath, Mayor Monroe, and the House
of the Good Shepherd, 58
Hehir, Sister Mary Thomasine, and
arrest in Florida, 213n57
Heilbrun, Carolyn G., on courage,
157n23, 214n69
Helper, and Amanda Berry Smith, 79
Hendrican, Margaret, 17
Henjum, Sister Edward Henjum, and
civil rights demonstration, 212n55
Hennessy, Richard, and care of emi-
grants, 32–33, 168n104
Hennessy Hotel (Ireland), 32
Henni, Bishop John (Milwaukee), and
Mother Agatha O'Brien, 2
hierarchy, in Catholic Church: and
Catholic sisters' distrust of, 152;
and nuns' place, 46, 70, 94, 159n9,
193n26, 197n3
Hillard, Raymond, 141
Hogan, Edmund M., on nuns in Irish
church, 159n9
Hoge, Jane: and Catholic sisters, 45;
and Chicago sanitary fair, 42
Holland, Mother Eleanor: and educa-
tion, 204–5n60; and Loretto Acad-
emy, 119, 121, 198n20
Holy Angels Parish and School, and
School Sisters of St. Francis, 98–102

SUELLEN HOY is guest professor of history at the University of Notre Dame. She is the author of many articles and books, including *Chasing Dirt: The American Pursuit of Cleanliness.* She lives with her husband, historian Walter Nugent, in Highland Park, Illinois.

The University of Illinois Press
is a founding member of the
Association of American University Presses.

———————————————————————————

Composed in 9.5/12.5 Trump Mediaeval
by Jim Proefrock
at the University of Illinois Press
Manufactured by Thomson-Shore, Inc.

University of Illinois Press
1325 South Oak Street
Champaign, IL 61820-6903
www.press.uillinois.edu